Soul Food

Soul Food

Stories to Nourish
the Spirit and the Heart

Edited by Jack Kornfield
and Christina Feldman

Foreword by
Jon Kabat-Zinn

HarperSanFrancisco
An Imprint of HarperCollins*Publishers*

FIRST EDITION

Library of Congress Cataloging-in-Publication Data

Soul food : stories to nourish the spirit and the heart / edited by Jack Kornfield and Christina Feldman ; foreword by Jon Kabat-Zinn. — 1st ed.
     Rev. ed. of : Stories of the spirit, stories of the heart. Includes bibliographical references and index.
     1. Parables. 2. Parables—Paraphrases, tales, etc. 3. Storytelling—Religious aspects. 4. Spiritual life. I. Kornfield, Jack. II. Feldman, Christina. III. Stories of the spirit, stories of the heart.
BL624.S755   1996
291.4'3 — dc20   96-11418
ISBN 0-06-251442-3 (pbk.)

96 97 98 99 00 ❖ RRD(H) 10 9 8 7 6 5 4 3 2 1

To our children

Caroline Waterman Kornfield
Sara Lichen Rusling
Arran Sean Rusling

and to the
Child of the Spirit in all of us

Contents

The Universe is made of stories,
not atoms.

Muriel Rukeyser

Foreword

by Jon Kabat-Zinn

OUR VERY LIVES ARE STORIES. BUT SOMETIMES we don't know what our own story is as it unfolds. We may have only a vague sense that our story is unique. It's worthy of some contemplation. Perhaps we would do well to meditate on our life path, to ask periodically such questions as "Who am I?" "Where am I going?" "What is my heart-path?" Then listen carefully to what emerges out of stillness and silence and over time. For each of our lives is a singular story, woven together of many different substories, plots, currents, and times. Having at least an inkling of our story allows us to be more the author and less the victim of our own life. Sometimes hearing stories from another time or another culture inspires us and serves to guide us in the ongoing weaving of our own story-tapestry.

Stories are as ancient as the mind itself. We might say that language developed so we could tell our stories. Stories are how we organize our thoughts, preserve them in memory, share them with others, and pass on the lineage of the community and its experiences. What happened down the road is a story. So is how to find a good place to dig for tasty roots. Culture itself is a story. History, of course, is also story. Only culture and history are many stories, not one. And even one story, if it is a good one, is different each time it is told. For stories reflect the mind itself, and the mind itself is always changing, like the surface of the ocean. When the story is a good one, then teller, listeners, and the story itself (or the mind of the reader and the story) all merge into one inseparable whole. In such moments, magic arises and the true work of the story gets under way. The mind slows down and opens, and the story goes under the skin and enters the heart. This was perhaps more so in olden times, when stories were told mostly at night, sitting around a fire, when the world of darkness overtook us and brought to a close the work of the day and of the hands, ushering in the world of imagination and some quiet and receptivity in the mind.

All great works of literature have stories to tell. The Odyssey, the Iliad, *Hamlet* and *King Lear, The Divine Comedy, Beowulf,* the Aeneid, *Huckleberry Finn, Pride and Prejudice.* Every great poem tells a story, paints a picture in the mind, invites many more, ignites passion and resonances in the listener, and in that way nourishes, transforms, and enriches the world.

The lives and messages of the world's religions live in story. The Bible is a fantastic collection of stories. The life of Jesus is a story. His teachings are all told in story form. So are the life and teachings of the Buddha. The life of Muhammad, the Ramayana, the Bhagavad Gita, and Gilgamesh are all stories.

All science is story, too, and strives to be. Science wants to know nature's story. What is the universe trying to tell us? How can we listen better to it and see beyond the veils of appearance to other levels of order and interconnectedness? We have the story of the big bang, the story of the double helix, the story of Gregor Mendel growing his pea plants in the monastery garden, the story of Marie Curie and the discovery of radium, the story of evolution, of cosmology, of the universe and the solar system. We organize our understanding in stories. We always have, and we likely always will.

The stories gathered together here and very aptly entitled *Soul Food* are teaching stories in the highest sense of the word *teaching*. They are offered to us, and organized with very fine introductory commentaries, by two of the world's most skillful and sensitive teachers of Buddhist meditation, Jack Kornfield and Christina Feldman. Over time, Jack and Christina have used many of these stories as part of their teaching, to inspire, to reveal, to awaken. They often tell them to groups of people during extended meditation retreats at the end of a long day as part of an evening talk. Each day, the retreatants engage in hard inner work, exploring stillness in mind and body, dwelling for long periods of time in silence and cultivating a refined, moment-to-moment, if possible nonreactive, nonjudging, awareness known as *mindfulness*.

Told in such a context, to minds ripe for hearing, these stories can go straight into the heart of the listener and help it to open; they can go straight into the mind and help it to see and understand some aspect of itself better. Ultimately, whether we are on retreat or not, or for that matter, whether we meditate formally or not, these stories can help us to know ourselves better and to cultivate our best qualities of mind and heart. They serve as mirrors into which we are invited to look, mirrors of imagination, of cleverness, of wisdom, of compassion, that bring out our own best qualities and truly feed our souls.

Now Christina and Jack have made their favorite stories available for all. As editors, they have carefully selected wonderful teaching stories from all traditions. Some are very short, virtual snapshots of one element or another of wisdom. Others are longer and more fully developed as stories. But regardless of length, all carry some deep potion for your mind and heart.

And if you have a meditation practice, recurrent visits to your favorites, and to those you may not know, sometimes chosen at random, sometimes by particular theme, can be of great use in developing and deepening your practice. Actually, you could put it the other way around and entertain the notion that certain of these stories might be waiting to choose you. Either way, many of these offerings will help ensure that your practice is appropriately loose and easy and fun-loving as well as wise and clear.

I love many of these stories and have had personal connections with some of them for many years. Some I heard for the first time on retreat with Jack or Christina. I think you will find that different stories will speak to you more directly at different points in your life. One of my all-time favorites in this collection is Helen Luke's version of Odysseus's final journey. She wrote it when she was in her late eighties, as part of her wonderful book, *Old Age*. Another is the Zen story of the Samurai who seeks to know the difference between heaven and hell and learns it in a surprising way.

But all of these stories are gems—there are Zen gems, Chassidic gems, Christian gems, Sufi gems, Native American gems—diamond wisdom from all traditions and all ages for us to take up with reverence and respect from time to time over the course of our lives and perhaps share with others.

Stories are like shy living creatures. They need to be handled gently, with respect. It is best not to overuse a story by telling it too frequently. Each has to be treated with reverence, used appropriately and at the right time, then put back in its case, stored away, to be called upon when necessary. Stories are a pharmacopoeia, a storehouse of culture and wisdom. Not only are they food for the soul. They are medicine for the soul as well. They need to be thought about, meditated on, revisited in silent contemplation.

And when read to someone else, they also serve as scaffolding for meaningful glances and pauses, for inflections of tone, the dropping of the voice, for the celebration of words and of our capacity for words and all they carry and point to. Taking this one step further, you might try learning some of these stories by heart and telling them to others. That way, you will befriend them even more deeply and discover what they are really about.

Soul Food offers us a bountiful menu. Many lives will be immeasurably enriched by its fare.

—Jon Kabat-Zinn
    February 1996
    Center for Mindfulness in Medicine, Health Care,
      and Society
    University of Massachusetts Medical Center
    Worcester, Massachusetts

Introduction

ONG BEFORE THE BIRTH OF FORMAL RELIGIONS, storytelling was the vehicle for sustaining age-old wisdom. Within the stories, legend, history, and profound truths about life found their expression. Stories introduced their listeners to a world of magic and mystery. Stories, too, have long been the traditional medium of teaching and learning. Great masters like Jesus and Buddha excelled in them, and shamans and elders of every tradition have captured their wisdom in stories around campfires and at tribal gatherings, drawing listeners worldwide to deeper visions of life with images and symbols.

This book is a collection of such teaching stories, drawn from the great traditions of the East and West, from Christian, Buddhist, Sufi, Zen, Chassid, Hindu, Native American, African, and other sources. Each story is alive, filled with the heart and inspiration of these traditions.

One of the central messages of these stories is their humor. Spiritual life is at times perceived as a solemn and serious business, devoid of humor and lightness. Some of us even approach the spiritual path as we would approach the taking of distasteful medicine. We are convinced that it is beneficial and healing to us, but no one can persuade us that it actually tastes good. Amid our earnestness and intensity, laughter appears almost sacrilegious. Yet there has always been a place for divine humor, for adding a little fizz to our own seriousness.

Listening to the stories of others, learning from them, brings a ray of light to our own understanding. These stories connect us with others, with men and women, animals and angels, beings of all times and cultures. In the stories of others we see ourselves reflected in a different form. We learn to laugh a little at our own absurdities and at the detours we find ourselves lost in. A good story creates a bridge for us from our particular life to the universal, connecting our individual life to the patterns and wonder of the whole.

The stories of the spiritual journeys of others nourish us, revealing profound psychological and spiritual realities, illuminating the inevitable difficulties and realizations of all who journey along with us. Stories show a path, shine a light on our way, teach us how to see, remind us of the greatest of human possibilities. We are invited to laugh, to awaken, to join our journey with others. Their stories are our stories—they have the power to touch us, move us, and inspire us.

The stories in this book are divided into three sections, each illustrating an aspect of the spiritual journey. Part I, "Opening to Possibilities," emphasizes the emergence of the inner vision that inspires us to begin our spiritual journey. Through our own life experience and through the example of great and simple people, we awaken to the possibilities of our own lives and hearts. We glimpse the transformation that is possible through the power of our own compassion, courage, integrity, and attention. Part II,

"Finding the Way," shows us the valleys and peaks we encounter as we begin to travel our spiritual path. The stories in this chapter help us to separate wisdom from folly, false ideals from the truth before us, and show the way to compassion, wisdom, and awakening. In Part III, "Living Our Truth," we learn what it means to embody integrity and compassion in our lives and how to touch the world around us through the simple love and wisdom that is born of our own experience.

As you read this book let yourself be empty, receptive, as though at the feet of a master or around an ancient campfire. Listen to the message of the story, the feel, the delight, the images, the wisdom. Take the message inside and let it resonate, let it touch whatever part of your being it will, and learn from all its levels. If you wish, let yourself see how it is true or not in your way of living. If it brings inspiration, listen so that its wisdom might be embodied in your own life. But most of all, enjoy the stories. Take them in like nectar, like honey wine, like song and poetry, comedy and gospel tale.

We are delighted to share this book with you. It has grown out of many years of our own spiritual practice, our wanderings, difficulties, understanding, and teaching. We have developed a great love and respect for stories of the spirit. Sharing these stories is a way of sharing our hearts and our wisdom. We hope they bring you understanding and delight.

I

Opening to Possibilities

THE PRICELESS GIFT OF ANY STORY LIES IN ITS power to spark a fire in our imagination. A great story has the capacity to transcend the boundaries of our personal world and introduce the universality of human experience. Through stories we learn that heartbreak and joy, grief and love, sacrifice and courage are not the territory of one time, or one culture, nor are they the blessing or curse of any one individual. Stories remind us how timeless and universal is the search to find peace and freedom, to live with love and courage, and to be free from conflict and pain.

Our imagination is touched by the tales and myths of people who have changed the world around them through the power of their own wisdom and love. We are inspired by the stories of spiritual leaders who teach a path of peace in the midst of hatred and violence. We are equally moved by the story of a child who learns to meet a life-threatening illness with grace or by the story of an impoverished refugee who finds forgiveness for the oppressor.

As we are touched by these stories, our imagination travels beyond the limits of our individual experience.

Our hearts open to feel the sorrow and courage of another person, to experience the world through the eyes of another, and to empathize with their struggle. We begin to see more clearly our own story reflected in the stories of others.

Timeless stories move us to look anew at our own lives. These great stories teach us not to despair, not to be swamped by sorrow or hopelessness; they remind us in clear and inspiring ways of our own possibilities and potential. The stories of others serve as examples, teaching us that the possibility of great courage, love, and compassion can be part of our own story.

We have all experienced moments of revelation, of profound opening. These moments seem to touch us in an unexpected fashion, yet they can make a transformative impression upon us. It may be a moment of walking in nature when the chatter of our mind suddenly stills, and in the silence we experience deep sensitivity and harmony. It may be a moment when, conversing with a troubled friend, we feel our judgments drop away and our hearts open. We know ourselves to be totally present, the barriers between self and other melt, and the natural radiance of our own compassion emerges. It may be a moment alone, when our need for busyness and the clamoring of our thoughts cease. In that stillness we experience an aloneness that knows no loneliness or alienation but that speaks of a rich completeness and oneness with the rhythms of the entire universe. These moments offer us a glimpse of our own possibilities.

From the benediction of these moments of stillness, we are reminded in a vivid way of what truly matters in our lives. These moments remind us of how important it is to live as awake, compassionate human beings. Possessions or credentials don't give a true sense of quality and value to our lives. Our lives are given quality by knowing that we have learned to love well, to live fully, and to let go.

The spiritual connection we seek and long for is present in any moment, our eyes and hearts need only open to it. There are a hundred right ways to travel the spiritual path and a thousand spiritual paths to travel. Each one of them has to do with the next step we take, the words we speak, the songs we sing, the ways we touch one another. No other person can tell us exactly how to live our life, no matter how wise or loving that person is. No one has ever lived our life before. We ourselves must learn how to live with integrity and wisdom. To live from what is true is to live from what is here already.

Freedom is simply the art of letting go and being fully open, honest, and loving toward the next moment, the next person, the fullness of life as it is. By living in this way, we can show the way to others, though we cannot free another being directly (for each of us must let go individually). We can teach and serve by how we are, how empty we are, how deeply we listen, how open our hearts have become. Freedom is contagious; love is, too.

The stories contained in this section describe the openings of masters and students, of past and present. If we can listen to them as if we were sitting at the feet of a great sage, they have the power to awaken the greatness of our own hearts. Reading these stories with an open heart, we come to understand that they reveal our own story in a different form. The universal wisdom reflected in these stories is an invitation to explore the possibilities within each of our hearts within each moment.

ONE

*Extraordinary
Possibilities and
the Greatness
of the Heart*

WE BEGIN WITH STORIES OF GREAT TRIUMPHS and revelations, not because they are impossible but because they are possible. They convey the power of love, faith, and courage. They speak of the capacity that deep compassion and integrity have to touch the hearts of others and to transform the world. If we read these stories wisely, we will not try to create saints or ideals from their message but will try to discover the same faith, wisdom, and courage within our own hearts.

We would do ourselves a great disservice to use the wisdom and example in these stories as a measure to judge our own imperfections and failings. Rather, these stories can inspire us to see beyond our frailties and doubts, to appreciate the strength and love that lie within us. Each one of us will be called upon to respond to hardship, sorrow, and loss. Each one of us will be profoundly touched by the pain and conflict that is part of the human experience. Our capacity to respond with grace and courage is the truth that is expressed in these stories.

There is a place within each of us that is the source of fearlessness, compassion, and integrity. It is this place that inspires us to reach out a hand of comfort to a friend in need, to intervene to prevent the infliction of pain upon another. It is this place that grieves at the pain in our world and rejoices in the happiness and love that is found. When we are vitally connected to our own hearts, we know that all living beings wish to be free from pain and to live in peace and freedom.

It is not just a saint who can forgive, not only Jesus or Buddha who can make great sacrifice. Compassion and love do not need grand gestures and dramatic expression. Our opportunities for love, forgiveness, and reverence are manifold. Each time we respond with love we create a world of peace and integrity. Every response is worthy, significant, each makes a difference.

The greatness of our hearts lies in not demanding proof that our responses of care and love make a difference. Our faith in love itself sustains us, the richness of our caring nurtures us. In not asking for confirmation, approval, or reward we are free to live simply in the spirit of reverence and love.

The stories in this chapter speak of this love and faith. They invite us to look anew at our own lives. What in our lives now could be healed by forgiveness? What discord and division exists that could be reconciled by patience and love? What conflicts could be ended by tolerance and compassion? What opportunities do we have to truly make a difference?

IT HAPPENED JUST A FEW YEARS AGO TO TWO YOUNG children in a family from Illinois. The eight-year-old daughter became ill and was diagnosed with a life-threatening blood disease. A search went out to find a donor of blood compatible with her own. As she weakened, they looked and no donor could be found. Then it was discovered that her six-year-old brother shared her rare blood type. The mother and their minister and doctor sat down with the boy to ask if he would be willing to donate his blood to save the life of his sister.

Much to their surprise he did not answer right away. He wanted some time to think about it. Six year olds can be quite thoughtful at times. After a few days he went to his mother and said, "Yes, I'll do it."

The following day the doctor brought both children to his clinic and placed them on cots next to each other. He wanted them to see how one was helping the other. First he drew a half pint of blood from the young boy's arm. Then he moved it over to his sister's cot and inserted the needle so her brother could see the effect. In a few minutes color began to pour back into her cheeks.

Then the boy motioned for the doctor to come over. He wanted to ask a question, very quietly.

"Will I start to die right away?" he asked.

You see, when he had been asked to donate his blood to save the life of his sister, his six-year-old mind understood the process literally. That's why he needed a few days to think about it.

And then he simply gave what is in the heart of every human being to give when we are truly connected.

Christian

❧❧

THIS STORY CONCERNS A MONASTERY THAT HAD fallen upon hard times. Once a great order, as a result of waves of antimonastic persecution in the seventeenth and eighteenth centuries and the rise of secularism in the nineteenth, all its branch houses were lost and it had become decimated to the extent that there were only five monks left in the decaying mother house: the abbot and four others, all over seventy in age. Clearly it was a dying order.

In the deep woods surrounding the monastery there was a little hut that a rabbi from a nearby town occasionally used for a hermitage. Through their many years of prayer and contemplation the old monks had become a bit psychic, so they could always sense when the rabbi was in his hermitage. "The rabbi is in the woods, the rabbi is in the woods again," they would whisper to each other. As he agonized over the imminent death of his order, it occurred to the abbot at one such time to visit the hermitage and ask the rabbi if by some possible chance he could offer any advice that might save the monastery.

The rabbi welcomed the abbot at his hut. But when the abbot explained the purpose of his visit, the rabbi could only commiserate with him. "I know how it is," he exclaimed. "The spirit has gone out of the people. It is the same in my town. Almost no one comes to the synagogue anymore." So the old abbot and the old rabbi wept together. Then they read parts of the Torah and quietly spoke of deep things. The time came when the abbot had to leave. They embraced each other. "It has been a wonderful thing that we should meet after all these years," the abbot said, "but I have still failed in my purpose for coming here. Is there nothing you can tell me, no piece of advice you can give me that would help me save my dying order?"

"No, I am sorry," the rabbi responded. "I have no advice to give. The only thing I can tell you is that the Messiah is one of you."

When the abbot returned to the monastery his fellow monks gathered around him to ask, "Well, what did the rabbi say?"

"He couldn't help," the abbot answered. "We just wept and read the Torah together. The only thing he did say, just as I was leaving—it was something cryptic—was that the Messiah is one of us. I don't know what he meant."

In the days and weeks and months that followed, the old monks pondered this and wondered whether there was any possible significance to the rabbi's words. The Messiah is one of us? Could he possibly have meant one of us monks here at the monastery? If that's the case, which one? Do you suppose he meant the abbot? Yes, if he meant anyone, he probably meant Father Abbot. He has been our leader for more than a generation. On the other hand, he might have meant Brother Thomas. Certainly Brother Thomas is a holy man. Everyone knows that Thomas is a man of light. Certainly he could not have meant Brother Elred! Elred gets crotchety at times. But come to think of it, even though he is a thorn in people's sides, when you look back on it, Elred is virtually always right. Often very right. Maybe the rabbi did mean Brother Elred. But surely not Brother Phillip. Phillip is so passive, a real nobody. But then, almost mysteriously, he has a gift for somehow always being there when you need him. He just magically appears by your side. Maybe Phillip is the Messiah. Of course the rabbi didn't mean me. He couldn't possibly have meant me. I'm just an ordinary person. Yet supposing he did? Suppose I am the Messiah? O God, not me. I couldn't be that much for You, could I?

As they contemplated in this manner, the old monks began to treat each other with extraordinary respect on the off chance that one among them might be the Messiah. And on the off, off chance that each monk himself might be the Messiah, they began to treat themselves with extraordinary respect.

Because the forest in which it was situated was beautiful, it so happened that people still occasionally came to visit the monastery to picnic on its tiny lawn, to wander along some of its paths, even now and then to go into the dilapidated chapel to meditate. As they did so, without even being conscious of it, they sensed this aura of extraordinary respect that now began to surround the five old monks and seemed to radiate out from them and permeate the atmosphere of the place. There was something strangely attractive, even compelling, about it. Hardly knowing why, they began to come back to the monastery more frequently to picnic, to play, to pray. They began to bring their friends to show them this special place. And their friends brought their friends.

Then it happened that some of the younger men who came to visit the monastery started to talk more and more with the old monks. After a while one asked if he could join them. Then another. And another. So within a few years the monastery had once again become a thriving order and, thanks to the rabbi's gift, a vibrant center of light and spirituality in the realm.

Chassid

⋙⋘

ONCE, THE BUDDHA WAS BORN AS A BANYAN DEER. When he was grown he became leader of the herd. He guided his herd wisely and led them to the heart of a secluded forest where, sheltered by the giant trees, they lived free from danger.

Then a new king came into power over the land. And, above all things, this king loved hunting. As soon as the sun rose he would mount his horse and lead his men on a furious chase through fields and meadows, forests and glens. Shooting his arrows madly, he would not leave off until the sun had set. Then the wagons rolled back to the palace behind him, filled now with deer, boar, rabbit, pheasant, monkey, leopard, bear, tiger, and lion. And the king was happy.

His people, however, were not pleased. Fields had been ruined by the royal hunt. Farmers and merchants had been forced to leave off their work in order to beat the jungles and drive the hidden beasts toward the waiting king and his men. Affairs of state, too, lay unattended.

The people, determined to bring all this to an end, devised a simple plan. They built a stockade deep in the forest. "We'll trap a herd or two of deer in this stockade," they said. "Then the king can hunt all he wants. Let him hunt to his heart's content. He won't ruin our fields or force us to leave our shops. Then let him be happy."

The stockade was built and two herds of deer were driven within its walls. The gates were closed and the delicate animals, charging and wheeling in frantic circles, sought some way out. But there was none. Exhausted at last, they stood trembling, awaiting their fate.

The men left happily to tell the king of their success.

One of the herds that had been captured was the herd of the Banyan Deer.

The Banyan Deer walked among his herd. Sunlight played on his many-branched antlers. His black eyes shone and his muzzle was wet. "The blue sky is overhead. Green grass grows at our feet," he told the others. "Do not give up. Where there is life, there is hope. I will find a way." And so he strove to ease their fears.

Soon the king arrived to view the newly captured herds. He was pleased. He strung his bow in preparation for the hunt. Noticing the two deer kings below he said, "The leaders of both herds are magnificent animals. No one is to shoot them. They shall be spared." Then, standing on the wall, looking down over the stockade, he sent his arrows flying into the milling herds. The deer became frantic. Racing wildly they injured one another with horns and hooves as they sought to escape the deadly rain of arrows.

And so it went. Every few days the king and his courtiers would return to the stockade. And every few days more of the gentle deer were killed. Many others were wounded by the flying arrows. Still others were injured in the effort to escape.

The king of the Banyan Deer met with the leader of the other herd. "Brother," he said, shaking his antlered head sadly, "we are trapped. I've tried every way, but all are barred against us. The pain our subjects suffer is unbearable. As you know, when the arrows fly, many get badly hurt just trying to stay alive. Let us hold a lottery. Each day all the deer, one day from your herd, one day from mine, must pick a straw. Then, the one single deer on whom the lottery falls will go stand near the wall just below the king. That one deer must offer itself to be shot. It is a terrible solution, but at least this way we can keep many from needless injury and pain."

And the leader of the other herd agreed.

The next day, when the king and his courtiers arrived, they found one trembling deer standing directly below them. Its legs and body were shaking but it held its head high. "What is this?" said the king. "Ah, I see. These are noble deer indeed! They have chosen that one deer alone shall die rather than that they all should suffer from our hunt. Those deer kings have wisdom." A heaviness descended on the king's heart. "We will accept their terms," he announced. "From now on shoot only the one deer that stands below." And unstringing his bow, he descended from the stockade wall and rode back in silence to the palace.

That night the king tossed and turned, a radiant deer pacing through his dreams.

One day the lot fell on a pregnant doe. She went to her king, the leader of the other herd, and said, "I will willingly go and fulfill the lottery once my fawn is safely born. But if I go now, both I and my unborn child will die. Please spare me for now. I do not ask for myself but for the sake of the child that is soon to be born."

But the leader of that herd said, "The law is the law. I cannot spare you. The lottery has fallen on you and you must die. There are no exceptions. Justice demands that you go."

In desperation she ran to the Banyan Deer. She fell on her knees before him and begged for his aid. He listened quietly, observing her with wide and gentle eyes. "Rise, Sister," said the Banyan Deer, "and go free. You are right. The terms of the lottery require that only one need die. Therefore you shall be freed from the lottery until your fawn is born. I will see that it is so done."

Too overjoyed for words, the grateful doe bowed and then bounded away.

The Banyan Deer King rose to his feet. There was no other he could send to take her place. He had spared her, therefore he himself must replace her. How could it be otherwise?

He walked calmly, with great dignity, through his browsing herd.

They watched him as he moved among them. His great, curving antlers and strong shoulders, his shining eyes and sharp, black hooves, all reassured and comforted them. Never had their Banyan Deer King let them down. Never had he abandoned them. If there was a way he would find it. If there was a chance to save another, he would take it. Not once had he lorded it over them. He was a king indeed, and his whole herd took comfort in his presence.

The courtiers were waiting with bows drawn atop the stockade. When they saw it was the Deer King who had come to stand below they called out, "O King of the Banyan Deer, you know our king has spared you. Why are you here?"

"I have come so that two others need not die. Now shoot! You have your work and I have mine."

But, lowering their bows, they sent a message to the king. "Your Majesty, come with all speed to the stockade."

Not long after, the king arrived, riding like the wind, with his robes streaming behind him.

"What is it?" he called. "Why have you summoned me?"

"Come, your majesty," his men called. "Look!"

Dismounting from his horse, the king hurried up the rough wooden steps and looked down over the wall.

The Banyan Deer stood below. Then deer king and human king looked at one another.

"Banyan King," said the King of Men at last, "I know you. I have seen you gliding through the forests of my dreams. Why are you here? Have I not freed you from my hunt?"

"Great King," replied the Banyan Deer, "what ruler can be free if the people suffer? Today a doe with fawn asked for my aid. The lottery had fallen on her and both she and her unborn fawn were to die. The lottery requires that only one shall die. I shall be that one. I shall take her place. The lottery shall be fulfilled. This is my right and my duty as king."

A stone rolled from the king's heart. "Noble Banyan Deer," he said, "you are right. A king should care for the least of his subjects. It is a lesson I have been long in the learning but today, through your sacrifice, you have made it clear to me. So I shall give you a gift, a teacher's fee for the lesson you have taught me. You and your whole herd are freed. None of you shall be hunted again. Go and live in peace."

But the Banyan Deer said, "Great King, that is, indeed, a noble gift. But I cannot leave yet. May I speak further?"

"Speak on, Noble Deer."

"O King of Men, if I depart to safety with my own herd will that not mean that the remaining herd shall simply suffer all the more? Each day you shall kill only them. They will have no respite. A rain of arrows will fall upon them. While I desire, above all things, the safety of my people, I cannot buy it at the cost of increasing the suffering of others. Do you understand?"

The human king was stunned. "What?!" he exclaimed. "Would you, then, risk your own and your herd's freedom for others?"

"Yes," said the Banyan Deer, "I would. I will. Think of their anguish, Great King. Imagine their sufferings, and then let them too go free."

The King of Men paused and he pondered. At last he lifted his head and smiled. "Never have I seen such nobility or such resolute concern. How can I refuse you? You shall have your wish. The other herd too shall go free. Now, can you go off with your own herd and be at peace?"

But the Banyan Deer answered, "No, Great King, I cannot. I think of all the other wild, four-footed creatures. Like them, I have lived my life surrounded by dangers and by fears. How could I live in peace knowing the terrors they must endure? I beg you, Mighty King, have pity on them. There can be no peace unless they too are free."

The King of Men was again astonished. He had never imagined such a thing. He thought and thought, and slowly the truth of the Banyan Deer's words grew clear to him. It was true, he realized. There is no real peace unless its benefits extend to all.

"You are right, Great Deer," said the King of Men at last. "Never again, in all my realm, shall any four-footed creature be slain. They are all freed from my hunt—rabbit, boar, bear, lion, leopard, tiger, deer—all. Never again shall they fall to my huntsmen's arrows. So, my Teacher, have you now found peace?"

But the Banyan Deer said, "No, Great King, I have not. What, my Lord, of the defenseless ones of the air? The birds, Great King, live surrounded by a net of danger. Stones and arrows shall greet them now wherever they fly. They shall fall from the skies like a rain throughout your kingdom. They shall know such suffering as can hardly be imagined. O Great King, I beg you. Let them go free. Release them also."

"Great One," said the King of Men, "you drive a hard bargain and are determined, it seems, to make farmers of us all. But, yes, I shall free the birds. They may now fly freely throughout my realm. No man shall hunt them again. Then may they build their nests in peace. Now, are you satisfied? Are you at last at peace?"

"Great King," answered the Banyan Deer, "think if you will of the silent ones of your realm—the fish, my Lord. If I do not now speak for them, who will? While they swim the lakes, rivers, and streams of your land, hooks, nets, and spears will be ever poised above them. How can I have peace while they abide in such danger? Great King, I beg you, spare them as well."

"Noble Being," said the King of Men, tears trickling down his cheeks, "Compassionate One, never before have I been moved to think in such a way, but, yes, I do so agree. The fish, too, are of my kingdom, and they too shall be free. They shall swim throughout my land and no one shall kill them again.

"Now, all of you assembled courtiers and attendants," announced the king, "hear my words; this is my proclamation. See that it is posted throughout the land. From this day forth, all beings in my realm shall be recognized as my own dear subjects. None shall be trapped, hunted, or killed. This is my lasting decree. See to it that it is fulfilled.

"Now, tell me, Noble One," he said, turning to the Banyan Deer once more, "are you at peace?"

Flocks of birds flew overhead and perched, singing, from among the nearby trees. Deer grazed calmly on the green grass.

"Yes," said the Banyan Deer, "now I am at peace!" And he leaped up, kicking like a fawn. He leaped for joy—sheer joy! He had saved them all!

Then he thanked the king and, gathering his herd, departed with his herd back into the depths of the forest.

The king had a stone pillar set on the spot where he had spoken with the Banyan Deer. Carved upon it was the figure of a deer, encircled with these words: "Homage to the Noble Banyan Deer, Compassionate Teacher of Kings."

Then he too lived on, caring wisely for all things.

Early Buddhist

❧

I'M NINETY-TWO YEARS OLD, ALL RIGHT. I GET UP every morning at seven A.M. Each day I remind myself, "Wake up. Get up." I talk to my legs, "Legs, get moving. Legs, you're an antelope." It's a matter of mind over matter. You have to have the right spirit. And I'm out on the streets, seven-thirty A.M. sharp.

I'm wearing my Honorable Sanitation Commissioner badge they gave me from City Hall. I'm alert, I'm ready, I'm out there. And I got my whistle. My job is I help get parked cars off the street so they can bring in the sanitation trucks and the Wayne Broom, the big one—thirty grand for a broom! So when they show up, I go around blowing my whistle to get people to move their cars. I have a great time.

People are asleep. They're busy with businesses. They're busy taking time off from the businesses. They're busy having a good time. They're busy not having a good time. Whatever. I don't care. I blow my whistle. I'm all over the place.

I don't discriminate, either. I go after the sanitation men, too. The union got them a coffee break. Some coffee. They're having eggs, they're having bacon, they're having toast . . . they're having *French* toast. I kid them about it. And I go right into the restaurant and blow my whistle. They love it, they understand. Everybody loves it, everybody understands. It's the whistle that gets them. Sometimes I'm having such a laugh, I can't blow it. Then I get back to work. "Schleppers, get moving, let's go!"

This used to be a beautiful city. People cared. If you didn't pay your rent, the sheriff would come and put your furniture out on the street. But the poorest of the poor would come automatically and drop their pennies and nickels at your house and put you back into your apartment. That's neighborhood.

Now it's different. Things have gotten out of kilter— hard to say why. People seem to be lost in their own lives. I see them on the street, lost in their own thoughts. Not that I'm all that different. I'm a schlepp myself. I have as many bad habits as anyone. You should see my apartment. It's a mess. Me, Mr. Clean! But I'm trying. Let's try. It's all possible.

What can I tell you? I'm not a saint or a wise man. I'm not the Two-Thousand-Year-Old Man. I'm only the ninety-two-year-old man. Just a senior citizen. But what do I know that everybody else doesn't know? We know. I just go out there in the morning and blow my whistle. That's what *I* do. You do what you do. Me, I'm having a great time. Wonderful fun. And when people see how much fun I'm having, they have to laugh. What else can they do? Then I hit them with it: "Move your car!"

Contemplorary

❧❧

ABBOT ANASTASIUS HAD A BOOK WRITTEN ON VERY fine parchment which was worth eighteen pence, and had in it both the Old and New Testaments in full. Once a certain brother came to visit him, and seeing the book made off with it. So that day when Abbot Anastasius went to read his book, and found that it was gone, he realized that the brother had taken it. But he did not send after him to inquire about it for fear that the brother might add perjury to theft. Well, the brother went down into the nearby city in order to sell the book. And the price he asked was sixteen pence. The buyer said: Give me the book that I may find out whether it is worth that much. With that, the buyer took the book to the holy Anastasius and said: Father, take a look at this book, please, and tell me whether you think I ought to buy it for sixteen pence. Is it worth that much? Abbot Anastasius said: Yes, it is a fine book, it is worth that much. So the buyer went back to the brother and said: Here is your money. I showed the book to Abbot Anastasius and he said it is a fine book and is worth at least sixteen pence. But the brother asked: Was that all he said? Did he make any other remarks? No, said the buyer, he did not say another word. Well, said the brother, I have changed my mind and I don't want to sell this book after all. Then he hastened to Abbot Anastasius and begged him with tears to take back his book, but the Abbot would not accept it, saying: Go in peace, brother, I make you a present of it. But the brother said: If you do not take it back I shall never have any peace. After that the brother dwelt with Abbot Anastasius for the rest of his life.

Desert Fathers

A YOUNG MAN WHO HAD A BITTER DISAPPOINTMENT in life went to a remote monastery and said to the abbot: "I am disillusioned with life and wish to attain enlightenment to be freed from these sufferings. But I have no capacity for sticking long at anything. I could never do long years of meditation and study and austerity; I should relapse and be drawn back to the world again, painful though I know it to be. Is there any short way for people like me?" "There is," said the abbot, "if you are really determined. Tell me, what have you studied, what have you concentrated on most in your life?" "Why, nothing really. We were rich, and I did not have to work. I suppose the thing I was really interested in was chess. I spent most of my time at that."

The abbot thought for a moment, and then said to his attendant: "Call such-and-such a monk, and tell him to bring a chessboard and men." The monk came with the board and the abbot set up the men. He sent for a sword and showed it to the two. "O monk," he said, "you have vowed obedience to me as your abbot, and now I require it of you. You will play a game of chess with this youth, and if you lose I shall cut off your head with this sword. But I promise that you will be reborn in paradise. If you win, I shall cut off the head of this man: chess is the only thing he has ever tried hard at, and if he loses he deserves to lose his head also." They looked at the abbot's face and saw that he meant it: he would cut off the head of the loser.

They began to play. With the opening moves the youth felt the sweat trickling down to his heels as he played for his life. The chessboard became the whole world; he was entirely concentrated on it. At first he had somewhat the worst of it, but then the other made an inferior move and he seized his chance to launch a strong attack. As his opponent's position crumbled, he looked covertly at him. He saw a face of intelligence and sincerity, worn with years of austerity and effort. He thought of his own worthless life, and a wave of compassion came over him. He deliberately made a blunder and then another blunder, ruining his position and leaving himself defenseless.

The abbot suddenly leant forward and upset the board. The two contestants sat stupefied. "There is no winner and no loser," said the abbot slowly, "there is no head to fall here. Only two things are required," and he turned to the young man, "complete concentration, and compassion. You have today learnt them both. You were completely concentrated on the game, but then in that concentration you could feel compassion and sacrifice your life for it. Now stay here a few months and pursue our training in this spirit and your enlightenment is sure." He did so and got it.

Zen

In the Gospel story
where the apostles
get trapped
in that sudden and wild storm
on the Sea of Galilee,
we find a lesson
for today's peacemakers.

When the waves first rose
and the boat began to rock,
the apostles
worked hard and with hope
in order to survive
the storm raging around them.
But then they lost heart
and allowed the storm outside

to come inside.
It's easy to imagine
the apostles
as frantic, disconnected, out of control.
In their desperation
they waken
a peaceful Jesus
who questions their faith
and calms the storm
by projecting
   his inner stillness,
   his inner harmony,
   his inner peace.

Sometimes
we peacemakers
are more like the apostles.
We have allowed
the war around us
to become part of us.
Too often
we only worsen the situation
by projecting
our fear and guilt and despair.

What we want to do
is become like Jesus
—to have that still center
that nothing can disturb.
In that way
we are true peacemakers,
persons who project peace
wherever we go.

Pax Christi

WHEN THE BISHOP'S SHIP STOPPED AT A REMOTE island for a day, he determined to use the time as profitably as possible. He strolled along the seashore and came across three fishermen mending their nets. In pidgin English they explained to him that centuries before they had been Christianized by missionaries. "We are Christians!" they said, proudly pointing to one another.

The bishop was impressed. Did they know the Lord's Prayer? They had never heard of it. The bishop was shocked.

"What do you say, then, when you pray?"

"We lift eyes to heaven. We pray, 'We are three, you are three, have mercy on us.'" The bishop was appalled at the primitive, the downright heretical nature of their prayer. So he spent the whole day teaching them the Lord's Prayer. The fishermen were poor learners; but they gave it all they had, and before the bishop sailed away next day he had the satisfaction of hearing them go through the whole formula without a fault.

Months later the bishop's ship happened to pass by those islands again and the bishop, as he paced the deck saying his evening prayers, recalled with pleasure the three men on that distant island who were now able to pray, thanks to his patient efforts. While he was lost in the thought he happened to look up and notice a spot of light in the east. The light kept approaching the ship and, as the bishop gazed in wonder, he saw three figures walking on the water. The captain stopped the boat and everyone leaned over the rails to see this sight.

When they were within speaking distance, the bishop recognized his three friends, the fishermen. "Bishop!" they exclaimed. "We hear your boat go past island and come hurry hurry meet you."

"What is it you want?" asked the awe-stricken bishop.

"Bishop," they said, "we so, so sorry. We forget lovely prayer. We say, 'Our Father in heaven, holy be your name, your kingdom come. . .' then we forget. Please tell us prayer again."

The bishop felt humbled. "Go back to your homes, my friends," he said, "and each time you pray, say, 'We are three, you are three, have mercy on us!'"

Christian

❦

As a physician I had a man come into my practice with bone cancer. His leg was removed at the hip to save his life.

He was twenty-four years old when I started working with him and he was a very angry man with a lot of bitterness. He felt a deep sense of injustice and a very deep hatred for all well people, because it seemed so unfair to him that he had suffered this terrible loss so early in life.

I worked with this man through his grief and rage and pain using painting, imagery, and deep psychotherapy. After working with him for more than two years there came a profound shift. He began "coming out of himself." Later he started to visit other people who had suffered severe physical losses and he would tell me the most wonderful stories about these visits.

Once he visited a young woman who was almost his own age. It was a hot day in Palo Alto and he was in running shorts so his artificial leg showed when he came into her hospital room. The woman was so depressed about the loss of both her breasts that she wouldn't even look at him, wouldn't pay attention to him. The nurses had left her radio playing, probably in order to cheer her up. So, desperate to get her attention, he unstrapped his leg and began dancing around the room on one leg, snapping his fingers to the music. She looked at him in amazement, and then burst out laughing and said, "Man, if you can dance, I can sing."

It was a year following this that we sat down to review our work together. He talked about what was significant to him and then I shared what was significant in our process. As we were reviewing our two years of work together, I opened his file and there discovered several drawings he had made early on. I handed them to him. He looked at them and said, "Oh, look at this." He showed me one of his earliest drawings. I had suggested to him that he draw a picture of his body. He had drawn a picture of a vase, and running through the vase was a deep black crack. This was the image of his body and he had taken a black crayon and had drawn the crack over and over again. He was grinding his teeth with rage at the time. It was very, very painful because it seemed to him that this vase could never function as a vase again. It could never hold water.

Now, several years later, he came to this picture and looked at it and said, "Oh, this one isn't finished." And I said, extending the box of crayons, "Why don't you finish it?" He picked a yellow crayon and putting his finger on the crack he said, "You see, here—where it is broken—this is where the light comes through." And with the yellow crayon he drew light streaming through the crack in his body. We can grow strong at the broken places.

Rachel Naomi Remen

❧❧

THIS STORY WAS TOLD TO ME BY LI PUNG, WHO is now an old man with a thin gray beard who sweeps the path to the Taoist temple outside the prosperous village of Feng Shr Li. The village was not always so prosperous. Indeed it stood on barren land with only a few of the most rudimentary huts for the three or four families who eked out a living grazing a few scrawny animals and planting seeds in the dry, bony soil with a prayer for their growth. Most often their prayers were not answered.

This desolation is not new to China. Oh, it is a sad story and an old one. You who have a chance to know what is befalling the last forests of our modern times should consider it well, for China was not always bereft of forests. Forests hold the soul of the land and the greenness of their trees breathes life back into the air that we breathe together. The fluttering of their leaves like the white barked Chinese aspen has given rise to our greatest Chinese poetry. A thousand years ago, Li Po walked through such magical forests and meditated there until his heart was clear and his thoughts flew away like clouds before the wind. He wrote:

> We sat together, the forest and I
> Merging into silence
> Until only the forest remained.

Those among us fortunate enough to have entered a great and beautiful forest even once in our life cannot forget such a memory, the spring in our feet, the vibrancy of our breath and the joy of the cells of our body.

But now the forests of China are dead. They have been dead for five hundred years or a thousand years or two thousand years. There are so many of us. We have cut them down to build homes, for cooking and for warmth, to clear the land for yet one more field. And our land has become barren. The soil has run into our rivers. The ancient and winding yellow river was not always so, but for centuries now it has flowed yellow like our tears with soil eroding year after year from our barren lands.

Even young children know something is wrong, never seeing a great forest or hearing the cries of birds in its treetops and stopping for the noises of unseen animals. These children know something is missing. They hear ancient stories of the wolves and bear that lived in the forests, the stories of wild pig and Chinese mountain tiger. Their hearts too must long for a time when the forests were alive and when human life was more fully alive.

But all is not lost. The village of Feng Shr Li sits at the foot of the Feng Shu valley, which is again filled with glades of bamboo and running streams. Beyond them a whole range of low hills and mountains in the distance is covered by the sweet scent of Chinese forest. One day, my friend, Li Pung, sat down from his sweeping and told me how this forest returned.

At the end of the last century, there lived in this valley a man who the Taoists now revere as a dragon (which for the Taoists means the Spirit come alive on earth). Li Pung tells me his name was Tam Yang Bun and he was born in a desolate village half a province from here near the Lo Chu riverbed. Now they say that as he grew up he loved to visit the old Taoist temple along the dry riverbank of the Lo Chu. But he was a dutiful son as we are taught to be (those were still the days of the Confucian system that lasted here for more than two thousand years). As a dutiful son, he worked the land for his parents and being gifted with a mind of brightness began to write poetry and read at a young age. Sensing his potential, his parents hired a tutor to visit as was the custom in those days, to prepare for the Confucian examinations. Taking the lowest level at age twelve, he showed promise and the county itself supported his further studies. He passed successfully the medium and higher level examinations. Had he been born of a good family he might even have gone to the capitol to stand for the examinations known as the Emperor's Blessings. But he was not and so was prepared to work for the local magistrate.

A marriage was arranged to a lovely young woman from several villages away. The pigs were offered as is our local custom, an appropriate wedding ensued, and for one year they lived happily, soon graced by a young child.

Then the sorrows came. First his young child, Most Precious Gift, died of pneumonia and his father, though not old, died in the influenza epidemic that same year. His wife stricken with grief became thin and pale and she too died within a year. His old mother sought refuge in a small Taoist nunnery at the foot of the Tai Shung mountains and he was left with his heart as desolate as the lands around him. He could not return to his old home village. He left the magistrate, taking a few clothes and several volumes of Taoist poetry, disappearing up into the mountains.

Li Pung says he first met Tam Yang Bun when, as a young man, he went off walking and hunting in those desolate mountains beyond the Taoist temple that is now his home. He had walked far into the mountains after hearing at a farmhouse of a strange Taoist priest who was seen occasionally living far beyond the settlement. As he walked far into Feng Shu valley, he came upon an amazing sight—one whole part of the hillside was filled with young and beautifully growing Chinese shen trees, their delicate leaves fluttering in the breeze. He couldn't understand how this young and beautiful forest had begun so far up in the hills. He sat down with a certain joy among the saplings and saw a Chinese ground squirrel run behind the rocks nearby. For where the forest had begun to grow, the animals who came with it had begun to take shelter.

In the distance he heard a *ching-ching* and then nothing, and then a *ching-ching* again and then nothing. Rousing himself, he walked toward the sound and that is when he first met Tam Yang Bun.

Though thin and simply clad, Tam Yang Bun gave off an air that was neither blank nor impoverished. There was a grace and economy in his movements and a stillness about him that belied his strength. His skin was dark from the sun and eyes bright and steady. He could have been any age from thirty-five to seventy-five, but this is often the case with those Taoist priests who have studied the immortal arts. Tam Yang Bun looked at Li Pung steadily for a minute or two while he approached and then returned to his work. He was carrying a curved wooden staff, a Taoist divining rod with a long brass point at its lower end. He would walk several paces along the hillside and then *ching-ching,* the staff opened a hole in the earth at a small level spot or place where the earth seemed receptive. Into this he dropped one or two of the small shen tree pods, gently covering the hole with a sweep of his foot, moving several paces away to *ching-ching* in another spot. It was steady, peaceful work and you could see that Tam Yang Bun had already planted a series of long rows along this hillside.

Li Pung sat and watched him for nearly an hour when finally he stopped and sat on a rock outcropping to rest. Li Pung brought his satchel of food to share, glutinous rice balls and vegetable paste, and offered them to Tam Yang Bun. They shared the lunch in peaceful silence. Finally Li Pung asked if he might stay with Tam Yang Bun for the afternoon. Tam Yang Bun replied simply by handing him a sack of shen tree pods with a great smile. Li Pung asked several more questions and, as an answer each time, received more silence than words. When Li Pung asked if

Tam Yang Bun had planted the entire young and beautiful forest in these hills and how long it had taken, Tam Yang Bun finally laughed and said: "The earth replenished herself with the help of the Tao."

This was to be the first of many encounters with Tam Yang Bun but Li Pung did not know it at the time. He knew nothing of Tam Yang Bun's life which would be revealed to him many years later. He only knew that he felt a peace and steadiness in this man's presence, steady like warm sunlight and receptive like mountain stream water entering dry earth. He sensed there was some simple power working here through the shen pods and the land and the *ching-ching* of the wood and brass pole and he knew it was part of the Tao he had sought.

Li Pung visited several times in the next few years. Once on a cold winter day, he came upon Tam Yang Bun standing like an enormous bird in the crane posture wearing only a modest bathing cloth. In the cold air, his deep and directed breathing sent a pulsating cloud in front of him. As Li Pung got closer he could see the shining of Tam Yang Bun's eyes and a remarkable glow upon his skin.

Tam Yang Bun taught him some of the secrets of caring for the forest. He showed him how to soak the shen tree pods in a spring for two days to soften them for planting and rapid growth. He created a small orchard and an upland nursery for hundreds of new saplings. Always when Li Pung returned, the forest was growing and new hillsides were covered with saplings. The streams seemed fuller with moisture and the young forest rustled with wildlife as if the animals had felt the hospitality return again to the land. Mouse deer were sighted and other animals from the high mountains began to return to the hills around Feng Shu valley. Li Pung felt in this forest as if he were entering a graceful and ancient Chinese scroll, the watercolors of mountains and wilderness painted by the masters of old.

Li Pung, still a young man, then moved to one of the eight central provinces to continue his studies of the Analects and philosophies of the middle kingdom. Even as he studied, the last of the Confucian examinations were being held and from a distance came news of the Boxer Rebellion. There were rumors of gunboats and of wars over tea and opium as some great new forces swept over the land of China.

Soon the new nation was in chaos, the armies of warlords were fighting from many sides and many factions. Revolution completed its process and Sun Yat Sen was made president. It was during this period that Li Pung was to be married. He played a small role in the revolution and spent a short time in the revolutionary student movement, long enough to know he did not have to follow the ways of his parents, nor take the bride assigned to him by traditional village custom. He recognized that what his parents wanted of him did not fit his true nature.

With such upheaval in China, Li Pung longed to return to his home. He did so and found his village much unchanged but strangely more prosperous. The streams that had been small or nonexistent had more water coursing through them. There were new dikes and water was led across newly planted fields, somehow more fertile than he remembered. The land was softer, more alive and less desolate. Up in the hills, Tam Yang Bun continued his work as if the great rebellion had not happened. He continued his planting of several large hillsides, of a whole mountainside, then moving on to other land further back in the valley. He had now added Chinese alder, whose tender bark makes fine food for the increasing numbers of small deer and other animals, to the forests. It was not many days before Li Pung climbed into these mountains to look for his friend. The shade and moisture of the trees had somehow grown and brought with them their sisters, the clouds, and rivulets of water moved in the ground where the forest had matured, a moisture that brought the entire land alive again. As usual, Tam Yang Bun said little to Li Pung, but shared most generously his balance and timeless spirit. The forest was growing by hundreds of rai in several directions and, on some days, Tam Yang Bun took Li Pung on long walks to care for the areas of new growth.

Descending to his village, Li Pung felt drawn to the Taoist temple. Leaving the world of examinations and revolutions behind, he formally entered the temple and commenced his study of the Way. Over the first several years, the handful of monks there completed his training in the eight forms and began to demonstrate the unlearning which marks the art of the Tao. He heard the stories of Lao-tzu and Chuang-tzu and saw them brought alive by the monks in the Taoist kitchen and garden, in their mixing of herbs and in their economy of movement. He learned the Taoist postures and energy circulation meditation.

' Li Pung studied under the two oldest teachers of the temple and gradually made it his home. When Li Pung's parents died, he performed the ceremony to honor his ancestors and then committed his days to the Taoist order. For twenty-one years Li Pung lived in that temple. He would occasionally walk up into the mountains and visit Tam Yang Bun when he could find him. Some were now calling Tam Yang Bun by a new name, Mountain Tao. Others called him a tree spirit. The forests continued to grow.

When the next wave of revolution swept China with the Japanese invasion, there came the destruction of the

Emperor himself. China was again in great disarray and Li Pung stayed cloistered in the temple those years, wrapping himself in the practices of the Tao. When an interlude of peace descended on the land, Li Pung walked into Feng Shu valley to look for Tam Yang Bun. He was amazed at how beautifully the forest had developed, how dense the trees had become, and how Chinese maple, red-crested woodpeckers, civet cats, and even tracks of wild boar could be seen among the trees. He was also astonished to see the beginnings of several new villages below the valley. The land was no longer desolate and the streams flowed clear and fresh. Li Pung climbed into the mountains. He saw a poem written on a rock as he climbed, a favorite of the ancient master, Cold Mountain:

> When people see me,
> they all say, "he's a bit crazy,"
> not much to look at,
> dressed in rags and hides.
> Seated among the clouds,
> wandering like the moon on water,
> all I can say to those I meet,
> "try and make it to Cold Mountain."

He knew he was on the right trail.

Remarkably, Tam Yang Bun was planting the day he arrived. He could tell by the *ching-ching* in the distance. When he encountered his old friend, they embraced and Li Pung knew it was time to come and live with his master. He stayed with Tam Yang Bun for seven years and was taught to eat the herbs of the forest and the Taoist exercises of drawing the cream of heaven down through the limbs of the body. Every third moon they performed a ceremony to make the oldest trees honorary monks of the Taoist temple. And in his years in the mountains, Li Pung learned the story of Tam Yang Bun's early sorrows and his mastery of the Tao. He learned from Tam Yang Bun's own teachers, the wind, the rocks, and the trees. He learned a harmony so deep it could not be called by any name. The two men lived together in the Tao and *ching-ching* became their music. They lived as Lao-tzu taught,

> The spirit of the valley never dies, it is called
> the subtle and the profoundly receptive.
> To hold and fill to overflowing is not as good
> as to stop in time.
> The best of humans is like water. Water is
> good, it benefits all things and does not
> compete with them. The wise man places
> himself in the background and finds him-
> self in the foreground.
> He lets go of the spirit and the spirit moves
> through him.

Then Li Pung fell ill and could not remain in the mountains. Even the Tao has its seasons and difficulties. He returned to the monastery. Now over ten thousand rai had been reclaimed and planted. The new villages were prospering, small dikes and paddies shone in the morning sun. Goats and pigs squealed under the houses and there was the laughter of children as new families thrived on this once desolate land. The village had built a fine new school and the children were already accustomed to white rice from the paddy, forgetting the days when glutinous mountain rice was all that would grow. There was a singing like springtime from the streams.

I, myself, who have been telling you this story was born at the end of Mao's great triumph. It is a sad triumph for me because few are left of our five million monks of the Taoist and Buddhist way. But a few old men like Master Li Pung were allowed to remain in the temples and some-how as a young boy, I too was called there. My heart went to join him and learn the way of Tao. So I have lived with him these last eight years and heard the stories and practiced the eight treasures. Several times I have climbed into the forest to look for Tam Yang Bun but there has been no sign of him. I thought perhaps he had died but then one day in the far distance, I heard the sound *ching-ching* of the immortal Mountain Way. And now I have decided to go into the mountains. It is also my Way. I write this story for you as I leave. Li Pung has taught me the secret of soaking shen tree pods and shown me the fire herbs that bring body warmth in winter. Sometimes I feel there is not much honor left for the Tao in our temples and I am called to these mountains, to the animals that roam there, to the sweetness of the forest valleys.

I know there is desolation where you live also. I know that your forests have been lost and that many of your friends do not know who they are. But the earth will not always be desolate and the Tao has its cycle of return. Perhaps one of you who reads this story will know the spirit of the immortals in your heart and go off to the mountains to replant the forests of this earth.

Taoist

TWO

The Courage
Within Us

EVERY GREAT JOURNEY, WHETHER AN ATTEMPT TO scale a mountain or to awaken the spirit, calls for great courage and steadfastness. To fulfill any significant quest or possibility in our lives we need to call upon inner resources of fearlessness, dedication, and perseverance. For in every great journey we enter into unfamiliar territory, and inevitably fear, doubt, and uncertainty will be occasional companions in our travels. Yet we must travel on.

Few great journeys are completed without the occasional detour or diversion. Again and again we make new beginnings in our lives, initiate new directions. The very unfamiliarity of our travels means that there are few signposts we can rely upon for reassurance. Inevitably there are times when we lose our way, make mistakes, or flounder in doubts about our ability to complete our journey. Part of bringing our journey to completion is learning how to accept difficulty with graciousness, how to grow through the mistakes we make. It is our own courage that allows us to find a place of serenity and truth amid the storms and difficulties.

It is the courage of the warrior that sustains us through these moments of darkness. Don Juan, a great Yaqui shaman, spoke of the difference between an ordinary person and a warrior, saying that to an ordinary person everything in life is seen as either a blessing or a curse, whereas to a warrior everything is a challenge. In embarking on great journeys and making new beginnings, we, too, are called upon to learn how to be a warrior—but a warrior with a heart. The qualities of the inner warrior that will serve us well on our journey are the qualities of focus, courage, and perseverance. The qualities of acute awareness and inner trust are fundamental to our journey's completion. A true warrior must learn to nurture these qualities and yet be beyond concern with either winning or losing.

This chapter tells of those who have been transformed by the difficulties and challenges they have faced and who have discovered how to touch the world around them with the power of their love and courage. Through extending an openhearted welcome to difficulties, we, too, can learn to love more deeply and to see more clearly. The power of our courage opens our eyes to the discovery of light amid darkness, a freshness of vision.

The stories that follow can inspire us to look at our own journey. What are the hardships and obstacles we are struggling with in our journey at this moment in our lives? How do we meet failure, loss, and disappointment? Can we open our hearts to accept with grace and love the inevitable challenges? What are the opportunities to discover new depths of wisdom and compassion in the face of difficulty?

A BROTHER CAME TO ABBA POEMEN AND SAID: Abba, a variety of thoughts are coming into my mind and I am in danger. The old man took him out in the air and said, "Open your robe and take hold of the wind." And he answered, "No, I cannot do it." The old man said, "If you cannot do it, neither can you prevent those thoughts from coming in. But what you should do is to stand firm against them."

Desert Fathers

❧❧

DURING A TIME OF CIVIL WAR IN KOREA, A CERTAIN general led his troops through province after province, overrunning whatever stood in his path. The people of one town, knowing that he was coming and having heard tales of his cruelty, all fled into the mountains. The general arrived in the empty town with his troops and sent them out to search the town. Some of the soldiers came back and reported that only one person remained, a Zen priest. The general strode over to the temple, walked in, pulled out his sword, and said, "Don't you know who I am? I am the one who can run through you without batting an eye."

The Zen master looked back and calmly responded, "And I, sir, am one who can be run through without batting an eye." The general, hearing this, bowed and left.

Zen

❧❧

THIS IS A STORY TOLD OF MOTHER TERESA OF CALcutta. After praising her extraordinary work, an interviewer for the BBC remarked that in some ways service might be a bit easier for Mother Teresa than for us ordinary householders. After all, she had no possessions, no car, no insurance, and no husband. "This is not true," she replied at once. "I am married, too." She held up the ring that nuns in her order wear to symbolize their wedding to Christ. Then she added, "And he can be very difficult sometimes!"

Christian Contemporary

IN THE SPIRITUAL COMMUNITY THAT G. I. GURDJIEFF led in France, an old man lived there who was the personification of difficulty—irritable, messy, fighting with everyone, and unwilling to clean up or help at all. No one got along with him. Finally, after many frustrating months of trying to stay with the group, the old man left for Paris. Gurdjieff followed him and tried to convince him to return, but it had been too hard, and the man said no. At last Gurdjieff offered the man a very big monthly stipend if he returned. How could he refuse? When he returned everyone was aghast, and on hearing that he was being paid (while they were being charged a lot to be there), the community was up in arms. Gurdjieff called them together and after hearing their complaints laughed and explained: "This man is like yeast for bread." He said, "Without him here you would never really learn about anger, irritability, patience, and compassion. That is why you pay me, and why I hire him."

Sufi

A ZEN MASTER WAS INVITED TO A GREAT CATHOLIC monastery to give instructions in Zen practice. He exhorted the monks there to meditate and try to solve their koan or Zen question with great energy and zeal. He told them that if they could practice with full-hearted effort, true understanding would come to them. One old monk raised his hand. "Master," he said, "our way of prayer is different than this. We have been meditating and praying in the simplest fashion without effort, waiting instead to be illuminated by the grace of God. In Zen is there anything like this illuminating grace that comes to one uninvited?" he asked. The Zen master looked back and laughed. "In Zen," he said, "we believe that God has already done his share."

Zen

R ECKON A MILLION LITTLE CRITTERS LIVE ALONG the spring branch.

If you could be a giant and could look down on its bends and curves, you would know the spring branch is a river of life.

I was the giant. Being over two feet tall, I squatted, giant-like, to study the little marshes where trickles of the stream eddied off into low places. Frogs laid eggs; big crystal balls of jelly that had pollywogs dotted all through them . . . waiting for the time to eat their way out.

Rock minnows darted to chase musk bugs scuttering across the stream. When you held a musk bug in your hand, it smelled real sweet and thick.

Once I spent a whole afternoon collecting some musk bugs, just a few in my pocket, for they are hard to catch. I took them to Granma, as I knew she loved sweet smells. She always put honeysuckle in her lye soap when she made it.

She was more excited about the musk bugs than I was, might near. She said she had never smelled anything so sweet and couldn't figger how she had missed out on knowing about musk bugs.

At the supper table she told Granpa about it before I could, and how it was the brandest new thing she had ever smelled. Granpa was struck dumfounded. I let him smell them and he said he had lived seventy odd years, total unaware of such a smell.

Granma said I had done right, for when you come on something that is good, first thing to do is share it with whoever you can find; that way, the good spreads out to where no telling it will go. Which is right.

I got pretty wet, splashing in the spring branch, but Granma never said anything. Cherokees never scolded their children for having anything to do with the woods.

I would go far up the spring branch, wading the clear water, bending low through the green feather curtains of the weeping willows that hung down, trailing branch tips in the current. Water ferns made green lace that curved over the stream and offered holding places for the little umbrella spiders.

These little fellers would tie one end of a thin cable to the fern branch, then leap into the air, spilling out more cable in an umbrella and try to make it across to a fern branch on the other side. If he made it, he would tie the cable and jump back—back and forth—until he had a pearly looking net spread over the spring.

These were gritty little fellers. If they fell in the water, they got swept along in rapids and had to fight to stay on top and make it to the bank before a brook minnow got them.

I squatted in the middle of the spring branch and watched one little spider trying to get his cable across. He had determined that he was going to have the widest pearl net anywheres up and down the whole spring branch; and he picked a wide place. He would tie his cable, jump in the air and fall in the water. He'd get swept downstream, fighting for his life, crawl out on the bank and come back to that same fern. Then he'd try again.

The third time he come back to the fern and walked out on the end and laid down, crossing his front arms under his chin, to study the water. I figured he was might near give out—I was, and my bottom was numbing cold from squatting in the spring branch. He laid there thinking and studying. In a minute he got a thought, and commenced to jump up and down on the fern. Up and down. The fern got to rising and falling. He kept at it, jumping to move the fern down and riding it back up. Then, of a sudden, when the fern rose high, he jumped, letting out his umbrella—and he made it.

He was fired up proud and leapt around after he made it, until he nearly fell off. His pearl net become the widest I ever saw.

I got to know the spring branch, following it up the hollow: the dip swallows that hung sack nests in the willows and fussed at me until they got to know me—then they would stick out their heads and talk; the frogs that sung all along the banks, but would hush when I moved close, until Granpa told me that frogs can feel the ground shake when you walk. He showed me how the Cherokee walks, not heel down, but toe down, slipping the moccasins on the ground. Then I could come right up, and set down beside a frog and he would keep singing.

Following the spring branch was how I found the secret place. It was a little ways up the side of the mountain and hemmed in with laurel. It was not very big, a grass knoll with an old sweet gum tree bending down. When I saw it, I knew it was my secret place, and so I went there a whole lot.

Ol' Maud taken to going with me. She liked it too, and we would sit under the sweet gum and listen—and watch.

Ol' Maud never made a sound in the secret place. She knew it was secret.

Once in the late afternoon me and ol' Maud was sitting with our backs against the sweet gum and watching when I saw a flicker of something move a ways off. It was Granma. She had passed not far from us. But I figured she hadn't seen my secret place atall or she would of said something.

Granma could move quieter than a whisper through wood leaves. I followed her and she was root gathering. I caught up to help, and me and Granma set down on a log to sort the roots out. I reckined I was too young to keep a secret, for I had to tell Granma about my place. She wasn't surprised—which surprised me.

Granma said all Cherokees had a secret place. She told me she had one and Granpa had one. She said she had never asked, but she believed Granpa's was on top of the mountain, on the high trail. She said she reckined most everybody had a secret place, but she couldn't be certain, as she had never made inquiries of it. Granma said it was necessary. Which made me feel right good about having one.

Granma said everybody has two minds. One of the minds has to do with the necessaries for body living. You had to use it to figure how to get shelter and eating and such like for the body. She said you had to use it to mate and have young'uns and such. She said we had to have that mind so as we could carry on. But she said we had another mind that had nothing to do with such. She said it was the spirit mind.

Granma said if you used the body-living mind to think greedy or mean; if you was always cuttin' at folks with it and figuring how to material profit off'n them ... then you would shrink up your spirit mind to a size no bigger'n a hickor'nut.

48

Granma said that when your body died, the body-living mind died with it, and if that's the way you had thought all your life there you was, stuck with a hickor'-nut spirit, as the spirit mind was all that lived when everything else died. Then, Granma said, when you was born back—as you was bound to be—then, there you was, born with a hickor'nut spirit mind that had practical no understanding of anything.

Then it might shrink up to the size of a pea and could disappear, if the body-living mind took over total. In such case, you lose your spirit complete.

That's how you become dead people. Granma said you could easy spot dead people. She said dead people when they looked at a woman saw nothing but dirty; when they looked at other people they saw nothing but bad; when they looked at a tree they saw nothing but lumber and profit; never beauty. Granma said they was dead people walking around.

Granma said that the spirit mind was like any other muscle. If you used it, it got bigger and stronger. She said the only way it could get that way was using it to understand, but you couldn't open the door to it until you quit being greedy and such with your body mind. Then understanding commenced to take up, and the more you tried to understand, the bigger it got.

Natural, she said, understanding and love was the same thing; except folks went at it back'ards too many times, trying to pretend they loved things when they didn't understand them. Which can't be done.

I see right out that I was going to commence trying to understand practical everybody, for I sure didn't want to come up with a hickor'nut spirit.

Granma said your spirit mind could get so big and powerful that you would eventually know all about your past body lives and would get to where you could come out with no body death atall.

Granma said I could watch some of how it worked from my secret place. In the spring when everything is born (and always, when anything is born, even an idea), there's fret and fuss. There's spring storms like a baby borning in blood and pain. Granma said it was the spirits kicking up a fuss at having to get back into material forms again.

Then there was the summer—our growed-up lives—and autumn when we got older and had that peculiar feeling in our spirits of being back in time. Some folks called it nostalgia and sadness. The winter with everything dead or seeming to be, like our bodies when they die, but born again just like the spring. Granma said the Cherokees knew, and had learned it long ago.

Granma said I would come to know that the old sweet gum tree in my secret place had a spirit too. Not a spirit of humans, but a tree spirit. She said her Pa had taught her all about it.

Granma's Pa was called Brown Hawk. She said his understanding was deep. He could feel the tree-thought. Once, she said, when she was a little girl, her Pa was troubled and said the white oaks on the mountain near them were excited and scared. He spent much time on the mountain, walking among the oaks. They were of much beauty, tall and straight. They wasn't selfish, allowing ground for sumach and persimmon, and hickory and chestnut to feed the wild things. Not being selfish gave them much spirit and the spirit was strong.

Granma said her Pa got so worried about the oaks that he would walk amongst them at night, for he knew something was wrong.

Then, early one morning, as the sun broke the mountain ridge, Brown Hawk watched while lumbermen moved through the white oaks, marking and figuring how to cut all of them down. When they left, Brown Hawk said, the white oaks commenced to cry. And he could not sleep. So he watched the lumbermen. They built a road up to the mountain over which to bring their wagons.

Granma said her Pa talked to the Cherokees and they determined to save the white oaks. She said at night, when the lumbermen would leave and go back to the settlement, the Cherokees would dig up the road, hacking deep trenches across it. The women and children helped.

The next morning, the lumbermen came back and spent all day fixing the road. But that night, the Cherokees dug it up again. This went on for the next two days and nights; then the lumbermen put up guards on the road with guns. But they could not guard all the road, and the Cherokees dug trenches where they could.

Granma said it was a hard struggle and they grew very tired. Then one day, as the lumbermen were working on the road, a giant white oak fell across a wagon. It killed two mules and smashed the wagon. She said it was a fine, healthy white oak and had no reason to fall, but it did.

The lumbermen gave up trying to build the road. Spring rains set in . . . and they never came back.

Granma said the moon waxed full, and they held a celebration in the great stand of white oaks. They danced in the full yellow moon, and the white oaks sang and touched their branches together, and touched the Cherokee. Granma said they sang a death chant for the white oak who had given his life to save others, and she said the feeling was so strong that it almost picked her up off the mountain.

"Little Tree," she said, "these things you must not tell, for it will not help to tell them in this world that is the white man's. But you must know. And so I have told you."

I knew then why we only used the logs that the spirit had left for our fireplace. I knew the life of the forest . . . and the mountains.

Granma said that her Pa had such understanding that she knew he would be strong . . . where he would know, in his next body life. She said she hoped soon she would be strong, too; then she would know him, and their spirits would know.

Granma said that Granpa was moving closer to the understanding without knowing it, and they would be together, always, their spirits knowing.

I asked Granma, reckin if I could get that way so I wouldn't be left behind.

She taken my hand. We walked a long way down the trail before she answered. She said for me always to try to understand. She said I would get there too, and I might even be ahead of her.

I said I didn't care a thing in the world about being ahead. It would suit me might near total if I could just catch up. It was kind of lonesome, always being left behind.

Forrest Carter

❧❧

ONCE, TRUTH AND FALSEHOOD MET AT A CROSS-roads, and after they had greeted each other, Falsehood asked Truth how the world went with him. "How goes it with me?" said Truth. "Each year worse than the last." "I can see the plight you are in," said Falsehood, glancing at Truth's ragged clothes, "Why, even your breath stinks." "Not a bite has passed my lips these three days," said Truth. "Wherever I go, I get troubles, not only for myself, but for the few who love me still. It's no way to live, this." "You have only yourself to blame," said Falsehood to him. "Come with me. You'll see better days, dress in fine clothes like mine, and eat plenty, only you must not gainsay anything I say."

Truth consented, just that once, to go and eat with Falsehood because he was so hungry he could hardly keep upright. They set out together and came to a great city, went into the best hotel, which was full of people, and sat and ate of the best. When many hours had gone by, and most of the people had gone, Falsehood rapped with his fist on the table, and the hotelkeeper himself came up to see to their wants, for Falsehood looked like a great nobleman. He asked what they desired.

"How much longer am I to wait for the change from the sovereign I gave the boy who sets the table?" said Falsehood. The host called the boy, who said that he had had no sovereign. Then Falsehood grew angry and began to shout, saying he would never have believed that such a hotel would rob the people who went in there to eat, but he would bear it in mind another time, and he threw a sovereign at the hotelkeeper. "There," he said, "bring me the change."

Fearing that his hotel would get a bad name, the hotelkeeper would not take the sovereign, but gave change from the reputed sovereign of the argument, and boxed the ears of the boy who could not remember taking the coin. The boy began to cry and protest that he had not had the sovereign, but as no one believed him, he sighed deeply and said, "Alas, where are you, unhappy Truth? Are you no more?"

"No, I'm here," said Truth, through clenched teeth, "but I had not eaten for three days, and now I may not speak. You must find the right of it by yourself, my tongue is tied."

When they got outside, Falsehood burst out laughing and said to Truth, "You see how I contrive things?"

"Better I should die of hunger," said Truth, "than do the things you do." So they parted forever.

Traditional Fable

AMMA SYNCLETICA SAID: IN THE BEGINNING, THERE is struggle and a lot of work for those who come near to God. But after that, there is indescribable joy. It is just like building a fire: at first it's smoky and your eyes water, but later you get the desired result. Thus we ought to light the divine fire in ourselves with tears and effort.

Desert Fathers

A MAN WALKING THROUGH THE FOREST SAW A FOX that had lost its legs and wondered how it lived. Then he saw a tiger come in with game in its mouth. The tiger had its fill and left the rest of the meat for the fox.

The next day God fed the fox by means of the same tiger. The man began to wonder at God's greatness and said to himself, "I too shall just rest in a corner with full trust in the Lord and he will provide me with all I need."

He did this for many days but nothing happened, and he was almost at death's door when he heard a voice say, "O you who are in the path of error, open your eyes to the truth! Follow the example of the tiger and stop imitating the disabled fox."

Sufi

"MULLA, MULLA, MY SON HAS WRITTEN FROM THE Abode of Learning to say that he has completely finished his studies!"

"Console yourself, madam, with the thought that God will no doubt send him more."

Sufi

❧

I HAVE ONLY THREE ENEMIES. MY FAVORITE ENEMY, the one most easily influenced for the better, is the British Empire. My second enemy, the Indian people, is far more difficult. But my most formidable opponent is a man named Mohandas K. Gandhi. With him I seem to have very little influence.

Mahatma Gandhi

❧

THE FOLLOWING IS EXCERPTED FROM THE TRUE *tale called "The Relation of Cabeza de Vaca as it was written to His Majesty, The King of Spain." In it he recounts a remarkable journey on foot across the continent from Florida to Mexico City in the sixteenth century. This tale was widely circulated at that time. Cabeza de Vaca must also have sensed that he was writing through the centuries to the greater human audience. I have added some lines here that frame his narrative and allow him to speak to us directly. Eighty percent of the narrative is still his own, and I can only hope he would be pleased with that which has been added.*

To His Majesty, The King of Spain:

As a result of the expeditions I have undertaken on your behalf as your loyal subject, and interested in the benefit of the world at large, I entrust to your throne this letter of import for the future. If you find it of value, Your Majesty, kindly place it among your royal documents to be preserved and revealed. Perhaps it will be of some benefit to your subjects in the new world some centuries hence.

In the name of your Majesty the King, and God,
Núñez Cabeza de Vaca

To the Descendants of Those Who Have Settled the New World:

When you read this letter it will have been nearly five hundred years since the first voyage of Christopher Columbus. Many of us followed in his footsteps inspired by conquest, by fame, by greed, or by a sense of adventure. In 1528, not long after Columbus, in the name of his Majesty, the King of Spain, I set sail in an expedition of over four hundred men, eighty horses, four ships, and a brigantine. My own rank was as Lord Treasurer of the expedition, headed by Panfilo de Navarez. Thus we headed for the New World.

In the eight years of journey that I have recounted to His Majesty, there is much to be remembered by future generations of Europeans who settle this land. In seeking a new home, we must suffer great uprooting and sorrow. Yet, if we seek a true home, we must find it first in our hearts. Otherwise, grave danger awaits. Although ambition and love of action are common to all, there are great inequalities of fortune, the result not only of conduct and accident but coming in the providence of God. In this way, we who sought to conquer this land have perforce learned differently, that to bring all these new peoples to be Christians, we must act like Christians ourselves. To bring people to be followers of Christ and to the obedience of his Imperial Majesty, it must be won by kindness which is a way certain, and no other is.

Prior to the expedition I had seen my share of the ways of man. I fought in the Battle of Ravenna, and in 1521 under the Duke of Medine-Sidonia I learned well the ways of human destruction. But it was in eight years of being naked and often hungry, of walking with three companions from Florida to Mexico City, across the entire continent of the new world, that I learned the power of the Christian teachings and the certainty to which they must be followed in the face of all that life brings us. This is the only way to create a new world.

I myself undertook this expedition by royal authority, firmly trusting in my conduct, my sovereign, and fidelity to God. While in all honesty my own ambition can be included in my motivation, I have learned so strongly that nothing good can come of such ambition, and the desire to conquer must be translated to conquering one's heart with the help of God. I only hope that those of you now living in this new land can yourselves take this to heart.

No expedition that had gone into the new world before us could have found itself in more dire straits than our own, or come to an end alike forlorn and fatal. We reached the coast of Florida with Governor Panfilo de Navarez after having lost half of our ships and men in a great hurricane while harboring in Cuba. Not long after we landed, we debarked with as many men in armor and horses as the boats that remained could contain. The great storms continued and many others of us died. The remaining were so lean and fatigued, that for the time there was little we could do to help one another. Our horses and armor proved of no avail against the swamps of Florida and the arrows of the Indians; our ships and ambitions proved of no avail against the great storms. As if that was not enough, the governor, our commandant, in his greed and ignorance, force-marched us through the swamps to the town of Apalachen. We had found pieces of linen, woolen cloth and bunches of feathers which appeared like those of Mexico. There were likewise traces of gold. Our governor then had the ships burned behind us, fancying himself Cortez, but we were entering a country of which we had no account and already had encountered such tragedy and adversity, so many storms and so great loss of men and ships since leaving Spain, that perhaps all senses had been lost to us and lost to the governor.

No matter what is said of battle and expedition, and no matter with what armor we prepare ourselves, our hearts are never prepared for the loss of our companions nor protected from the tragedies that follow our mistaken motivations. We must learn a new way of endeavor. I myself would have opposed the march and remained behind, and thus my courage would have been called into question, but I chose rather to risk my life and follow than put my honor in such position.

In short order on our march we came to a great river which we passed with great difficulty by using rafts and swimming. On the other side there appeared as many as two hundred natives. In conversing by signs, we attempted to force them to take us to a town, whereupon they insulted us with their gestures. We seized several and continued our traveling. On the seventeenth of June a chief approached, borne on the back of other Indians, covered with a painted deer skin. A great many people attended him, playing on flutes of reed. By signs we were given to understand we were going to Apalachen. We gave him beads and hawk bells and other articles of barter.

Apalachen was a swampy and squalid settlement of forty small houses made of thatch and wood. It was surrounded by large mangroves and bodies of water in

which so many trees had fallen as to render travel difficult and dangerous. In the town we found stores of maize
and a round small maize field. There were skins of deer
of three kinds, rabbits, hares, bears, lions and wild beasts.
In the surrounding waters there were ducks, mallards,
night herons and partridges abounding as well as many
falcons, sparrow hawks, merlins, and various other fowl.

About two hours after our arrival at Apalachen, the
Indians who fled from there came to us in peace, but
were retained by our governor, causing great conflict,
and a large number of them returned for battle the next
day. This was the last period of good food that we found.
We left Apalachen and our continued marches through
the swamps on horses and armor every day brought the
death of more of our men. The poverty of the land and
the unfavorable accounts of the Indians continually making war on us was such that at the end of twenty-five
days we had lost half our remaining men. The horses
doing no good, the governor commanded our cavalry to
dismount and charge the Indians on foot. The Indians in
Florida are archers. They go naked, are of admirable
proportions and great strength. In such trials many of
our men were wounded and our good armor was of no
avail. There were those who swore they had seen red
oaks the thickness of the lower part of the leg, pierced
from side to side by arrows. This is not so much to be
wondered at, considering the power and skill in which
the Indians are able to project them.

Through the misdeeds of our governor, we found
ourselves back at the coast not far from where our ships
had been burned. Disease and hunger had killed many
of us and the horses had been consumed one by one during our long march back. In great sorrow, the forty of us
remaining endeavored to build five small boats, caulked
with the fiber of palmetto and pitched with resin. We

launched these boats into the sea and after several days fell nearly mad for the need of fresh water. A storm arose and our thirst became so excessive that it put us to the extremity of swallowing salt water by which some of the men became so crazed that they suddenly died. The suffering and toils among us grew. How little hope we had of relief.

Under the storms a handful of us crawled ashore and were tended by kindly Indians. We commended ourselves to God and were taken by the next gathering of Indians to a small home where we were given something to eat. By the end of this period almost all our men were lost. The Indians fled in canoes, leaving us sorrowful and much dejected. We walked along the shore for some days and at one sunset the Indians seeing that we had not gone came to bring us food. When the Indians saw us in a plight so different from what it was before, they were alarmed and turned back.

I went toward them and called, and they returned much frightened. I gave them to understand by signs that our boats had sunk and many of our number had drowned. There on the beach before them they saw two who had died. The Indians, in sight of what had befallen us in our state of suffering, melancholy and destitution, sat down among us, and from the sorrow and pity they felt, they all began to lament so earnestly, that they might have been heard at a distance. It was strange to see these men, wild and untaught, howling like hoots over our misfortune which caused in us an increase of feeling and a livelier sense of our own calamity.

The Indians then took us to their habitations with many fires and began to hold dances which followed the wailing in order to cheer and soothe us as strangers, that we might less feel our loss. It is a duty, they communicated, among their people to mourn with friends in bereavement, and an act of respect. We Europeans and those in future centuries ahead might benefit by this deep empathy among humans that would be the basis for a greater and more fortunate culture, would it not.

We stayed with these Indians for not many days until their food ran out. The fish no longer yielded anything, and the houses being open to cold, the rest of our people began to die. A small party of our men left on the beach, though Christians in name, came to such extremity that they ate of our own dead. The body of the last one only was found unconsumed. This produced great distress among the Indians and much censure. They would have doubtless destroyed us survivors had not a disease of the bowels visited them as well. They ran away from us and we began to march through the swamps.

Finally there were but a few of us wandering, bleary, and we came to near starvation ourselves. We had lost everything, our ships, our armor, our horses, our protection and our friends. Indeed, our very clothes and much of our body had been taken from us. I'm unable to give suitable words to many of these privations and sufferings, so difficult indeed were they, but truly the worst shocks came to our souls as we saw the veneer of what we called civilization stripped from us, layer after layer, until we became cannibals, eating amongst ourselves. What had been Spanish gentlemen had shown itself to be a party of greed and ignorance and we marched causing destruction to ourselves and others until nothing of our old life was left. This we had done in the name of Christ. The moments of generosity of the savages, weeping with us and feeding us, was an illumination of the true human spirit. And I must say that with that spirit absent, no amount of ambition and adventuresomeness is worthy of us or is of any benefit. Heed this well as you settle and develop the new world.

Here we were, naked, stripped of everything we had relied on in our life. This was an inconceivable situation and yet one that became the forerunner of great renewal, for it is in weathering loss and leaving behind the old, that something new and indestructible can be born in us in the name of the spirit. This I found only through great privation.

Perhaps it is only in such circumstances that a man finds what is of true value. Perhaps when we have let go of all things, then the power of the spirit is free to move in us.

A period of extreme famine began for us and for the Indians all, for men, women and children. As food was scarce, disease increased among the tribes. The small band we were with traveled in a northerly direction. Now there were only four of us left, myself, Alonzo, Andreas and the black Moor. We were taken to an island where we feared to be given up completely or worse yet killed for the burden we caused upon the community. To see ourselves as a burden upon the community of Indians was an extraordinary vision, we who had come to convert and conquer and instruct. Thus it was that we prayed for their support.

The Indians kept food from us and instead brought us a number of their sick. They indicated that if we wished to eat we must cure the disease first. We had been observing their physicians, their practitioners cured by blowing on the sick, and with that breath and imposing of hands cast out infirmity. We grew hungrier and more concerned for our survival. Finally, in desperation we began to heal the only way we knew possible. Our method was to bless the sick, breathing upon them, and reciting Ave Maria, praying with all the earnestness to our Lord that he would give good health. To our astonishment, in His clemency he brought that to those whom we supplicated directly after we made the sign of the blessed cross over them. For this, the Indians treated us kindly and deprived themselves of food that they might give to us. Yet, so protracted was the hunger we experienced, many times we were three days without eating.

We traveled a long time suffering the cold and hunger with them and healing as best we could. The mosquitoes were poisoned and inflamed us. Passing through thickets our skin was broken and bleeding. At times we were treated like slaves. Many times they threw lumps of mud at us and put their arrows to our hearts saying they were inclined to kill us. Then they would demand further healing, and we hid from them our desire to go on.

When the seasons changed, there were berries to eat, and as the weather changed we were able to account to ourselves the great privations and conditions through which we had passed. Alonzo told me how his party of soldiers from whom I had been separated during our last storm had one by one begun to die of cold and hunger and that the lieutenant governor abused them severely and in the end that a number were killed through fighting with one another by blows of clubs and sword. I cannot say what made us different from the Indians who kept us. It is with shame that I think of what we call our Christian behavior and only wish that those who read this account might consider their lives in this light. In fact, by now we had experienced great generosity from the Indians. It was in our poverty and hunger that we began to learn the true meaning of faith.

The need for healing became so greatly necessary for our survival that even the Moor who had little sense for it had become avid in his prayer. It is said that faith heals all wounds. It was only in such fearsome circumstances that we were able to learn the true power of this faith. If you have not yet learned it in your life, perhaps coming to the new world has been of no avail to you.

After some period with these Indians, we commended ourselves to God and set forth to escape. Coming upon another tribe, the Indians came to us and one told Alonzo that he had a great pain in his head, begging him to cure him. After he made over him a sign of the cross and commended him to God, he instantly said that all the pain left and he went home bringing us fruit and pieces of venison. As a report of such healing spread, many came to us that night sick, that we should heal them, each bringing gifts of venison. We gave great thanks to God, for every day went on increasing his compassion and his gifts. After the sick were attended to, the Indians began to dance and sing, rejoicing, which continued for three days.

We asked the Indians about country farther on and they answered that the country ahead was very cold and there was little food. We set out alone for days of great hunger. For warmth we made four fires in the form of the cross and gathered bundles of straw to cover ourselves in the hole. Our feet were bare and bled a good deal, yet through the mercy of God the wind did not blow hard on us; otherwise we should have died. In all our labors our solace was to think of the sufferings of our redeemer Jesus Christ, and in the blood he shed for us, and to consider how much greater was the torment he sustained from his thorns than we did from the thorns and shrubs that tore at our skin.

In a few days we encountered many Indians who brought persons with cramps and unwell. They came that we might cure them. Each offered their bows and arrows and Alonzo particularly received them. We all prayed and God bestowed his mercy so that all got up well and sound, strong as though they had never had a disorder. This caused great admiration and the Indians, taking their friends in health, traveled westward with us.

There was fright among us that our prayers would fail us, not out of doubt in the Lord, who had brought us so far and so fulfilled our faith, but rather doubt in ourselves, being timid and believing that our sins would inevitably weigh and hinder us in performing cures. From this we could do nothing but deepen our prayers and devotions.

One day many Indians brought us to one of their chiefs. The persons around him were weeping and his house was prostrate, a sign that the one who dwelt there had died. When I arrived I found his eyes rolled up and his pulse gone, having all the appearance of death. I removed the mat with which he was covered and supplicated our Lord as fervently as I could that he would be pleased to give help to him. After this blessing, breathing, and a sign of the cross many times, the natives brought me his bow and offered me food.

The natives took me to cure many others who were sick. Then several Indians arrived reporting that he who had been dead and for whom I had prayed had gotten up and walked, had eaten and spoken with them. This caused great wonder and fear. Throughout the land the people talked of nothing else. Thus began an amazing period of our travels.

We crossed the continent, being passed from tribe to tribe, and people came to see us from many parts. They said that we were truly children of the sun. All those whom we treated told us they left well, and so great was their confidence that they would be healed by the power of the Lord that this indeed was the case.

A man was brought to me who had been wounded by an arrow and the point of that shaft was lodged in his heart. Probing the wound with a knife I opened the breast and at last drew the arrowhead forth. With the bone of a deer as a needle I made two stitches and with hair through the skin I stopped the flow. The wound I made appeared like the seam in the palm of the hand. After some days the whole town came to look at it for our fame spread far and wide and the customary dances and festivities followed and a place of privilege with them. For a long time now our whole understanding had shifted, and the Indians whom we had at first viewed as pagans and enemies were transformed in our eyes. Gradually they took upon a life to us that became valuable and honorable, as we took upon a life to them.

In each village we were received as great healers and the Indians came to take the measure of us. They are the most watchful in danger of any people I ever knew. If they fear an enemy they are awake all night long, and if they perceive anything of concern their bows are strung in an instant. I believe these people see and hear better and have keener senses than any other in the world. They are great in hunger, thirst and cold as if they were made for the endurance of these more than other men by nature and habit.

For those who follow me soon or in centuries after I wish to repeat these tales that they may learn the customs and values and benefits of living among these people which they will not find inconsiderable in such event. Take care and regard what you find in this new land.

We left there and traveled through so many sorts of people of such diverse languages memory fails to recall them. And ever as we went with Indians from one village, as was custom, they robbed and took from the new village, yet so many followers renewed themselves, that all that was missing was quickly replenished. Frequently we were accompanied by three or four thousand persons. And as we had to breathe upon and sanctify all food and drink for them, and grant permission, our very fortune became one of the last and greatest of our trials. Those of you who are seeking fame and fortune must beware of this, for the blessings which the Lord provides us in simplicity, are they not great enough for our hearts.

Under these difficult conditions we continued travel through mountains, towns, villages and tribes. And as I previously recounted to His Majesty, strange customs and remarkable insights arose. Always we were carried on the miraculous power of our prayer, by moonlight on desolate mountains, the passage of great and turbulent rivers, and always the healing and blessing. By now our arrival created such blessings that adjacent tribes who previously had been in battle with one another immediately made friends that they might come to meet us and bring to us what they possessed. In this way, we left all the land behind us at peace. We taught all the inhabitants by signs which they understood, that in heaven there was a man called God who had created the sky and the earth; him we worshipped and had for our master; that we did what he commanded; and from his hand came all good. So ready of apprehension did we find them that had we had the use of language to make ourselves perfectly understood we should have left them all Christians, and yet in some way these people had about them such a goodness as we did through the grace of our Lord in healing as if they were true Christians among us.

Finally, after eight years we passed through a territory which brought us signs of Europeans, and the natives became fearful. They related how the Christians at times had come through the land destroying and burning towns, carrying away half the men and all the women and boys as slaves. We found them so alarmed, they dared not remain anywhere, nor could they plant the earth, but preferred to die rather than live in the dread of such cruel usage and slavery they had received.

We began to fear that those Indians who had fought against these Christians would now treat us badly and revenge on us the conduct of their enemies, but when our Lord was pleased to bring us there, they began to respect us as the others had done and even somewhat more. Thus it was that I realized that to bring all these people to be Christians, they must be won by kindness which is a way certain and no other is.

We indicated that we wished to meet with the Christians and they took us to the edge of a range of mountains after dispatching messengers that instructed the rest of the Indians to march with us. Yet many fled, fearing that the Christians would kill them or make them slaves. Finally, we overtook four of them who were riding on horseback. They were astonished at the sight of us, strangely dressed as we were in the company of Indians. They stood staring at me a length of time so confounded that they neither hailed me nor drew near to make an inquiry. I bade them to take me to their leader.

After we had conversed, he stated to me that he was completely undone, that for a long time he had not been able to take any Indians. He knew not which way to turn, and his men had begun to experience hunger and fatigue. We sent our messengers to the Indians who came six hundred strong, bringing us all the maize in their possession in pots closed with clay. They brought us whatever else they had, but we wishing only to have provisions, gave the rest to the Christians that they might divide among themselves.

After this we had a great argument, for they wished to make slaves of the Indians we brought. To us this was unthinkable and we began to see with horror the so-called Christian ways which we were bringing into this new land. The Indians remained apprehensive and our countrymen became jealous of us. When we spoke with the Indians, they had become confused. Our Christian countrymen in their jealousy explained to the Indians that we had been lost and were now persons of mean conditions and small force, while they on horseback were lords of the land who must be obeyed and served. The Indians cared little for what was told to them and conversing among themselves said that the Christians lied; that we four had come whence the sun rises, and they from where it goes down. We had healed the sick, they killed the sound; that we had come naked and barefoot while they arrived in clothing on horses with lances; that we were not covetous or possessive of anything but all that was given to us we were directly returned to give, while the others had only the purpose to rob whomsoever they found, bestowing nothing on anyone. Even to the last I could not convince the Indians that we too were of the Christians, and only with great effort we got them back to their own residences and arranged for their protection from enslavement by our Christian brothers.

The Indians taking their leave told us that they would do whatever we suggested and would even build a town for us if the Christians would treat them well. This I affirm most positively, and if it has not been so, it is the fault of the Christians. God in his infinite mercy would be most pleased if these nations should be thoroughly and voluntarily subject to the Lord who has created and redeemed us all.

I must tell you that in two thousand leagues of travel on land, in boats and water, walking unceasingly for eight years with the natives, we found neither sacrifices nor idolatry, and we wept for the misunderstandings and slavery that was brought to them.

In the end we rode to Mexico City accompanied by twenty mounted men through a hundred leagues of country entirely devastated and filled with enemies. It was necessary we should have such protection. This was what was created in the name of conversion and conquest. Think of this, you who live in the land of the new world, and remember it. I, for one, found it the greatest and most heartfelt pain to confront the armored conquerors of which I had been among their number eight years before. It was as if I had died and been given rebirth anew as the child of the spirit that our Lord has spoken of, and what I could see of our civilization was neither Christian nor pleasant.

While the governor entertained us graciously and gave of some of his clothing for our use, I could not wear any for some time, nor could I stand to be closed in the dark walls of a house. For a long time I was unable to wear shoes, they brought such heaviness and pain to my feet. Most deeply I regarded the loss of the openness of my senses, the smell and taste of the sun and the winds and the openness of the land on which we had passed. I deeply regretted the end of the camaraderie and the spirit of the Lord which had carried us from one village to another and which had protected us and all those with whom we had traveled.

It was horrifying to see that among those of my countrymen who traveled in the name of the Lord, this spirit was almost entirely absent. The power of greed, the notions of conquest and slavery, and the desire for gold were tangible and repugnant to me. So apparent was the danger and destruction they were causing that I declared out loud to the commandant and Your Majesty that no Indian should be reduced to slavery and that they could not hope for the favor of God in their expeditions if they deprived the natives of their liberty.

We had come to conquer, to enslave, and to use the people and the land and all therein, yet I learned so profoundly while barefoot and possessing nothing that it is not ours to own, that it is all the land of the Lord alone, and that we are simply given it as caretakers. How much suffering will come from our greed and selfishness I cannot tell. Among the Christians there was little desire to even assist one another, yet we called ourselves gentlemen. What kind of world will come from this I do not know, but this I can say: That greed and possession is not the way; that enslavement and destruction of the land will bring nothing but great sufferings; and that in creating a new world all things are possible but these things must be done from the spirit of the Christian heart. In no other way can we honor Christ on this earth.

Christian Spanish

THREE

A Little
Attention Makes All
the Difference

THE SECRET OF BEGINNING A LIFE OF AWARENESS and sensitivity lies in our willingness to pay attention. Our growth as conscious human beings is marked not so much by grand gestures as by extending loving attention to the minutest particulars of our lives. Every relationship, every thought, every gesture is blessed with meaning through the wholehearted attention we bring to it.

In the complexities of our minds and lives we easily forget the power of attention, yet without attention we live only on the surface of existence. It is just simple attention that allows us to listen truly to the song of a bird, to see deeply the glory of an autumn leaf, to touch the heart of another and be touched. We need to be fully present in order to love a single thing wholeheartedly. We need to be fully awake in this moment if we are to receive and respond to the learning inherent in it.

We may think of our lives as an endless stretch of time that extends beyond the horizon. We are easily lost in the memories of our past and the fantasies of our future. We tell ourselves that we have time to postpone opening our hearts, to defer our quest for connectedness. But our lives are unpredictable and our days uncertain. We don't know what time we will have. What other place can we begin to live with love and wisdom but here, what other time can we begin to open our hearts fully but now?

Attention is sensitivity, attention is connectedness. The attention we bring to this moment reveals both the joys and sorrows of our world. Wisdom inspires us not to retreat from this pain but to ask ourselves how we can participate in the healing of our earth, our communities, our world. We often discover that the greatest healing can lie within the smallest gestures; a loving touch, a caring word, the gift of a compassionate heart allow us to extend ourselves beyond the boundaries of our personal worlds.

Attention is also the vehicle that connects us with the changing rhythms of our own thoughts, feelings, and yearnings. Learning to listen inwardly without judgment or resistance is to begin to understand ourselves—it is the source of wisdom. Such attention can begin only in this moment we find ourselves in.

The gift of the stories within this chapter lies in their power to remind us of the difference our own attention can make. Who can we love today? What have we neglected to bring attention to in this moment in our lives? Are we truly listening, fully seeing? Is our heart open in this moment?

ZEN STUDENTS ARE WITH THEIR MASTERS AT LEAST ten years before they presume to teach others. Nan-in was visited by Tenno, who, having passed his apprenticeship, had become a teacher. The day happened to be rainy, so Tenno wore wooden clogs and carried an umbrella. After greeting him, Nan-in remarked: "I suppose you left your wooden clogs in the vestibule. I want to know if your umbrella is on the right or left side of the clogs."

Tenno, confused, had no instant answer. He realized that he was unable to carry his Zen every minute. He became Nan-in's pupil, and he studied six more years to accomplish this every-minute Zen.

Zen

A MODERN MASTER DESCRIBED HOW THE BUDDHA had encouraged his monks by stating that those who practiced diligently would surely be enlightened in seven days or, if not in seven days, then in seven months or seven years. A young American monk heard this and asked if it was still true. The master, Achaan Chah, promised that if the young monk was continuously mindful without break for only seven days, he would be enlightened.

Excitedly the young monk started his seven days, only to be lost in forgetfulness ten minutes later. Coming back to himself, he again started his seven days, only to become lost once more in mindless thought—perhaps about what he would do after his enlightenment. Again and again he began his seven days, and again and again he lost his continuity of mindfulness. A week later, he was not enlightened but had become very much aware of his habitual fantasies and wandering of mind—a most instructive way to begin his practice on the Path to real awakening.

Buddhist

ONE DAY IT OCCURRED TO A CERTAIN EMPEROR THAT if he only knew the answers to three questions, he would never stray in any matter.

What is the best time to do each thing?
Who are the most important people to work with?
What is the most important thing to do at all times?

The emperor issued a decree throughout his kingdom announcing that whoever could answer the questions would receive a great reward. Many who read the decree made their way to the palace at once, each person with a different answer.

In reply to the first question, one person advised that the emperor make up a thorough time schedule, consecrating every hour, day, month, and year for certain tasks and then follow the schedule to the letter. Only then could he hope to do every task at the right time.

Another person replied that it was impossible to plan in advance and that the emperor should put all vain amusements aside and remain attentive to everything in order to know what to do at what time.

Someone else insisted that, by himself, the emperor could never hope to have all the foresight and competence necessary to decide when to do each and every task and what he really needed was to set up a Council of the Wise and then to act according to their advice.

Someone else said that certain matters required immediate decision and could not wait for consultation, but if he wanted to know in advance what was going to happen he should consult magicians and soothsayers.

The responses to the second question also lacked accord.

One person said that the emperor needed to place all his trust in administrators, another urged reliance on priests and monks, while others recommended physicians. Still others put their faith in warriors.

The third question drew a similar variety of answers.

Some said science was the most important pursuit. Others insisted on religion. Yet others claimed the most important thing was military skill.

The emperor was not pleased with any of the answers, and no reward was given.

After several nights of reflection, the emperor resolved to visit a hermit who lived up on the mountain and was said to be an enlightened man. The emperor wished to find the hermit to ask him the three questions, though he knew the hermit never left the mountains and was known to receive only the poor, refusing to have anything to do with persons of wealth or power. So the emperor disguised himself as a simple peasant and ordered his attendants to wait for him at the foot of the mountain while he climbed the slope alone to seek the hermit.

Reaching the holy man's dwelling place, the emperor found the hermit digging a garden in front of his hut. When the hermit saw the stranger, he nodded his head in greeting and continued to dig. The labor was obviously hard on him. He was an old man, and each time he thrust his spade into the ground to turn the earth, he heaved heavily.

The emperor approached him and said, "I have come here to ask your help with three questions: When is the best time to do each thing? Who are the most important people to work with? What is the most important thing to do at all times?"

The hermit listened attentively but only patted the emperor on the shoulder and continued digging. The emperor said, "You must be tired. Here, let me give you a hand with that." The hermit thanked him, handed the emperor the spade, and then sat down on the ground to rest.

After he had dug two rows, the emperor stopped and turned to the hermit and repeated his three questions. The hermit still did not answer, but instead stood up and pointed to the spade and said, "Why don't you rest now? I can take over again." But the emperor continued to dig. One hour passed, then two. Finally the sun began to set behind the mountain. The emperor put down the spade and said to the hermit, "I came here to ask if you could answer my three questions. But if you can't give me any answer, please let me know so that I can get on my way home."

The hermit lifted his head and asked the emperor, "Do you hear someone running over there?" The emperor turned his head. They both saw a man with a long white beard emerge from the woods. He ran wildly, pressing his hands against a bloody wound in his stomach. The man ran toward the emperor before falling unconscious to the ground, where he lay groaning. Opening the man's clothing, the emperor and hermit saw that the man had received a deep gash. The emperor cleaned the wound thoroughly and then used his own shirt to bandage it, but the blood completely soaked it within minutes. He rinsed the shirt out and bandaged the wound a second time and continued to do so until the flow of blood had stopped.

At last the wounded man regained consciousness and asked for a drink of water. The emperor ran down to the stream and brought back a jug of fresh water. Meanwhile, the sun had disappeared and the night air had begun to turn cold. The hermit gave the emperor a hand in carrying the man into the hut where they laid him down on the hermit's bed. The man closed his eyes and lay quietly. The emperor was worn out from a long day of climbing the mountain and digging the garden. Leaning against the doorway, he fell asleep. When he rose, the sun had already risen over the mountain. For a moment he forgot where he was and what he had come here for. He looked over to the bed and saw the wounded man also looking around him in confusion. When he saw the emperor, he stared at him intently and then said in a faint whisper, "Please forgive me."

"But what have you done that I should forgive you?" the emperor asked.

"You do not know me, your majesty, but I know you. I was your sworn enemy, and I had vowed to take vengeance on you, for during the last war you killed my brother and seized my property. When I learned that you were coming alone to the mountain to meet the hermit, I resolved to surprise you on your way back and kill you. But after waiting a long time there was still no sign of you, and so I left my ambush in order to seek you out. But instead of finding you, I came across your attendants, who recognized me, giving me this wound. Luckily, I escaped and ran here. If I hadn't met you I would surely be dead by now. I had intended to kill you, but instead you saved my life! I am ashamed and grateful beyond words. If I live, I vow to be your servant for the rest of my life, and I will bid my children and grandchildren to do the same. Please grant me your forgiveness."

The emperor was overjoyed to see that he was so easily reconciled with a former enemy. He not only forgave the man but promised to return all the man's property and to send his own physician and servants to wait on the man until he was completely healed. After ordering his attendants to take the man home, the emperor returned to see the hermit. Before returning to the palace the emperor wanted to repeat his three questions one last time. He found the hermit sowing seeds in the earth they had dug the day before.

The hermit stood up and looked at the emperor. "But your questions have already been answered."

"How's that?" the emperor asked, puzzled.

"Yesterday, if you had not taken pity on my age and given me a hand with digging these beds, you would have been attacked by that man on your way home. Then you would have deeply regretted not staying with me. Therefore the most important time was the time you were digging in the beds, the most important person was myself, and the most important pursuit was to help me. Later, when the wounded man ran up here, the most important time was the time you spent dressing his wound, for if you had not cared for him he would have died and you would have lost the chance to be reconciled with him. Likewise, he was the most important person, and the most important pursuit was taking care of his wound. Remember that there is only one important time and that is Now. The present moment is the only time over which we have dominion. The most important person is always the person with whom you are, who is right before you, for who knows if you will have dealings with any other person in the future. The most important pursuit is making that person, the one standing at your side, happy, for that alone is the pursuit of life."

Leo Tolstoy

A HASID COMPLAINED TO RABBI WOLF THAT CERtain persons were turning night into day, playing cards. "That is good," said the zaddik. "Like all people they want to serve God and don't know how. But now they are learning to stay awake and persist in doing something. When they have become perfect in this, all they need to do is turn to God—and what excellent servants they will make for him then!"

Chassid

Lord Shantih once came to a pond and stopped to look at his reflection in the still water.

"Is this reflection me?" he asked his companion.

"No, my Lord. It is but an image of you."

"And how does the water hold my image?"

"It holds you," said the companion, "with a skin like a mirror."

"And where," said Lord Shantih, "do we touch, this pond and I?"

His companion reached in the water and splashed Lord Shantih in the face.

Thomas Wiloch

Ryōkan never preached to or reprimanded anyone. Once his brother asked Ryōkan to visit his house and speak to his delinquent son. Ryōkan came but did not say a word of admonition to the boy. He stayed overnight and prepared to leave the next morning. As the wayward nephew was lacing Ryōkan's straw sandals, he felt a warm drop of water. Glancing up, he saw Ryōkan looking down at him, his eyes full of tears. Ryōkan then returned home, and the nephew changed for the better.

Zen

The whole family went out to dinner one evening. Menus were passed to all including Molly, the eight-year-old daughter. The conversation was an "adult" one so Molly sat ignored. When the waiter took orders, he came to Molly last.

"And what do you want?" he asked.

"A hot dog and a soda," she said.

"No," said her grandmother, "she'll have the roast chicken dinner, carrots, and mashed potatoes."

"And milk to drink," chimed in her father.

"Would you like ketchup or mustard on your hot dog?" asked the waiter as he walked away, taking the parents aback.

"Ketchup," she called out. She then turned to her family and added, "You know what? He thinks I'm real!"

Contemporary

❧❧

ONCE, LONG AGES AGO, THE BUDDHA WAS BORN as a friendly little parrot. He lived happily in the forest and delighted in flying among the tangled branches of the huge forest trees. Wherever he went, he greeted other creatures with joy. He was a happy bird, glad to be alive and glad to have been given the gift of flight.

One day the skies over his forest home darkened and, without warning, a terrible storm thundered down, flashing and roaring among the ancient trees. The wind howled, lightning crackled, and one old tree burst into flames. Soon the whole forest began to blaze as sparks blew everywhere. Terrified animals ran wildly in every direction, seeking safety from the burning flames and choking, acrid smoke.

When the little parrot smelled the smoke, he flung himself out bravely into the fury of the storm, crying out loudly as he flew, "Fire! Fire! Run to the river!" But though the animals heard his voice and many did make it to the safety of the river, what could the others do, trapped as they were by the flames and smoke? So, rather than flying off to safety himself, he continued circling over the raging fire, seeking some means of helping those who were trapped below.

A desperate idea came to him. Darting down to the river that flowed at the forest's edge, he dipped his body and wings into the dark water and then flew back to the fire, which was now raging like an inferno. Unmindful of the leaping flames, he dropped down low and rapidly shook his wings, releasing the few precious drops of water which still clung to his feathers. They tumbled down like little jewels into the heart of the blaze. Again he flew to the river and dipped in body and wings and again he flew back over the flames. Again and again he flew between the river and the forest, many, many times. His feathers grew greasy and ragged and black and his eyes burned red as coals. His lungs ached and his mind danced dizzily with the spinning sparks, but still the brave little parrot flew on. "What, after all, can a bird do in times like these," he said to himself, "but fly? So fly I shall. And I won't stop if there's even a chance I can save a single life."

Now some of the godly beings of the higher realms, relaxing in their palaces of ivory and gold, saw the little parrot below them as he flew among the leaping flames. Between mouthfuls of sweet foods, they pointed him out. And some of them began to laugh. "What a foolish little bird!" they said. "Trying to put out a raging fire with just a few sprinkles of water from his wings. Who ever heard of such a thing. Why, it's absurd!"

But one of the gods found himself strangely moved by what he saw. Taking the form of a golden eagle, he let himself be drawn down into the parrot's fiery path.

The little parrot was just nearing the flames again when suddenly a huge eagle with eyes like molten gold appeared at his side. "Go back, little bird! Your task is hopeless!" pronounced the eagle in a solemn and majestic voice. "What can a few drops of water do against a blaze like this? Turn around and save yourself before it is too late!"

But the little parrot would not listen. He only continued to fly doggedly on through the flames. He could hear the great eagle flying above him now as the heat grew fiercer, still calling out, "Stop! Stop! Foolish little parrot! Save yourself! Save yourself!"

But the little parrot only continued on. "Why, I don't need a great, shining eagle to give me advice like that!" he thought to himself. "My own mother, the dear bird, could have told me such things long ago. Advice," he coughed, "I don't need advice. I just need someone to pitch in and help!"

And the great eagle, seeing the little parrot flying so steadily on through the searing flames, thought with shame of his own privileged kind. He could see the carefree gods looking down from above as if life was just a game for others to live. He could hear their laughter still echoing, while many creatures cried out in fear and pain from the flames just below. All at once, he no longer wanted to be a god or an eagle or anything else. He simply wanted to be like that brave little parrot, and to help.

"I will help!" he said. And, flushed with these new feelings, he began to weep. Streams and streams of sparkling tears poured from his eyes and washed down in waves like cooling rain upon the fire, upon the forest, upon the animals, and upon the little parrot himself.

Deluged with the god's shimmering tears, the flames died down and the smoke began to clear. The little parrot himself, washed and bright, rocketed above the sky like a little feathered sun. He laughed aloud, "Now that's more like it!" Tears dripped quietly from all the burned branches and scorched buds, which began to send forth green shoots and stems and leaves.

Teardrops sparkled on the parrot's wings, too, and dropped down like petals upon the burned and blackened ground. Green grass began to push up from among the still glowing cinders.

Then all the animals looked at one another in amazement. All were whole and well. Up in the clear blue sky they could see their friend, the little parrot, looping and soaring and flying happily on and on. "Hurray!" they suddenly cried, "Hurray for the brave little parrot and for this sudden, miraculous rain!"

Early Buddhist

❧❧

ONE OF THE BEST EXAMPLES OF THE ATTENTIVE heart came after Gandhi's death, when the whole Gandhian movement was in disarray. Within a year or two of the establishment of India, a number of Gandhi's followers decided to have a nationwide meeting to see how best to continue his work. They hoped to convince one elder, Vinoba Bhave, Gandhi's closest disciple and heir apparent, to lead this conference, but he declined. "We cannot revive the past," he stated. After much pleading, they finally convinced Vinoba to lead their gathering, but only on the condition, as he requested, that it be postponed for six months, giving him enough time to walk on foot from where he lived to the meeting site, halfway across India, and listen as he went.

He began to walk from village to village. As he stayed in each village, he would call a spiritual meeting as Gandhi had done. He would listen to their problems and at times advise the villagers. Naturally, he walked through a series of very poor villages, there being many of them in India. In one, many people spoke of their hardship, of their hunger and how little food they had to eat. He asked them, "Why don't you grow your own food?" But most of them were untouchables, and they said, "We would grow our own food, sir, but we have never been allowed to own land." Upon reflection, Vinoba promised them that when he returned to Delhi he would speak to Prime Minister

Nehru and see if a law could be passed giving land to the poorest villagers in India.

The village went to sleep, but Vinoba, struggling with the problem, did not rest that night. In the morning he called the villagers together and apologized. "I know government too well," he said. "Even if after several years I am able to convince them to pass a law granting land, you may never see it. It will go through the states and provinces, the district head man and the village head man, and by the time the land grant reaches you, with everyone in the government taking their piece, there probably will be nothing left for you." This was his honest but sad predicament. "I wish I knew what to do," he said.

Then one rich villager stood up and said, "I have land. How much do these people need?" There were sixteen families, each needing five acres apiece, so Vinoba said, "Eighty acres," and the man, deeply inspired by the spirit of Gandhi and Vinoba, offered eighty acres. Vinoba replied, "No, we cannot accept it. You must first go home and speak with your wife and children who will inherit your land." The man went home, got permission, and returned saying, "Yes, we will give eighty acres of our land." That morning eighty acres of land were given to the poorest families in the village.

The next day Vinoba walked to another village and heard the plight of hunger and landlessness from its lowest caste members. In the meeting he recited the tale of the previous village, and from his story another rich landowner was inspired. He offered 110 acres for twenty-two desperately poor families and again was directed to get permission from his family. Within the day the land was granted to the poor at a meeting and celebration.

Village by village, Vinoba held meetings and continued this process until he reached the council several months later. In the course of his walk, he had collected over twenty-two hundred acres of land for the poorest families along the way. He told this story to the council, and out of it, many joined him to start the great Indian Land Reform Movement. For fourteen years that followed, Vinoba Bhave and thousands of those inspired by him walked through every state, every province, and most districts of India. Without any government complications or red tape, they collected over ten million acres of land for the hungriest and most impoverished villagers.

This was one of the greatest peaceful transfers of land in modern history. And it all began with an open mind and an attentive heart.

Hindu

FOUR

*Finding Light
in the
Darkness*

IN HUMAN LIFE WE LOOK FOR HAPPINESS AND understanding to bring light into our lives and our hearts. Often we look to the future or to some set of ideals, searching for the key to our wholeness and happiness as if it were somewhere else. Yet the place to find wholeness, light, and well-being is here and now, even in the midst of our difficulties.

There are moments in each of our lives when our personal world is filled with darkness. Tragedy, loss, bereavement, rejection, and failure are all common experiences. There is no living being who can avoid being touched by pain, no defense strong enough to make us invulnerable to the unpredictability of life's changes.

At times, attuning ourselves to the condition of the world we live in, we begin to believe we have entered into an age of darkness. We are appalled and horrified by the collective human capacity for violence and exploitation, or we despair over the seemingly inevitable destruction of our planet. We become distressed by the suspicion and alienation that are too often the hallmarks of human relationships.

A sense of our own vulnerability can leave us feeling overwhelmed and powerless. The insecurity born of these feelings then leads us to anger, blame, self-protection, and hostility. We may even attempt to anesthetize ourselves to life's experience, and in this numbness our isolation and pain increases.

In times of such darkness we find ourselves longing for an ideal future or seeking miraculous formulas to protect us from pain and conflict. It is not easy for us to accept that there is no cure for living. Seeking a perfection that conforms to our images or our imagination, we miss the perfection and the mystery that is here before us every day—the rising of the sun, the beating of the heart, the changing of the seasons, the miracle of human speech.

There is an art to learning how to live with life's challenges and hardships, to discover light amid darkness, and to heal ourselves and the world around us. Like any other art, the art of living in peace calls for both great love and discipline. We must be willing not to turn away from or shun the shadows in our lives but to turn toward them. This is the first and most significant step, for in turning, we begin to cast away our fears, despair, and self-doubt. It is not darkness that is our opponent but our rejection and denial of it. It is in our greatest difficulties that we find the world's everlasting, unquenchable light. As Saint John of the Cross said, "If a person wishes to be sure of the road they tread upon, they must close their eyes and walk in the dark." There we find true compassion and greatness of spirit.

As we turn toward the specific shadows in our own lives with an open heart and a clear and focused mind, we cease resisting and begin to understand and to heal. In order to do this, we must learn to feel deeply, not so much opening our eyes as opening the inner senses of the body and the heart. This means listening closely to the mystery that is right in front of us rather than to the ideas we have about things. As the great Tibetan doctor shows in this chapter, the power to listen with one's fingertips reveals the music of the body and the music of the spheres. This listening and opening sets our life free. Learning to listen with sensitivity, we discover new depths of calmness, new resources of energy and effectiveness. The shadows we regard as adversaries then become our most profound teachers. We learn to meet them with grace and serenity.

In that calmness we begin to understand that peace is not the opposite of challenge and hardship. We understand that the presence of light is not a result of darkness ending. Peace is found not in the absence of challenge but in our own capacity to be with hardship without judgment, prejudice, and resistance. We discover that we have the energy and the faith to heal ourselves, and the world, through an openheartedness in this moment.

The stories in this chapter tell of people who are beacons of light, like the young blind boy who discovers that all things are illuminated by an inner light, that they exude a radiance, and that in a most fundamental way what we are is light. Our true nature, our basic goodness shines when we stop looking elsewhere and discover that what we seek has been here all along.

We might ask ourselves, Who or what do we see as an adversary, an enemy in our lives? What obstacles or hardships are we struggling with, are we denying? Look at the darkest period of your life or at one of the greatest difficulties you currently face. What have you resisted in that difficulty or darkness? What have you not accepted that is true? How might you discover the wisdom of a Buddha or the heart of Jesus if you could accept what is actually before you, difficult though it may be? What freedom and light could come to your spirit in the middle of these very difficulties? Is there another way of being with darkness? How can we extend an openhearted welcome and grace? How can we see our shadows anew, in the light of awareness and compassion? It is here that we begin to heal.

MULLA NASRUDIN WAS OUTSIDE ON HIS HANDS and knees below a lantern when a friend walked up. "What are you doing, Mulla?" his friend asked. "I'm looking for my key. I've lost it." So his friend got down on his hands and knees too and they both searched for a long time in the dirt beneath the lantern. Finding nothing, his friend finally turned to him and asked, "Where exactly did you lose it?" Nasrudin replied, "I lost it in the house, but there is more light out here."

Sufi

❧❧

ON THE BULLETIN BOARD IN THE FRONT HALL OF the hospital where I work, there appeared an announcement. "Yeshi Dhonden," it read, "will make rounds at six o'clock on the morning of June 10." The particulars were then given, followed by a notation: "Yeshi Dhonden is Personal Physician to the Dalai Lama." I am not so leathery a skeptic that I would knowingly ignore an emissary from the gods. Not only might such sangfroid be inimical to one's earthly well-being, it could take care of eternity as well. Thus, on the morning of June 10, I join the clutch of whitecoats waiting in the small conference room adjacent to the ward selected for the rounds. The air in the room is heavy with ill-concealed dubiety and suspicion of bamboozlement. At precisely six o'clock he materializes, a short, golden, barrelly man dressed in a sleeveless robe of saffron and maroon. His scalp is shaven, and the only visible hair is a scanty black line above each hooded eye.

He bows in greeting while his young interpreter makes the introduction. Yeshi Dhonden, we are told, will examine a patient selected by a member of the staff. The diagnosis is unknown to Yeshi Dhonden as it is to us. The examination of the patient will take place in our presence, after which we will reconvene in the conference room, where Yeshi Dhonden will discuss the case. We are further informed that for the past two hours Yeshi Dhonden has purified himself by bathing, fasting, and prayer. I, having breakfasted well, performed only the most desultory of ablutions, and given no thought at all to my soul, glance furtively at my fellows. Suddenly we seem a soiled, uncouth lot.

The patient had been awakened early and told that she was to be examined by a foreign doctor, and had been asked to produce a fresh specimen of urine, so when we enter her room, the woman shows no surprise. She has long ago taken on that mixture of compliance and resignation that is the facies of chronic illness. This was to be but another in an endless series of tests and examinations. Yeshi Dhonden steps to the bedside while the rest stand apart, watching. For a long time he gazes at the woman, favoring no part of her body with his eyes, but seeming to fix his glance at a place just above her supine form. I, too, study her. No physical sign or obvious symptom gives a clue to the nature of her disease.

At last he takes her hand, raising it in both of his own. Now he bends over the bed in a kind of crouching stance, his head drawn down into the collar of his robe. His eyes are closed as he feels for her pulse. In a moment he has found the spot, and for the next half hour he remains thus, suspended above the patient like some exotic golden bird with folded wings, holding the pulse of the woman beneath his fingers, cradling her hand in his. All the power of the man seems to have been drawn down into this one purpose. It is palpation of the pulse raised to the state of ritual. From the foot of the bed, where I stand, it is as though he and the patient have entered a special place of isolation, of apartness, about which a vacancy hovers, and across which no violation is possible. After a moment the woman rests back upon her pillow. From time to time she raises her head to look at the strange figure above her, then sinks back once more. I cannot see their hands joined in a correspondence that is exclusive, intimate, his fingertips receiving the voice of her sick body through the rhythm and throb she offers at her wrist. All at once I am envious—not of him, not of Yeshi Dhonden for his gift of beauty and holiness, but of her. I want to be held like that, touched so, *received*. And I know that I, who have palpated a hundred thousand pulses, have not felt a single one.

At last Yeshi Dhonden straightens, gently places the woman's hand upon the bed, and steps back. The interpreter produces a small wooden bowl and two sticks. Yeshi Dhonden pours a portion of the urine specimen into the bowl and proceeds to whip the liquid with two sticks. This he does for several minutes until a foam is raised. Then, bowing above the bowl, he inhales the odor three times. He sets down the bowl and turns to leave. All this while, he has not uttered a single word.

As he nears the door, the woman raises her head and calls out to him in a voice at once urgent and serene. "Thank you, doctor," she says, and touches with her other hand the place he had held on her wrist, as though to recapture something that had visited there. Yeshi Dhonden turns back for a moment to gaze at her, then steps into the corridor. Rounds are at an end.

We are seated once more in the conference room. Yeshi Dhonden speaks now for the first time, in soft Tibetan sounds that I have never heard before. He has barely begun when the young interpreter begins to translate, the two voices continuing in tandem—a bilingual fugue, the one chasing the other. It is like the chanting of monks. He speaks of winds coursing through the body of the woman, currents that break against barriers, eddying. These vortices are in her blood, he says. The last spendings of an imperfect heart. Between the chambers of the heart, long, long before she was born, a wind had come and blown open a deep gate that must never be opened. Through it charge the full waters of her river, as the mountain stream cascades in the springtime, battering, knocking loose the land, and flooding her breath. Thus he speaks, and now he is silent.

"May we now have the diagnosis?" a professor asks.

The host of these rounds, the man who knows, answers.

"Congenital heart disease," he says. "Interventricular septal defect, with resultant heart failure."

A gateway in the heart, I think. That must not be opened. Through it charges the full waters that flood her breath. So! Here then is the doctor listening to the sounds of the body to which the rest of us are deaf. He is more than a doctor. He is priest.

I know ... I know ... the doctor to the gods is pure knowledge, pure healing. The doctor to man stumbles, most often wounds; his patient must die, as must he. Now and then it happens, as I make my own rounds, that I hear the sounds of his voice, like an ancient Buddhist prayer, its meaning long since forgotten, only the music remaining. Then a jubilation possesses me, and I feel myself touched by something divine.

Richard Selzer

WHEN WE ARE WILLING TO REST WITH TRUST ON this earth, the great force of life will begin to move through us. I saw this force of life in the midst of tremendous desolation some years ago in the dry and barren land of the Cambodian refugee camps, which I had visited to assist the refugees. After the Cambodian holocaust only parts of families had survived—a mother and three children, an old uncle and two nephews—and each was given a little bamboo hut about four feet wide, six feet long, and five feet high. In front of each hut was a little patch of land perhaps no bigger than one square yard. After only a few months of camp life, next to most of the huts in their little squares of ground, people had planted gardens. They would have a squash plant with two or three small squash on it, or a bean plant, or some other vegetable. The plants were very carefully tended, with little bamboo stakes for support. The tendrils of a bean plant would wind around the stake and up over the roof of the house.

Every day each refugee family would walk a mile and stand for half an hour in a long line at the pit well at the far end of the camp and carry back a bucket of water for their plants. It was a beautiful, beautiful thing to see these gardens in the middle of this camp in the dry season, when you could barely believe that anything would grow on such a hot barren field.

As these war-shattered families planted and watered their tiny gardens, they awakened the unstoppable force of life. So can we! No matter what inner difficulty or outer suffering we may experience, in tending to the darkness with compassion we will discover this same unstoppable life force.

Buddhist

IT WAS A GREAT SURPRISE TO ME TO FIND MYSELF blind, and being blind was not at all as I imagined it. Nor was it as the people around me seemed to think it. They told me that to be blind meant not to see. Yet how was I to believe them when I saw? Not at once, I admit. Not in the days immediately after the operation. For at that time I still wanted to use my eyes. I followed their usual path. I looked in the direction where I was in the habit of seeing before the accident, and there was anguish, a lack, something like a void which filled me with what grown-ups call despair.

Finally, one day, and it was not long in coming, I realized that I was looking in the wrong way. It was as simple as that. I was making something very like the mistake people make who change their glasses without adjusting themselves. I was looking too far off, and too much on the surface of things.

This was much more than a simple discovery, it was a revelation. I can still see myself in the Champ de Mars, where my father had taken me for a walk a few days after the accident. Of course I knew the garden well, its ponds, its railings, its iron chairs. I even knew some of the trees in person, and naturally I wanted to see them again. But I couldn't. I threw myself forward into the substance which was space, but which I did not recognize because it no longer held anything familiar to me.

At this point some instinct—I was almost about to say a hand laid on me—made me change course. I began to look more closely, not at things but at a world closer to myself, looking from an inner place to one further within, instead of clinging to the movement of sight toward the world outside.

Immediately, the substance of the universe drew together, redefined and peopled itself anew. I was aware of a radiance emanating from a place I knew nothing about, a place which might as well have been outside me as within. But radiance was there, or, to put it more precisely, light. It was a fact, for light was there.

I felt indescribable relief, and happiness so great it almost made me laugh. Confidence and gratitude came as if a prayer had been answered. I found light and joy at the same moment, and I can say without hesitation that from that time on light and joy have never been separated in my experience. I have had them or lost them together.

I saw light and went on seeing it though I was blind. I said so, but for many years I think I did not say it very loud. Until I was nearly fourteen I remember calling the experience, which kept renewing itself inside me, "my secret," and speaking of it only to my most intimate friends. I don't know whether they believed me but they listened to me for they were friends. And what I told them had a greater value than being merely true, it had the value of being beautiful, a dream, an enchantment, almost like magic.

The amazing thing was that this was not magic for me at all, but reality. I could no more have denied it than people with eyes can deny that they see. I was not light myself, I knew that, but I bathed in it as an element which blindness had suddenly brought much closer. I could feel light rising, spreading, resting on objects, giving them form, then leaving them.

Withdrawing or diminishing is what I mean, for the opposite of light was never present. Sighted people always talk about the night of blindness, and that seems to them quite natural. But there is no such night, for at every waking hour and even in my dreams I lived in a stream of light.

Without my eyes light was much more stable than it had been with them. As I remember it, there were no longer the same differences between things lighted brightly, less brightly, or not at all. I saw the whole world in light, existing through it and because of it.

Colors, all the colors of the rainbow, also survived. For me, the child who loved to draw and paint, colors made a celebration so unexpected that I spent hours playing with them, and all the more easily now they were more docile than they used to be.

Light threw its color on things and on people. My father and mother, the people I met or ran into in the street, all had their characteristic color which I had never seen before I went blind. Yet now this special attribute impressed itself on me as part of them as definitely as any impression created by a face. Still, the colors were only a game, while light was my whole reason for living. I let it rise in me like water in a well, and I rejoiced.

I did not understand what was happening to me, for it was so completely contrary to what I heard people say. I didn't understand it, but no matter, since I was living it. For many years I did not try to find out why these things were going on. I only tried to do so much later, and this is not the time to describe it.

A light so continuous and so intense was so far beyond my comprehension that sometimes I doubted it. Suppose it was not real, that I had only imagined it. Perhaps it would be enough to imagine the opposite, or just something different, to make it go away. So I thought of testing it out and even of resisting it.

At night in bed, when I was all by myself, I shut my eyes. I lowered my eyelids as I might have done when they covered my physical eyes. I told myself that behind these curtains I would no longer see light. But the light was still there, and more serene than ever, looking like a lake at evening when the wind has dropped. Then I gathered up all my energy and will power and tried to stop the flow of light, as I might have tried to stop breathing.

What happened was a disturbance, something like a whirlpool. But the whirlpool was still flooded with light. At all events I couldn't keep this up very long, perhaps only for two or three seconds. When this was going on I felt a sort of anguish, as though I were doing something forbidden, something against life. It was exactly as if I needed light to live—needed it as much as air. There was no way out of it. I was the prisoner of light. I was condemned to see.

As I write these lines, I have just tried the experiment again, with the same result, except that with the years the original source of light has grown stronger.

At eight I came out of this experiment reassured, with the sense that I was being reborn. Since it was not I who was making the light, since it came to me from outside, it would never leave me. I was only a passageway, a vestibule for this brightness. The seeing eye was in me.

Still there were times when the light faded, almost to the point of disappearing. It happened every time I was afraid.

If, instead of letting myself be carried along by confidence and throwing myself into things, I hesitated, calculated, thought about the wall, the half-open door, the key in the lock; if I said to myself that all these things were hostile and about to strike or scratch, then without exception I hit or wounded myself. The only easy way to move around the house, the garden or the beach was by not thinking about it at all, or thinking as little as possible. Then I moved between obstacles the way they say bats do. What the loss of my eyes had not accomplished was brought about by fear. It made me blind.

Anger and impatience had the same effect, throwing everything into confusion. The minute before I knew just where everything in the room was, but if I got angry, things got angrier than I. They went and hid in the most unlikely corners, mixed themselves up, turned turtle, muttered like crazy men and looked wild. As for me, I no longer knew where to put hand or foot. Everything hurt me. This mechanism worked so well that I became cautious.

When I was playing with my small companions, if I suddenly grew anxious to win, to be first at all costs, then all at once I could see nothing. Literally I went into fog or smoke.

I could no longer afford to be jealous or unfriendly, because, as soon as I was, a bandage came down over my eyes, and I was bound hand and foot and cast aside. All at once a black hole opened, and I was helpless inside it. But when I was happy and serene, approached people with confidence and thought well of them, I was rewarded with light. So is it surprising that I loved friendship and harmony when I was very young?

Armed with such a tool, why should I need a moral code? For me this tool took the place of red and green lights. I always knew where the road was open and where it was closed. I had only to look at the bright signal which taught me how to live.

It was the same with love, but let us see how. The summer after the accident my parents took me to the seashore. There I met a little girl my own age. I think she was called Nicole. She came into my world like a great red star, or perhaps more like a ripe cherry. The only thing I knew for sure was that she was bright and red.

I thought her lovely, and her beauty was so gentle that I could no longer go home at night and sleep away from her, because a part of my light left me when I did. To get it all back I had to find her again. It was just as if she were bringing me light in her hands, her hair, her bare feet on the sand, and in the sound of her voice.

How natural that people who are red should have red shadows. When she came to sit down by me between two pools of salt water under the warmth of the sun, I saw rosy reflections on the canvas of the awnings. The sea itself, the blue of the sea, took on a purple tone. I followed her by the red wake which trailed behind her wherever she went.

Now if people should say that red is the color of passion, I should answer quite simply that I found that out when I was only eight years old.

How could I have lived all that time without realizing that everything in the world has a voice and speaks? Not just the things that are supposed to speak, but the others, like the gate, the walls of the houses, the shade of trees, the sand and the silence.

Still, even before my accident, I loved sound, but now it seems clear that I didn't listen to it. After I went blind, I could never make a motion without starting an avalanche of noise. If I went into my room at night, the room where I used to hear nothing, the small plaster statue on the mantelpiece made a fraction of a turn. I heard its friction in the air, as light a sound as the sound of a waving hand. Whenever I took a step, the floor cried or sang—I could hear it making both these sounds—and its song was passed along from one board to the next, all the way to the window, to give me the measure of the room.

If I spoke out suddenly, the windowpanes, which seemed so solid in their putty frames, began to shake, very lightly of course but distinctly. This noise was on a higher pitch than the others, cooler, as if it were already in contact with the outside air. Every piece of furniture creaked, once, twice, ten times, and made a trail of sounds like gestures as minutes passed. The bed, the wardrobe, the chairs were stretching, yawning, and catching their breath.

When a draft pushed against the door, it creaked out "draft." When a hand pushed it, it creaked in a human way. For me there was no mistaking the difference. I could hear the smallest recession in the wall from a distance, for it changed the whole room. Because this nook, that alcove was there, the wardrobe sang a hollower song.

It was as though the sounds of earlier days were only half real, too far away from me, and heard through a fog. Perhaps my eyes used to make the fog, but at all events my accident had thrown my head against the humming heart of things, and the heart never stopped beating.

You always think of sounds beginning and ending abruptly. But now I realized that nothing could be more false. Now my ears heard the sounds almost before they were there, touching me with the tips of their fingers and directing me toward them. Often I seemed to hear people speak before they began talking.

Sounds had the same individuality as light. They were neither inside nor outside, they were passing through me. They gave me my bearings in space and put me in touch with things. It was not like signals that they functioned, but like replies.

I remember well when I first arrived at the beach two months after the accident. It was evening, and there was nothing there but the sea and its voice, precise beyond the power to imagine it. It formed a mass which was so heavy and so limpid that I could have leaned against it like a wall. It spoke to me in several layers all at once. The waves were arranged in steps, and together they made one music, though what they said was different in each voice. There was rasping in the bass and bubbling in the top register. I didn't need to be told about the things that eyes could see.

At one end there was the wall of the sea and the wind rustling over the sand. At the other there was the retaining wall, as full of echoes as a talking mirror. What the waves said they said twice over.

People often say that blindness sharpens hearing, but I don't think this is so. My ears were hearing no better, but I was making better use of them. Sight is a miraculous instrument offering us all the riches of physical life. But we get nothing in this world without paying for it, and in return for all the benefits that sight brings we are forced to give up others whose existence we don't even suspect. These were the gifts I received in such abundance.

I needed to hear and hear again. I multiplied sounds to my heart's content. I rang bells. I touched walls with my fingers, explored the resonance of doors, furniture and the trunks of trees. I sang in empty rooms, I threw pebbles far off on the beach just to hear them whistle through the air and then fall. I even made my small companions repeat words to give me plenty of time to walk around them.

But most surprising of all was the discovery that sounds never came from one point in space, and never retreated into themselves. There was the sound, its echo, and another sound into which the first sound melted and to which it had given birth, altogether an endless procession of sounds.

Sometimes the resonance, the hum of voices all around me, grew so intense that I got dizzy and put my hands over my ears, as I might have done by closing my eyes to protect myself against too much light. That is why I couldn't stand racket, useless noises or music that went on and on. A sound we don't listen to is a blow to body and spirit, because sound is not something happening outside us, but a real presence passing through us and lingering unless we have heard it fully.

I was well protected from these miseries by parents who were musicians, and who talked around our family table instead of turning on the radio. But all the more reason for me to say how important it is to defend blind children against shouting, background music and all such hideous assaults. For a blind person, a violent and futile noise has the same effect as the beam of a searchlight too close to the eyes of someone who can see. It hurts. But when the world sounds clear and on pitch, it is more harmonious than poets have ever known it, or than they will ever be able to say.

Every Sunday morning, an old beggar used to play three tunes on his accordion in the courtyard of our apartment house. This poor sour music, punctuated at intervals by the metallic scraping of rails from the streetcars on the avenue nearby—these in the silence of a lazy morning created a thousand dimensions in space; not just the steep drop into the court and the parade of the streets on the ground, but as many paths from house to house and court to roof as I could hold with my attention. With sound I never came to an end, for this was another kind of infinity.

At first my hands refused to obey. When they looked for a glass on the table, they missed it. They fumbled around the door knobs, mixed up black and white keys at the piano, fluttered in the air as they came near things. It was almost as if they had been uprooted, cut off from me, and for a time this made me afraid.

Fortunately, before long I realized that instead of becoming useless they were learning to be wise. They only needed time to accustom themselves to freedom. I had thought they were refusing to obey, but it was all because they were not getting orders, when the eyes were no longer there to command them.

But more than that it was a question of rhythm. Our eyes run over the surfaces of things. All they require are a few scattered points, since they can bridge the gap in a flash. They "half see" much more than they see, and they never weigh. They are satisfied with appearances, and for them the world glows and slides by, but lacks substance.

All I needed was to leave my hands to their own devices. I had nothing to teach them, and besides, since they began working independently, they seemed to foresee everything. Unlike eyes, they were in earnest, and from whatever direction they approached an object they covered it, tested its resistance, leaned against the mass of it and recorded every irregularity in its surface. They measured it for height and thickness, taking in as many dimensions as possible. But most of all, having learned that they had fingers, they used them in an entirely new way.

When I had eyes, my fingers used to be stiff, half dead at the ends of my hands, good only for picking up things. But now each one of them started out on its own. They explored things separately, changed levels and, independently of each other, made themselves heavy or light.

Movement of the fingers was terribly important, and had to be uninterrupted because objects do not stand at a given point, fixed there, confined in one form. They are alive, even the stones. What is more they vibrate and tremble. My fingers felt the pulsation distinctly, and if they failed to answer with a pulsation of their own, the fingers immediately became helpless and lost their sense of touch. But when they went toward things, in sympathetic vibration with them, they recognized them right away.

Yet there was something still more important than movement, and that was pressure. If I put my hand on the table without pressing it, I knew the table was there, but knew nothing about it. To find out, my fingers had to bear down, and the amazing thing is that the pressure was answered by the table at once. Being blind I thought I should have to go out and meet things, but I found that they came to meet me instead. I have never had to go more than halfway, and the universe became the accomplice of all my wishes.

If my fingers pressed the roundness of an apple, each one with a different weight, very soon I could not tell whether it was the apple or my fingers which were heavy. I didn't even know whether I was touching it or it was touching me. As I became part of the apple, the apple became part of me. And that was how I came to understand the existence of things.

As soon as my hands came to life they put me in a world where everything was an exchange of pressures. These pressures gathered together in shapes, and each one of the shapes had meaning. As a child I spent hours leaning against objects and letting them lean against me. Any blind person can tell you that this gesture, this exchange, gives him a satisfaction too deep for words.

Touching the tomatoes in the garden, and really touching them, touching the walls of the house, the materials of the curtains or a clod of earth is surely seeing them as fully as eyes can see. But it is more than seeing them, it is tuning in on them and allowing the current they hold to connect with one's own, like electricity. To put it differently, this means an end of living in front of things and a beginning of living with them. Never mind if the word sounds shocking, for this is love.

You cannot keep your hands from loving what they have really felt, moving continually, bearing down and finally detaching themselves, the last perhaps the most significant motion of all. Little by little, my hands discovered that objects were not rigidly bound within a mold. It was form they first came in contact with, form like a kernel. But around this kernel objects branched out in all directions.

I could not touch the pear tree in the garden just by following the trunk with my fingers, then the branches, then the leaves, one at a time. That was only a beginning, for in the air, between the leaves, the pear tree still continued, and I had to move my hands from branch to branch to feel the currents running between them.

At Juvardeil, in the holidays, when my small peasant friends saw me doing these magic dances around the trees and touching the invisible, they said I was like the medicine man, the man with an old secret who heals the sick by mesmerism, sometimes at a distance, and by methods not recognized by medical science. Of course, my young friends were wrong, but they had a good excuse, and today I know more than one professional psychologist who, for all his scientific knowledge, cannot account for these incongruous motions.

With smell it was the same as it was with touch—like touch an obvious part of the loving substance of the universe. I began to guess what animals must feel when they sniff the air. Like sound and shape, smell was more distinctive than I used to think it was. There were physical smells and moral ones, the latter, so important for living in society.

Before I was ten years old I knew with absolute certainty that everything in the world was a sign of something else, ready to take its place if it should fall by the way. And this continuing miracle of healing I heard expressed fully in the Lord's Prayer I repeated at night before going to sleep. I was not afraid. Some people would say I had faith, and how should I not have it in the presence of the marvel which kept renewing itself? Inside me every sound, every scent, and every shape was forever changing into light, and light itself changing into color to make a kaleidoscope of my blindness.

I had entered a new world, there was no doubt about it, but I was not its prisoner. All the things I experienced, however remarkable and however remote from the everyday adventures of a child my age, I did not experience in an inner void, a closed chamber belonging to me and no one else. They took place in Paris during the summer and fall of 1932, in the small apartment near the Champ de Mars, and on a beach on the Atlantic, between my father and mother and, toward the end of the year, a new little brother who had been born.

What I mean to say is that all these discoveries of sound, light, smell, and visible and invisible shapes established themselves serenely and solidly between the dining-room table and the window on the court, the bric-a-brac on the mantelpiece and the kitchen sink, right in the midst of the life of other people and without being put out of countenance by them. These perceptions were not phantoms which came bringing disorder and fear into my real life. They were realities and, to me, the simplest of them all.

But it is time to make it clear that, along with many marvelous things, great dangers lie in wait for a blind child. I am not speaking of physical dangers, which can well be circumvented, nor of any danger which blindness itself brings about. I am speaking of dangers which come from the inexperience of people who still have their eyes. If I have been so fortunate myself—and I insist that I have—it is because I have always been protected from perils of that sort.

You know I had good parents, not just parents who wished me well, but ones whose hearts and intelligence were open to spiritual things, for whom the world was not composed exclusively of objects that were useful, and useful always in the same fashion; for whom, above all, it was not necessarily a curse to be different from other people. Finally, mine were parents willing to admit that their way of looking at things, the usual way, was perhaps not the only possible one, and to like my way and encourage it.

That is why I tell parents whose children have gone blind to take comfort. Blindness is an obstacle, but only becomes a misery if folly is added. I tell them to be reassured and never to set themselves against what their small boy or girl is finding out. They should never say: "You can't know because you can't see"; and as infrequently as possible, "Don't do that, it is dangerous." For a blind child there is a threat greater than all the wounds and bumps, the scratches and most of the blows, and that is the danger of isolation.

When I was fifteen I spent long afternoons with a blind boy my own age, one who went blind, I should add, in circumstances very like my own. Today I have few memories as painful. This boy terrified me. He was the living image of everything that might have happened to me if I had not been fortunate, more fortunate than he. For he was really blind. He had seen nothing since his accident. His faculties were normal, he could have seen as well as I. But they had kept him from doing so. To protect him, as they put it, they had cut him off from everything, and made fun of all his attempts to explain what he felt. In grief and revenge, he had thrown himself into a brutal solitude. Even his body lay prostrate in the depths of an armchair. To my horror I saw that he did not like me.

Tragedies like this are commoner than people think, and all the more terrible because they are avoidable in every case. To avoid them, I repeat that it is enough for sighted people not to imagine that their way of knowing the world is the only one.

At the age of eight everything favored my return to the world. They let me move around, they answered all the questions I asked, they were interested in all my discoveries, even the strangest. For example, how should I explain the way objects approached me when I was walking in their direction? Was I breathing them in or hearing them? Possibly, though that was often hard to prove. Did I see them? It seemed not. And yet, as I came closer, their mass was modified, often to the point of defining real contours, assuming a real shape in space, acquiring distinctive color, just as it happens where there is sight.

As I walked along a country road bordered by trees, I could point to each one of the trees on the road, even if they were not spaced at regular intervals. I knew whether the trees were straight and tall, carrying their branches as a body carries its head, or gathered into thickets and partly covering the ground around them.

This kind of exercise soon tired me out, I must admit, but it succeeded. And the fatigue did not come from the trees, from their number or shape, but from myself. To see them like this I had to hold myself in a state so far removed from old habits that I could not keep it up for very long. I had to let the trees come toward me, and not allow the slightest inclination to move toward them, the smallest wish to know them, to come between them and me. I could not afford to be curious or impatient or proud of my accomplishment.

After all, such a state is only what one commonly calls "attention," but I can testify that when carried to this point it is not easy. The same experiment tried with the trees along the road I could practice on any objects which reached a height and breadth at least as great as my own: telegraph poles, hedges, the arches of a bridge, walls along the street, the doors and windows in these walls, the places where they were set back or sloped away.

As with the sense of touch, what came to me from objects was pressure, but pressure of a kind so new to me that at first I didn't think of calling it by that name. When I became really attentive and did not oppose my own pressure to my surroundings, then trees and rocks came to me and printed their shape upon me like fingers leaving their impression in wax.

This tendency of objects to project beyond their physical limits produced sensations as definite as sight or hearing. I only needed a few years to grow accustomed to them, to tame them somewhat. Like all blind people, whether they know it or not, these are the senses I use when I walk by myself either outdoors or through a house. Later I read that they call this sense "the sense of obstacles," and that some kinds of animals, bats, for instance, are highly endowed with it.

According to many traditions of the occult, man has a third eye, an inner eye, generally called "the eye of Siva," located in the middle of his forehead, an eye which he can bring to life in certain conditions by certain exercises. Finally, the researches undertaken by the French writer and member of the Academy Jules Romains have demonstrated the existence of visual perception outside the retina, situated in certain nervous centers of the skin, particularly in the hands, the forehead, the nape of the neck and the chest. I hear that more recently this kind of research has been carried on with success by physiologists, especially in the U.S.S.R.

But whatever the nature of the phenomenon, I experienced it from childhood, and its effects seem to me much more important than its cause. The indispensable condition for accurately pointing out trees along the road was to accept the trees and not try to put myself in their place.

All of us, whether blind or not, are terribly greedy. We want things only for ourselves. Even without realizing it, we want the universe to be like us and give us all the room in it. But a blind child learns very quickly that this cannot be. He has to learn it, for every time he forgets that he is not alone in the world he strikes against an object, hurts himself and is called to order. But each time he remembers he is rewarded, for everything comes his way.

Jacques Lusseyran

MULLA NASRUDIN DECIDED TO START A FLOWER garden. He prepared the soil and planted the seeds of many beautiful flowers. But when they came up, his garden was filled not just with his chosen flowers but also overrun by dandelions. He sought out advice from gardeners all over and tried every method known to get rid of them but to no avail. Finally he walked all the way to the capital to speak to the royal gardener at the sheik's palace. The wise old man had counseled many gardeners before and suggested a variety of remedies to expel the dandelions but Mulla had tried them all. They sat together in silence for some time and finally the gardener looked at Nasrudin and said, "Well, then I suggest you learn to love them."

Sufi

A SINGLE MOTHER I ADMIRE TOLD ME HOW SHE struggled for years to raise her four children alone, with little money and no free time. It seemed she was doing all she could do. Then quite unself-consciously the energy of the great mother of compassion filled her when her youngest daughter, at fourteen, was paralyzed as a result of an accident. Her daughter couldn't speak or move. The doctors at the hospital said they didn't think there was much chance for her to ever move again. Yet her mother knew that her daughter was still conscious inside. As mothers do, she felt deep in her being that her daughter could be rehabilitated. The mother moved into the hospital room and began working with her daughter. She spent a year in the hospital and two years after that at home almost every day with the daughter, just picking up the girl's hand, putting it down, picking it up and putting it down, moving something in front of her eyes, back and forth, day after day, until her daughter's hands and eyes began to move again. After three years the girl was well enough to return to school. Now full grown, she has finished law school and is about to be married. Such generosity cannot be forced; it moves through us when we are deeply connected and deeply empty. Such compassion moves through us as a grace, bringing together a tenderness and fearlessness that could never come by any other means.

Contemporary

FIVE

Compassion and
the Need to Touch
One Another

MORE THAN ANY OTHER HUMAN NEED, PER- haps even more than food and shelter, we human beings, born of other human beings, nur- tured by and connected to them, need to touch one an- other. We need to stay in contact and acknowledge our interdependence and love in order to live in a sacred way. Think about your own life, of the times that you have deeply touched another person and what that has meant to you, of the times of difficulty when you have al- lowed another person to touch you, to help you. It is not with our righteousness or our ideas that we solve the ills of the world but with the power of our kindness and our capacity to be intimate with one another. By seeing through the veils of our stories and dramas we come to know one another's pain and sorrow.

Compassion is that singular quality of heart that has the power to transform resentment into forgiveness, ha- tred into friendliness, anger into loving-kindness. It is this most precious quality of our being that allows us to extend warmth, sensitivity, and openness to the world around us and to ourselves rather than be burdened by prejudice, hostility, and resistance. It is a quality far more profound than pity. It is a deep, heartfelt caring for the dignity, well-being, and integrity of every single life in our world—from the smallest creature to the most powerful person.

No being in this world is exempt from the need for compassion, for no being is exempt from pain. In moments of suffering—death, sickness, loss—it is not prescriptions, formulas, and advice that we yearn for. We are healed by the loving presence of another. One great account in this chapter shows how much more a kind touch can do than all the great power of a master trained in martial arts. The greatest of human arts, kindness, is really very simple, and yet with it comes tremendous integrity and dignity for ourselves and for others. There is no barrier or obstacle that enough loving-kindness and compassion cannot overcome. Our capacity to embody this, simple though it is, is the spiritual strength that can change the world around us.

Love is not for cowards; it is not a weakness but a great strength. At times in our own pain and difficulty we may feel unable to find enough compassion to hold even ourselves, never mind others. Yet life continues to present us with countless moments that call for us to find greater and greater depths of compassion. The compassion that is needed can come from unexpected sources—from the wind or from the animals, as in the dolphin story in this chapter. Or we may lose our connection with it in busyness, ambition, or pride, only to find it again after we stumble and reconnect with the earth. It is always very simple, a touching of ourselves and those around us with kindness, seeing them as if for the last moment, forgiving what has disappointed us, and loving fully. In this living compassion remarkable changes happen.

We know what it feels like to live with anger, hatred, and alienation. We know, too, what it feels like to be filled with love, friendliness, and warmth and the power those feelings have to connect us. Our own stories are our greatest teachers; they reveal to us what we need to nurture in our hearts and the ill will we must let go of. To learn from our stories is not to ask how we can learn to be compassionate but to appreciate that we cannot afford to live without compassion. No matter how justified our anger and resentment seems to be, we must open our hearts to the words of Mahatma Gandhi, "An eye for an eye is a terrible way to blind the world."

Compassion is not some future goal. Nor is it necessarily a result of great spiritual effort. Opportunities to extend compassion, to open our heart and touch the heart of another or of ourself, are manifold. These opportunities lie in those moments we find ourselves reacting with hatred, rejection, and prejudice. In these moments we must ask ourselves if we really need to travel the pathways of alienation and pain or if it is possible to find within ourselves the forgiveness and care that allows us to touch the heart of another.

As you read this chapter, close your eyes and reflect at some point. Look back over your life and recall or picture two good deeds you have done, two things you feel happy about having done. Even if you were to die today, you would know they were good. When you see them, discover, as every person does, how simple they were— the moments when we were there for another person to say, "I love you," to touch their pain with our kindness, the courage and the simple power to be truly present with another person. These are the moments that matter in a human life.

The stories of forgiveness and compassion in this chapter can inspire us to look anew at our own lives, to ask ourselves where healing lies in our own relationships. We must ask ourselves without judgment but with kindness and sensitivity, Where are we holding resentment, prejudice, and anger in our hearts? Can we let go? Can we let the natural radiance of our own compassion emerge and touch the heart of another? Can we look even at those who have created suffering and violence in our life or in the world and see them as their mothers must have when they were children? Can we see the underlying pain and confusion and fear that creates the violence that they have spread, and see through all of that to the fundamental longings every human being shares? This is the basis of the transformation of heart.

GRANPA AND GRANMA HAD AN UNDERSTANDING, AND so they had a love. Granma said the understanding run deeper as the years went by, and she reckined it would get beyond anything mortal folks could think upon or explain. And so they called it "kin."

Granpa said back before his time "kinfolks" meant any folks that you understood and had an understanding with, so it meant "loved folks." But people got selfish, and brought it down to mean just blood relatives; but that actually it was never meant to mean that.

Granpa said when he was a little boy his Pa had a friend who ofttimes hung around their cabin. He said he was an old Cherokee named 'Coon Jack, and he was continually distempered and cantankerous. He couldn't figure out what his Pa saw in old 'Coon Jack.

He said they went irregular to a little church house down in a hollow. One Sunday it was testifying time, when folks would stand up, as they felt the Lord called on them, and testify as to their sins and how much they loved the Lord.

Granpa said at this testifying time, "'Coon Jack stood up and said, 'I hear tell they's some in here been talking about me behind my back. I want ye to know that I'm awares. I know what's the matter with ye; ye're jealous because the Deacon Board put me in charge of the key to the songbook box. Well, let me tell ye; any of ye don't like it, I got the difference right here in my pocket.'"

Granpa said, shore enough, 'Coon Jack lifted his deer shirt and showed a pistol handle. He was stomping mad.

Granpa said that church house was full of some hard men, including his Pa, who would soon as not shoot you if the weather changed, but nobody raised an eyebrow. He said his Pa stood up and said, "'Coon Jack, every man here admires the way ye have handled the key to the songbook box. Best handling ever been done. If words has been mistook to cause ye discomfort, I here and now state the sorrow of every man present."

'Coon Jack set down, total mollified and contented, as was everybody else.

On the way home, Granpa asked his Pa why 'Coon Jack could get away with such talk, and Granpa said he got to laughing about 'Coon Jack acting so important over the key to the songbook box. He said his Pa told him, "Son, don't laugh at 'Coon Jack. Ye see, when the Cherokee was forced to give up his home and go to the Nations, 'Coon Jack was young, and he hid out in these mountains, and he fought to hold on. When the War 'tween the States come, he saw maybe he could fight that same guvmint and get back the land and homes. He fought hard. Both times he lost. When the War ended, the politicians set in, trying to git what was left of what we had. 'Coon Jack fought, and run, and hid, and fought some more. Ye see, 'Coon Jack come up in the time of fighting. All he's got now is the key to the songbook box. And if 'Coon Jack seems cantankerous . . . well, there ain't nothing left for 'Coon Jack to fight. He never knowed nothing else."

Granpa said, he come might near crying fer 'Coon Jack. He said after that, it didn't matter what 'Coon Jack said, or did . . . he loved him, because he understood him.

Granpa said that such was "kin," and most of people's mortal trouble come about by not practicing it; from that and politicians.

I could see that right off, and might near cried about 'Coon Jack myself.

Forrest Carter

❦

THE TRAIN CLANKED AND RATTLED THROUGH THE suburbs of Tokyo on a drowsy spring afternoon. Our car was comparatively empty—a few housewives with their kids in tow, some old folks going shopping. I gazed absently at the drab houses and dusty hedgerows.

At one station the doors opened, and suddenly the afternoon quiet was shattered by a man bellowing violent, incomprehensible curses. The man staggered into our car. He wore laborer's clothing, and he was big, drunk, and dirty. Screaming, he swung at a woman holding a baby. The blow sent her spinning into the laps of an elderly couple. It was a miracle that the baby was unharmed.

Terrified, the couple jumped up and scrambled toward the other end of the car. The laborer aimed a kick at the retreating back of the old woman but missed as she scuttled to safety. This so enraged the drunk that he grabbed the metal pole in the center of the car and tried to wrench it out of its stanchion. I could see that one of his hands was cut and bleeding. The train lurched ahead, the passengers frozen with fear. I stood up.

I was young then, some twenty years ago, and in pretty good shape. I'd been putting in a solid eight hours of aikido training nearly every day for the past three years. I liked to throw and grapple. I thought I was tough. Trouble was, my martial skill was untested in actual combat. As students of aikido, we were not allowed to fight.

"Aikido," my teacher had said again and again, "is the art of reconciliation. Whoever has the mind to fight has broken his connection with the universe. If you try to dominate people, you are already defeated. We study how to resolve conflict, not how to start it."

I listened to his words. I tried hard. I even went so far as to cross the street to avoid the *chimpira,* the pinball punks who lounged around the train stations. My forbearance exalted me. I felt both tough and holy. In my heart, however, I wanted an absolutely legitimate opportunity whereby I might save the innocent by destroying the guilty.

This is it! I said to myself, getting to my feet. *People are in danger and if I don't do something fast, they will probably get hurt.*

Seeing me stand up, the drunk recognized a chance to focus his rage. "Aha!" He roared. "A foreigner! You need a lesson in Japanese manners!"

I held on lightly to the commuter strap overhead and gave him a slow look of disgust and dismissal. I planned to take this turkey apart, but he had to make the first move. I wanted him mad, so I pursed my lips and blew him an insolent kiss.

"All right!" he hollered. "You're gonna get a lesson." He gathered himself for a rush at me.

A split second before he could move, someone shouted "Hey!" It was earsplitting. I remember the strangely joyous, lilting quality of it—as though you and a friend had been searching diligently for something, and he suddenly stumbled upon it. "Hey!"

I wheeled to my left; the drunk spun to his right. We both stared down at a little old Japanese. He must have been well into his seventies, this tiny gentleman, sitting there immaculate in his kimono. He took no notice of me, but beamed delightedly at the laborer, as though he had a most important, most welcome secret to share.

"C'mere," the old man said in an easy vernacular, beckoning to the drunk. "C'mere and talk with me." He waved his hand lightly.

The big man followed, as if on a string. He planted his feet belligerently in front of the old gentleman, and roared above the clacking wheels, "Why the hell should I talk to you?" The drunk now had his back to me. If his elbow moved so much as a millimeter, I'd drop him in his socks.

The old man continued to beam at the laborer. "What'cha been drinkin'?" he asked, his eyes sparkling with interest. "I been drinkin' sake," the laborer bellowed back, "and it's none of your business!" Flecks of spittle spattered the old man.

"Oh, that's wonderful," the old man said, "absolutely wonderful! You see, I love sake too. Every night, me and my wife (she's seventy-six, you know), we warm up a little bottle of sake and take it out into the garden, and we sit on an old wooden bench. We watch the sun go down, and we look to see how our persimmon tree is doing. My great-grandfather planted that tree, and we worry about whether it will recover from those ice storms we had last winter. Our tree has done better than I expected, though, especially when you consider the poor quality of the soil. It is gratifying to watch when we take our sake and go out to enjoy the evening—even when it rains!" He looked up at the laborer, eyes twinkling.

As he struggled to follow the old man's conversation, the drunk's face began to soften. His fists slowly un-clenched. "Yeah," he said. "I love persimmons too. . . ." His voice trailed off.

"Yes," said the old man, smiling, "and I'm sure you have a wonderful wife."

"No," replied the laborer. "My wife died." Very gently, swaying with the motion of the train, the big man began to sob. "I don't got no *wife*, I don't got no *home*, I don't got no *job*. I'm so *ashamed* of myself." Tears rolled down his cheeks; a spasm of despair rippled through his body.

Now it was my turn. Standing there in my well-scrubbed youthful innocence, my make-this-world-safe-for-democracy righteousness, I suddenly felt dirtier than he was.

Then the train arrived at my stop. As the doors opened, I heard the old man cluck sympathetically. "My, my," he said, "that is a difficult predicament, indeed. Sit down here and tell me about it."

I turned my head for one last look. The laborer was sprawled on the seat, his head in the old man's lap. The old man was softly stroking the filthy, matted hair.

As the train pulled away, I sat down on a bench. What I had wanted to do with muscle had been accomplished with kind words. I had just seen aikido tried in combat, and the essence of it was love. I would have to practice the art with an entirely different spirit. It would be a long time before I could speak about the resolution of conflict.

Terry Dobson

A BROTHER ASKED ABBA MATOES: WHAT SHALL I DO? My tongue causes me trouble and whenever I am among people, I cannot control it and I condemn them in all their good deeds and contradict them. What, therefore, shall I do? The old man answered him: If you cannot control yourself, go away from people and live alone. For this is a weakness—Those who live together with others ought not to be square, but round, in order to turn toward all. Further, the old man said: I live alone not because of my virtue, but rather because of my weakness. You see, those who live among people are the strong ones.

Desert Fathers

THERE'S A MONK THERE WHO WILL NEVER GIVE you advice, but only a question. I was told his questions could be very helpful. I sought him out. "I am a parish priest," I said. "I'm here on retreat. Could you give me a question?"

"Ah, yes," he answered. "My question is, 'What do they need?'"

I came away disappointed. I spent a few hours with the question, writing out answers, but finally I went back to him.

"Excuse me. Perhaps I didn't make myself clear. Your question has been helpful, but I wasn't so much interested in thinking about my apostolate during this retreat. Rather I wanted to think seriously about my own spiritual life. Could you give me a question for my own spiritual life?"

"Ah, I see. Then my question is, 'What do they RE-ALLY need?'"

Father Theophane

❧❧

IN THE MIDDLE OF THE GENTLE INDIAN NIGHT, AN intruder burst through the bamboo door of the simple adobe hut. He was a government vaccinator, under orders to break resistance against smallpox vaccination. Lakshmi Singh awoke screaming and scrambled to hide herself. Her husband leaped out of bed, grabbed an ax, and chased the intruder into the courtyard.

Outside, a squad of doctors and policemen quickly overpowered Mohan Singh. The instant he was pinned to the ground, a second vaccinator jabbed smallpox vaccine into his arm.

Mohan Singh, a wiry forty-year-old leader of the Ho tribe, squirmed away from the needle, causing the vaccination site to bleed. The government team held him until they had injected enough vaccine; then they seized his wife. Pausing only to suck out some vaccine, Mohan Singh pulled a bamboo pole from the roof and attacked the strangers holding his wife.

When two policemen rebuffed him, the rest of the team overpowered the entire family and vaccinated each in turn. Lakshmi Singh bit deep into one doctor's hand but to no avail.

When it was over, our vaccination team gathered in the small courtyard. Mohan Singh and his exhausted family stood by the broken door of their house. We faced each other silently across a cultural barrier, neither side knowing what to do next. Such an event—a night raid and forcible smallpox vaccination—was unprecedented.

Mohan Singh surveyed his disordered household, and reflected. For a moment or two he hesitated. Then he strode to his small vegetable plot and stooped to pluck the single ripe cucumber left on the vine. Following the hospitality creed of his tribe, he walked over to the puzzled young Indian doctor whom his wife had bitten and handed him the cucumber.

I had stood in the shadows trying to fathom the meaning of this strange encounter. Now I reached out to Zafar Hussain, a Muslim paramedical assistant assigned to me by the Indian government as guide and translator. What on earth was the cucumber for? Speaking in Hindi, Zafar passed my question along to one of the vaccinators, a Westernized Ho youth, who challenged Mohan Singh in the staccato rhythm of the tonal Ho language.

With great dignity, Mohan Singh stood ramrod straight. The whole village was awake now, people standing around the courtyard stage as the rising sun illuminated our unfolding drama. Measuring his words carefully, Mohan Singh began:

"My dharma [religious duty] is to surrender to God's will. Only God can decide who gets sickness and who does not. It is my duty to resist your interference with his will. We must resist your needles. We would die resisting if that is necessary. My family and I have not yielded. We have done our duty. We can be proud of being firm in our faith. It is not a sin to be overpowered by so many strangers in the middle of the night.

"Daily you have come and told me it is *your* dharma to prevent this disease with your needles. We have sent you away. Tonight you have used force. You say you act in accordance with *your* duty. I have acted in accordance with mine. It is over. God will decide.

"Now I find you are guests in my house. It is my duty to feed guests. I have little to offer at this time. Except this cucumber."

I felt numb and torn. For an instant, I wondered if I was on the wrong side. Mohan Singh was so firm in his faith, yet there was not a trace of anger in his words. I scanned my teammates' faces, looking for someone to respond to Mohan Singh's challenge. All stared at the ground, humbled by the power of Mohan Singh's faith.

Lawrence Brilliant

REPORTS REACHED THE DALAI LAMA THAT A CERtain Master of Kung Fu was roaming the countryside converting young men to the study of violence. Though Tibetan by birth, this man had been raised in Peking and was said to have returned as a secret agent to astonish Tibetans with the superior power of the Chinese in such a way as to render the country open and eager for conquest.

The Master of Kung Fu had made his reputation by taking on eight fierce Lolo warriors who attacked him on a mountain pass, killing seven of them so quickly that the one with the broken legs who survived swore the marvelous voyager had met their attack with movements so swift he seemed merely to walk through them and continue peacefully on his way.

Wherever the Master of Kung Fu stopped, he gathered followers and admirers who were fascinated by the mystical beauty of his methods. The dance of destruction, which he was always glad to perform in slow motion before an audience in the marketplace, was said to be awesomely beautiful. Done swiftly, the dance could not be seen. The master would seem to be standing absolutely still. Only a rush of wind indicated that he had spun about, throwing out his arms and legs in such fashion as to leave at least a dozen of the young toughs who were trying to dodge him grabbing at the parts of their bodies he had playfully flicked with his hands or feet to indicate which bones he could have broken, which organs destroyed.

Against all Buddhist laws, there had been unnecessary slaughter of yaks in order to provide the many husky monks, who had abandoned their lamaseries and robes, with black leather outfits like the one the Master of Kung Fu wore from neck to ankle, his huge muscles making the costume tight as his own flesh.

These leather-sheathed disciples followed their master everywhere challenging one another to duels, many of which ended in death or crippling. The Regent and other advisers to the Dalai Lama were deeply concerned, especially after blasphemous rumors began circulating that the Master of Kung Fu was an incarnation of Shiva, Hindu god of destruction.

There would have been riots had they thrown the man in jail, since he had done nothing wrong. He had a perfect right to be in the country. Not since his brilliant defense against the Lolos had he seriously injured anyone. When government officials questioned his intentions, he said that he was a sincere religious mystic trying to communicate certain cosmic laws learned from his Chinese guru.

It was decided not to attack him publicly but, in conformity with old Tibetan customs when someone claims religious privilege for questionable acts, to invite him most courteously to visit the Dalai Lama.

Pleased with the invitation, the Master of Kung Fu strode into the Dalai Lama's ceremonial hall. Being only ten years old at the time, the young God-King could not help but be impressed with the marvelously potent vibrations he gave off. They reduced the monks and lamas present to womanish giggling and gasping. The Master of Kung Fu was indeed a handsome, dashing fellow with his thick blue-black hair falling down over the shoulders of his leather suit. His teeth flashed confidently under a handlebar mustache. He did not prostrate himself but merely bowed gallantly, then leaned back to fill his chest with air until his whole body seemed to swell, tighten, and gleam.

"Your Highness," he began, "I know why you asked me here and I want you to stop worrying. Ugliness is my only enemy. You're all beautiful people"—a titter from the monks—"and I wouldn't think of doing you harm."

"When you want to do harm," asked the Dalai Lama, "what kind of harm can you do?"

"Well, I don't want to see it as harm at all, Highness. I want to see it as help. I'm a lover of beauty is what I am, just like any enlightened man. And I know as well as you that you can't raise up beauty in this world without clearing out the ugliness first. You may not be able to see the results right now—in fact it may seem like just the opposite—but what I'm doing is I'm raising up beauty by training a special cadre of men to prepare the ground. That's why I like to do my recruiting from the lamaseries. There's too much ugliness in this world, much too much. Something's got to be done about it by people who can back their strength with moral zeal. I figure the place to start is right here in this country where I was born. I could use your help to get the job done."

"What exactly do you do?" asked the Dalai Lama.

"Royal Highness, the best way to show you would be for you to stand here in front of me while I do a little dance it took me some fifteen years to perfect. Though I can kill a dozen men instantly with this dance, have no fear. This will only be a demonstration of ugliness destruction. Without seeing these ugly forces destroyed—for my arms and legs move faster than the blades of a helicopter—you will experience the great quietness that comes afterward when they are stilled."

The Dalai Lama stood up and immediately felt as if a wind had blown flower petals across his body. He looked down but saw nothing. "You may proceed," he told the Master of Kung Fu.

"Proceed?" said the other, grinning jovially. "I've already finished. What you felt were my hands flicking across your body. If it please Your Highness, this was a demonstration in slow motion, extremely slow motion, of the way I could have destroyed the organs of your body one by one. With this knuckle, I could have severed the contact between your brain and your spine. With the tip of this finger, I could have left you impotent. With the edge of this hand, I could have made it impossible for you to excrete. With this toe, I could have broken your arm while breaking your leg in the same motion with my heel. Your eyes, ears, nose, throat, spleen, liver . . . you name it. I could have taken them all out during that one little dance."

Beaming with pride, he flexed his muscles and looked his body over, up and down, approvingly. "To achieve the great peace," he concluded, "there are demons inside and outside that need to be eradicated. They appear and disappear so rapidly you cannot see them, but I've learned to see them and I can catch them and kill them before they get away, just as you catch a fly."

"I do not catch flies," said the Dalai Lama. A murmur of approval went up from the assembled monks. "No," said the Dalai Lama, glad to hear that his comrades had not been entirely seduced, "we do not catch flies in Tibet."

The Master of Kung Fu seemed momentarily taken aback, but he puffed himself up once more and resumed: "Quite so. But there is much sickness in this land due to the flies. In China there is very little sickness since every man knows how to catch a fly. Your Highness, I was not brought up in the serene tranquillity of this palace but in the streets of a city much like your Lhasa only larger. In the city called Peking I looked at eyes muddied from staring through fumes of putrefaction at images of capitalistic lust. I heard mouths speak incessantly to presumed social inferiors in tones full of insult, contempt, dissimulation, and vengeance. I have known hearts to beat excitedly over the torture of innocent men. I have watched gluttons with bloated stomachs riding on the backs of starvelings. I have seen legs wobbling pathetically to hold up a body poisoned by chemicals. I have seen ears eagerly bending to rumor, gossip, false reports, and greedy evangelisms of all kinds. In short, I have witnessed corruption in every part of man's body and have taken it upon myself to destroy this corruption once and for all."

"And after it's destroyed?" asked the Dalai Lama.

"It is destroyed. Mine may only be an art of preliminaries but it *is* final. And I am its master."

"I know a master greater than you," said the Dalai Lama.

"Without wishing to offend Your Highness, I doubt that very much."

"Yes, I have a champion who can best you," insisted the boy king.

"Let him challenge me then, and if he bests me I shall leave Tibet forever."

"If he bests you, you shall have no need to leave Tibet." The Dalai Lama looked around to see if his monks were as confident as he was, but they all looked very disconsolate. The huge guards were looking away, hoping he wouldn't call on one of them; and the others were looking at the guards, obviously convinced that not one of them stood the slightest chance.

The Dalai Lama clapped his hands. "Regent," he said, "summon the Dancing Master, and while we're waiting let's have some tea."

The tea ceremony was just about over when the Regent returned with the Dancing Master. He was a wiry little fellow, half the size of the Master of Kung Fu and well past his prime. His legs were entwined with varicose veins and he was swollen at the elbows from arthritis. Nevertheless, his eyes were glittering merrily and he seemed eager for the challenge.

The Master of Kung Fu did not mock his opponent. "My own guru," he said, "was even smaller and older than you, yet I was unable to best him until last year. I could have finished him easily had I ever been able to touch him, but he moved too fast. Only last year did I finally catch him on the ear and destroy him, as I shall destroy you when you finally tire. To show that I know your methods and won't be tricked into exhausting my energy, I shall first let you strike me at will. Your frail little hands can do me no harm while I'm at full strength."

The two opponents faced off. The Master of Kung Fu was taking a jaunty, indifferent stance, tempting the other to attack.

The old Dancing Master began to swirl very slowly, his robes wafting around his head. His arms stretched out and his hands fluttered like butterflies toward the eyes of his opponent. The fingers settled gently for a moment upon the bushy eyebrows. The Master of Kung Fu drew back in astonishment. He looked around the great hall. Everything was suddenly vibrant with rich hues of singing color. The faces of the monks were radiantly beautiful. It was as if his eyes had been washed clean for the first time.

The fingers of the Dancing Master stroked the nose of the Master of Kung Fu and suddenly he could smell pungent barley from a granary in the city far below. He could smell butter melting in the most fragrant of teas, as the Dalai Lama, incomparably beautiful, sipped tea and watched him calmly. A flicking of the Dancing Master's foot at his genitals, and he was throbbing with desire. The sound of a woman singing through an open window filled him with exquisite yearning to draw her into his arms and caress her. He found himself removing his leather clothes until he stood naked before the Dancing Master, who was now assaulting him with joy at every touch.

His body began to hum like a finely tuned instrument. He could hear the great long horns resounding in a thousand rooms of the Potala, praising creation. He opened his mouth and sang like a bird at sunrise. It seemed to him that he was possessed of many arms, legs, and hands, and all wanted to nurture the blossoming of life.

The Master of Kung Fu began the most beautiful dance that had ever been seen in the great ceremonial hall of the Grand Potala. It lasted for three days and nights, during which time everyone in Tibet feasted and visitors crowded the doorways and galleries to watch.

Only when he finally collapsed at the throne of the Dalai Lama did he realize that another body was lying beside him. The old Dancing Master had died of exertion while performing his final and most marvelous dance. But he had died happily, having found the disciple he had always yearned for. The new Dancing Master of Tibet took the frail corpse in his arms and, weeping with love, drew the last of its energy into his body. Never had he felt so strong.

Pierre Delattre

At the third meal on the Sabbath, an intimate and holy gathering, the Hasidim at Rabbi Wolf's table carried on their conversation in a low voice and with subdued gestures so as not to disturb the zaddik who was deep in thought. Now, it was Rabbi Wolf's wish and the rule of his house that anyone could come in at any time, and seat himself at his table. On this occasion too, a man entered and sat down with the rest, who made room for him although they knew that he was an ill-bred person. After a time, he pulled a large radish out of his pocket, cut it into a number of pieces of convenient size, and began to eat with a great smacking of lips. His neighbors were unable to restrain their annoyance any longer. "You glutton," they said to him. "How dare you offend this festive board with your taproom manners?"

Although they had tried to keep down their voices, the zaddik soon noticed what was going on. "I just feel like eating a really good radish," he said. "I wonder whether anyone here could get me one?" In a sudden flood of happiness which swept away his embarrassment, the radish eater offered Rabbi Wolf a handful of the pieces he had cut.

Chassid

❧❧

[There was] a man who died and found himself in a beautiful place, surrounded by every conceivable comfort. A white-jacketed man came to him and said, "You may have anything you choose—any food—any pleasure—any kind of entertainment."

The man was delighted, and for days he sampled all the delicacies and experiences of which he had dreamed on earth. But one day he grew bored with all of it, and calling the attendant to him, he said, "I'm tired of all this. I need something to do. What kind of work can you give me?"

The attendant sadly shook his head and replied, "I'm sorry, sir. That's the one thing we can't do for you. There is no work here for you."

To which the man answered, "That's a fine thing. I might as well be in hell."

The attendant said softly, "Where do you think you are?"

Margaret Stevens

❧❧

I T WAS SUCH A CLEAR, SPARKLING DAY I COULDN'T resist the temptation to take my board onto the water even though my buddy hadn't been able to make it that day. I prided myself on my competence, my ability to read the wind and the currents. I didn't feel bound by the cautions I always gave to my friends never to windsurf alone. It was a glorious feeling to race through the water; I felt like I could go on forever as I watched the shoreline recede. I realized I was further out than I had ever been before but had no doubt I could make it back to shore. I realized how tired I was getting and started to turn toward the distant shoreline when it happened. The joint holding the rig to my board snapped and I was in the water, helpless. At first I wasn't very alarmed, figuring the rescue boat would see me and the worst that I would have to face would be their lecture about my foolishness in going out alone.

Hanging on to my board as I drifted, I could feel the power of the current dragging me further and further away from shore. I started to get colder and colder and more and more tired. I also began to feel afraid as I realized that no one had spotted me. I don't know how long I drifted. I felt as if I could hardly hold on any longer, but I knew that if I let go of my board I was finished. I hadn't

prayed in years but I began to pray now. "Someone, anyone, please help me! I don't want to drown, I don't want
to die alone."

Suddenly my board was bumped hard, and hard again.
I couldn't see anything I could be hitting but the bumps
kept coming, pushing me ever so slowly toward the shore.
The thought of sharks hit me, then I realized there were
no sharks in these waters. Beside me first a fin and then a
head broke through the surface. It was the eye of a dolphin. It sank beneath the water again and continued with
its slow and steady bumping. I could see the shoreline getting closer. All I could do, all I needed to do was hold on as
the dolphin guided me into the current that would carry
me to safety. I could hear shouts as the rescue crew spotted
me, I could feel the steady, sure pressure beneath me as the
dolphin continued to guide me. I kept babbling about the
dolphin that saved me.

When the boat reached me and the crew pulled me out
of the water I felt so many different feelings—exhaustion
but also such incredible exhilaration. I was safe, I was
alive, I was grateful. There are a lot of things I learned
from that day, about safety and fear. The most powerful
lesson I learned was about trust.

Contemporary

WHEN I LEFT NEW YORK HARBOR FOR PERU, I
instinctively felt I was making a journey that
would shape my life. It was 1951; I was robust and eager. I
wasn't even sure what my real mission would be. At that
point, there was just an empty lot.

It was 13,500 feet high, very cold and demanding. As a
Maryknoll sister, I was there to teach school. After a while
I became principal. I guess you could say I was a figure,

just by being in that role. Then the illness happened, quite suddenly, up there. The doctors said it was rheumatoid arthritis. They said it was ultimately a crippling disease. They said there was nothing really to do about it.

I went to see other doctors elsewhere, like in Panama, because I wanted to stay in South America. I wouldn't accept what they were telling me, what I was going to have to face. But it gradually became clear I should come back to the States for some treatment.

I got good care. However, the doctors said that gold injections would be the only help, but it would prevent me from going back to Peru. I didn't want them. I was going back. I was fighting it, fighting it all—the illness, my own reactions—self-pity, anger, discouragement, doubt. I wouldn't give in. But every day it seemed I was losing. Finally I felt I had to quit imposing my own will; that was a big step. I went to the doctors, and they said they could give me this medicine, and after a few months they'd see if I could get onto maintenance and go back to Peru. After all my anger and resistance, there seemed to be some kind of chance. But chance for what?

I had surgery at the Mayo Clinic, and I did a great deal of reflecting and praying in their chapel. There was a beautiful wooden statue of Christ there, with outstretched hands. I think that's why it had been chosen, to inspire the hands of surgeons and nurses. As it happened I was there to have my own hands operated on. I remember thinking that even though my hands were going to be broken and crooked, they would still be sacred to me. I'd use them to bring something to somebody, I didn't know what. My hands could be the compassionate hands of Christ as much as the hands of the doctors and nurses.

So I sought to be able to enter into the world of the sick, and to live with the mystery of suffering. I saw that I had to enter into my own experience of pain, and to face up to it, and to allow myself to be changed by it. Without that nothing could be done. I saw that healing comes with owning our wounds as the first step in moving beyond them.

I returned to Peru at a lower altitude. Almost everything had changed, especially my attitude toward the people I was working with. I could feel their terrible poverty and pain in a whole new way. In fact it seemed as if I was seeing it for the first time. How often I'd rushed around trying to solve people's problems without really seeing *them*—the pain in their faces, the insecure eyes, the nervous hands, all expressions of the hurt inside. It was only when suffering had actually touched *me* that I began to feel their condition.

The affirmation I got from them was so important: "You're the same person you were before. And even if you can't teach or do anything, we'd like you to stay." Just to see me get up and try to do something seemed to mean a great deal to them. We were meeting on a level where we all suffer. That became our ground.

And so my ministry changed. It became the ministry of walking together. Some of us with physical disabilities joined together to share our experiences. We were just being together, trying to understand what was possible for us, share what we could, examples of creativity. Our pain and weakness and deformity proved to be teachers of a great mystery, a small introduction into the kind of dying from which new spirit is born.

We found we had become more sensitive to others, more touched, more able to listen, moved more by feelings than by intellectual concepts. We discovered that the more we opened to the pain of others, the more we found ourselves in their service. Having been brought low, it was just a matter of standing humbly before others, and presenting a visible sign of hope by some silent testimony.

So we would simply walk about, as best we could. Many of the Peruvians we ran into with handicaps were deeply ashamed and hid. We would come to see them, and they would hide, in their own homes. But as we moved about, they would gradually come forth more.

I think of Juan, a polio victim at three, who had been hidden by his family in their small mud-brick house until we discovered him at the age of eight. His brother, Julio, took us home one day. There was Juan, his twisted legs underneath him, scooting around the small dirt patio on a circular piece of rubber. His mother was suspicious and didn't want us to stay. A handicapped child meant she was being punished for something. She was ashamed.

We returned on several occasions to visit Juan. One time we found him all alone. His family, with the rest of the town, had gone to a religious procession. Of course, he'd never seen one. So we borrowed a bicycle, put Juan on it, and joined the procession itself. It was his first time outside the house, the first time he'd looked at people from a level higher than the ground, his first procession.

His parents were momentarily annoyed, but their attitude changed gradually. When we thought it was right to raise the idea, we asked at the next town meeting if we could raise money to send Juan to Lima for physical rehabilitation. Everyone liked the idea and Juan went off to the big city.

He had a long, hard struggle, with much pain and effort. But one day he returned to the village. He was using braces and a cane. It was very hard for him. But as he began to walk down the streets to his home, people came out of their own homes. They appeared from all over. They were cheering and clapping and they followed him all the way home. It was so wonderful. It was Juan's second procession.

It's difficult. I have had many ups and downs. That's the thing about a progressive crippling disease: more and more pain and disability; it keeps on pushing you, making more demands, forcing you to greater discipline.

But I have seen much service born of suffering. And I see that our little suffering is not for ourselves. It can have impact throughout the world, that's how much our lives can mean, that's how much is possible. And I have been with people who would just cry over that message, cry and cry. And I have cried too.

Christian Contemporary

I KNEW THERE WERE MANY INTERESTING SIGHTS, BUT I didn't want any more of the LITTLE answers. I wanted the big answer. So I asked the guestmaster to show me the House of the Christian God.

I sat myself down, quite willing to wait for the big answer. I remained silent all day, far into the night. I looked Him in the eye. I guess He was looking me in the eye. Late, late at night I seemed to hear a voice, "What are you leaving out?" I looked around. I heard it again. "What are you leaving out?" Was it my imagination? Soon it was all around me, whispering, roaring, "What are you leaving out? WHAT ARE YOU LEAVING OUT?"

Was I cracking up? I managed to get to my feet and head for the door. I guess I wanted the comfort of a human face or a human voice. Nearby was the corridor where some of the monks live. I knocked on one cell.

"What do you want?" came a sleepy voice.

"What am I leaving out?"

"Me," he answered.

I went to the next door.

"What do you want?"

"What am I leaving out?"

"Me."

A third cell, a fourth, all the same.

I thought to myself, "They're all stuck on themselves." I left the building in disgust. Just then the sun was coming up. I had never spoken to the sun before, but I heard myself pleading, "What am I leaving out?"

The sun too answered, "Me." That finished me.

I threw myself flat on the ground. Then the earth said, "ME," too!

Father Theophane

SOME OLD MEN CAME TO SEE ABBA POEMEN, AND said to him: Tell us, when we see brothers dozing during the sacred office, should we pinch them so they will stay awake? The old man said to them: Actually, if I saw a brother sleeping, I would put his head on my knees and let him rest.

Desert Fathers

SIX

The Triumph
of the
Human Heart

IN EVEN THE WORST LANDSCAPE OF HUMAN DARK-
ness and difficulty there shine beacons of light. They
are not necessarily cast by particularly powerful or
holy people who possess grandiose strategies for changing the world. They most often radiate from ordinary
people who in their intimate encounters with tragedy,
injustice, and terror have been transformed and have
learned how to respond to the world with the simplicity
and power of their faith, love, and compassion. There is
no power greater than the power of love, no shadow that
can withstand the power of compassion, no demon that
can overwhelm the power of openheartedness. Through
their example our eyes are opened to the possibilities of
bringing light to our own shadows.

Whether we are in positions of power, like the king
in one story of this chapter, or in poverty, like the villager
of another, we will be tested. We will be asked to summon the spirit of greatness, of compassion, of openheartedness over and over again in our lives. Perhaps this is
what we are here for, to learn this single lesson. In the
end the strength that we have to fall back upon is not our

credentials or accomplishments or the ideals we hold but our humanness itself. Our basic ordinariness underlies all our attainments and experiences. The fact is that we, too, like the seasons and the sun and moon and all other living creatures, are born and die. We awake each morning and go to sleep each night; we eat and walk and feel in deep ways the preciousness and mystery of our very humanness.

We also hold within ourselves an extraordinarily precious gift—our capacity to be aware. This is the blessing that allows us to make choices, to sense the possibilities open to us. It empowers us to learn and grow through life's tests rather than be swallowed by them. The gift of our awareness allows us to nurture our capacities for forgiveness and understanding rather than be driven by self-protective instincts, hostility, and fear.

We have not yet plumbed the depths and possibilities of our own awareness. How close can we come to another person? How deeply can we feel the wind that seems only to brush us with its touch? How attuned can we be to the changing rhythms of our universe? What is the extent of freedom? The only thing that is certain about awareness is that it removes all distance, it shatters mistaken notions and superficiality, it connects us with the heart of all life. It allows us to meet the tests in our life with greatness of heart.

As you read the stories in this chapter, reflect on the challenges of your life. Bring to mind the times that you have been tested, and recall the forces that you have brought to those tests. What would it be like to touch those tests with your utter humanness, to be vulnerable and through that ultimate honesty to be strong and balanced in your heart? Has unworthiness, ambition, fear, or pride prevented you from learning from and growing through the challenges? What other qualities do you have to bring to those same challenges that would truly make a difference?

G RANPA TAUGHT ME TO HAND FISH. THIS WAS HOW, the second time in my five years of living with him, I nearly got killed. The first time, of course, was working in the whiskey trade when the tax law might near caught me. I was more than certain sure they would have taken me to the settlement and hanged me. Granpa said, more than likely they wouldn't have as he had never knowed such case to happen. But Granpa didn't see them. They wasn't chasing him. This time, however, Granpa nearly got killed too.

It was in the middle of the day, which is the best time to hand fish. The sun hits the middle of the creek and the fish move back under the banks to lie in the cool and doze.

This is when you lay down on the creek bank and ease your hands into the water and feel for the fish holes. When you find one, you bring your hands in easy and slow, until you feel the fish. If you are patient, you can rub your hands along the sides of the fish and he will lie in the water while you rub him.

Then you take one hold behind his head, the other on his tail, and lift him out of the water. It takes some time to learn.

This day, Granpa was laying on the bank and had already pulled a catfish out of the water. I couldn't find a fish hole, so I went a ways down the bank. I lay down and eased my hands into the water, feeling for a fish hole. I heard a sound right by me. It was a dry rustle that started slow and got faster until it made a whirring noise.

I turned my head toward the sound. It was a rattlesnake. He was coiled to strike, his head in the air, and looking down on me, not six inches from my face. I froze stiff and couldn't move. He was bigger around than my leg and I could see ripples moving under his dry skin. He was mad. Me and the snake stared at each other. He was flicking out his tongue—nearly in my face—and his eyes was slitted—red and mean.

The end of his tail began to flutter faster and faster; making the whirring sound get higher. Then his head, shaped like a big V, begun to weave just a little, back and forth, for he was deciding what part of my face to hit. I knew he was about to strike me but I couldn't move.

A shadow fell on the ground over me and the snake. I hadn't heard him coming atall but I knew it was Granpa. Soft and easy, like he was remarking about the weather, Granpa said, "Don't turn yer head. Don't move, Little Tree. Don't blink yer eyes." Which I didn't. The snake raised his head higher, getting ready to hit me. I thought he would not stop raising up.

Then, of a sudden, Granpa's big hand come between my face and the snake's head. The hand stayed there. The rattler drew up higher. He begun to hiss, and rattled a solid whirring sound. If Granpa had moved his hand . . . or flinched, the snake would have hit me square in the face. I knew it too.

But he didn't. The hand stayed steady as a rock. I could see the big veins on the back of Granpa's hand. There was beads of sweat standing out too, shining against the copper skin. There wasn't a tremble nor a shake in the hand.

The rattler struck, fast and hard. He hit Granpa's hand like a bullet; but the hand never moved atall. I saw the needle fangs bury up in the meat as the rattler's jaws took up half his hand.

Granpa moved his other hand, and grabbed the rattler behind the head, and he squeezed. The rattler come up off the ground and wrapped himself around and around Granpa's arm. He thrashed at Granpa's head with his rattling end, and beat him in the face with it. But Granpa wouldn't turn loose. He choked that snake to death with one hand, until I heard the crack of backbone. Then he throwed him on the ground.

Granpa set down and whipped out his long knife. He reached over and cut big slashes in his hand where the snake had bit. Blood was running over his hand and down his arm. I crawled over to Granpa . . . for I was weak as dishwater, and didn't think I could walk. I pulled myself to standing by holding onto Granpa's shoulder. He was sucking the blood out of the knife slash and spitting it on the ground. I didn't know what to do, so I said, "Thankee, Granpa." Granpa looked at me and grinned. He had blood smeared over his mouth and face.

"Helldamnfire!" Granpa said. "We showed that son of a bitch, didn't we?"

"Yes, sir," I said, feeling better about the whole thing. "We showed that son of a bitch." Though I couldn't rightly recall as having much to do with the showing.

Granpa's hand commenced to get bigger and bigger. It was turning blue. He taken his long knife and split the sleeve of his deer shirt. The arm was twice as big as his other one. I got scared.

Granpa taken off his hat and fanned his face. "Hot as hell," he said, "fer this time of year." His face looked funny. Now his arm was turning blue.

"I'm going for Granma," I said. I started off. Granpa looked after me and his eyes stared off, faraway.

"Reckin I'll rest a spell," he said, calm as syrup. "I'll be along directly."

I ran down the Narrows trail, and I guess maybe that nothing but my toes touched the ground. I couldn't see good, for my eyes was blinded with tears though I didn't cry. When I turned onto the hollow trail, my chest was burning like fire. I commenced to fall down, running down the hollow trail, sometimes in the spring branch, but I scrambled right up again. I left the trail and cut through briers and bushes. I knew Granpa was dying.

The cabin looked crazy and tilted when I run into the clearing, and I tried to yell for Granma . . . but nothing would come out. I fell through the kitchen door and right into Granma's arms. Granma held me and put cold water on my face. She looked at me steady and said, "What happened—where?" I tried to get it out. "Granpa's dying . . ." I whispered, "rattlesnake . . . creek bank." Granma dropped me flat on the floor, which knocked the rest of the wind out of me.

She grabbed a sack and was gone. I can see her now; full skirt, with hair braids flying behind and her tiny moccasin feet flying over the ground. She could run! She had not said anything, "Oh Lord!" or nothing. She never hesitated nor looked around. I was on my hands and knees in the kitchen door, and I hollered after her, "Don't let Granpa die!" She never slowed down, running from the clearing up the trail. I screamed as loud as I could, and it echoed up the hollow, "Don't let him die, Granma!" I figured, more than likely, Granma wouldn't let him die.

I turned the dogs out and they took off after Granma, howling and baying up the trail. I ran behind them, fast as I could.

When I got there, Granpa was laying flat out. Granma had propped his head up, and the dogs was circling around, whining. Granpa's eyes was closed and his arm was nearly black.

Granma had slashed his hand again and was sucking on it, spitting blood on the ground. When I stumbled up, she pointed to a birch tree. "Pull the bark off, Little Tree."

I grabbed Granpa's long knife and stripped the bark off the tree. Granma built a fire, using the birch bark to start it, for it will burn like paper. She dipped water out of the creek and hung a can over the fire and commenced to put roots and seeds into it; and some leaves that she had taken from the sack. I don't know all of what was used, but the leaves was lobelia, for Granma said that Granpa had to have it to help him breathe.

Granpa's chest was moving slow and hard. While the can was heating, Granma stood and looked around. I hadn't seen anything at all ... but fifty yards off, against the mountain, there was a quail nesting on the ground. Granma undid her big skirt and let it drop on the ground. She hadn't anything under it. Her legs looked like a girl's with long muscles moving under the copper skin.

She tied the top of the skirt together, and tied rocks around the bottom of the skirt. Then she moved on the quail's nest like a wind whisper. Just at the right time— she knew—the quail rose off the nest, and she threw the skirt over it.

She brought the quail back, and while it was still alive, she split it from breastbone to tail, and spraddled it, kicking, over Granpa's snake bite. She held the kicking quail on Granpa's hand for a long time, and when she took it off, the quail had turned green all over its inside. It was poison from the snake.

The evening wore on, and Granma worked over Granpa. The dogs set around us in a circle, watching. Nighttime fell, and Granma had me build up the fire. She said we had to keep Granpa warm and couldn't move him. She taken her skirt and laid it over him. I taken off my deer shirt and laid it on him too, and was taking off my britches, but Granma said that wasn't necessary, as my britches wasn't hardly big enough to cover one of Granpa's feet. Which they wasn't.

I kept the fire going. Granma had me build another fire near Granpa's head and so I kept them both going. Granma laid down by Granpa, holding close to him, for she said her body heat would help ... and so I laid by Granpa on the other side; though I reckined my body wasn't hardly big enough to heat up much of Granpa. But

Granma said I helped. I told Granma I didn't see hardly any way atall that Granpa would die.

I told her how it all happened, and that I reckined it was my fault for not watching. Granma said it wasn't anybody's fault, not even the rattlesnake's. She said we wasn't to place fault ner gain on anything that just happened. Which made me feel some better, but not much.

Granpa commenced to talk. He was a boy again, running through the mountains, and he told all about it. Granma said this was because he was recollecting while he was sleeping. He talked, off and on, all night. Just before dawn, he quieted and begun to breathe easy and regular. I told Granma the way I see it, there wasn't might near any way atall that Granpa could die now. She said he wasn't going to. So I went to sleep in the crook of his arm.

I woke at sunup . . . just as the first light topped the mountain. Granpa set up, all of a sudden. He looked down at me, and then at Granma. He said, "By God! Bonnie Bee, a feller can't lay his body down nowheres without you stripping buck naked and hunching at 'em."

Granma slapped Granpa's face and laughed. She rose and put on her skirt. I knew Granpa was all right. He wouldn't leave for home until he had skinned the rattler. He said Granma would make a belt for me, from its skin. Which she did.

We headed down the Narrows trail for the cabin, the dogs running ahead. Granpa was a little weak-kneed, and held Granma close, helping him to walk, I reckined. I trotted along behind them, feeling might near the best I had ever felt since coming to the mountains.

Though Granpa never mentioned putting his hand between me and the snake, I figured, next to Granma, more than likely Granpa kinned me more than anybody else in the world, even Blue Boy.

Forrest Carter

ONCE THERE WAS A KIND KING. HE WAS WEALTHY and respected and his kingdom was at peace. But he was not content. He was not happy. Sitting at the window of his throne room, he looked out over the well-trimmed lawns and tree-lined streets of his city, and out over the green fields of his land. He sighed. "I would like to really give," he said. "Life is short; even the virtuous gods do not live forever. Yet, though I have had my successes, I have not really given of myself." Now this was not exactly true. He had given his time, energy, and courage to the welfare of his country. He had listened patiently and kindly to the daily cares and problems of his people and had ruled them wisely. He had, in short, been a good king. But perhaps when one is good one hardly knows it oneself. At least that is how it seems to have been with this good King Sivi.

Shakra, king of the gods, heard this lament and thought to himself, "This King Sivi has led a good life so far. The gates of the heavens will certainly open to him when his years on earth are over. Yet he is now calling for a decisive test. The strong languish without challenge and, in the fields of goodness, Sivi is strong. Why, his many good deeds on earth have already built him extensive palaces and gardens here among us in which he will dwell for many thousands of earthly years. Still, a test is now in order. Aha," exclaimed Shakra, "I have it!"

Suddenly the king of the gods transformed himself. Where but a moment before—a moment, that is, by heavenly reckoning, which could equal two, or even three, earthly weeks—he had sat resplendent on his throne, wearing his robes and jeweled crown, there now perched two birds. One was a gentle, gray-eyed dove, which called in a soft, sweet melodious voice. The other was a fierce hawk, with yellow eyes, talons like knives, and a cruel, curved beak. The hawk ruffled his feathers and glared at the bright godly light of the upper realms. The dove cooed softly and, flapping her wings, darted down through the clouds. Faster and faster and faster raced the little shining dove. Down and down and down. And faster and faster and faster flew the golden-eyed hawk after her. Turning and twisting, they dove down toward the green earth and the marble palaces of King Sivi.

Soon the dove forgot that she had ever been just a thought in the mind of a god. The hawk too no longer remembered that he was but a god's dream. Now he flew after the little dove in deadly earnest, striving only to grasp the dove in his talons and to tear and devour her at last. So the little, gentle dove flew on in increasing terror as the moments of their deadly race sped by.

The dove spied an open window and, near exhaustion, sped through it. There sat King Sivi on his gold and sandalwood throne. The terrified dove darted to the king's side and perched, shaking, on the carved arm of his throne. "What is it, little bird?" asked the king in surprise. "What frightens you so? Can I help?"

"Oh, Lord," panted the dove, "a fierce hawk is after me. He wants to take my life."

"Don't worry. I will save you," said the king kindly. "I won't let him take you."

At that very moment, the hawk burst into the room. Drawing his wings together he swiftly perched upon the throne's other arm and saluted the king. "Great King," he said, "my lawful prey sits by you. I am weary with the chase. Give me the dove and I will depart in peace."

"I cannot give the dove to you," said the king. "I have promised her my protection."

"That is all very well," said the hawk, "but what of my rights? I am a hunting bird. Doves are my food. You have robbed me of what is lawfully mine and, without food, I shall starve this very night."

"Well, I can't let you starve," said the king with concern. "I'll give you some other food. Tell me what you need."

"I need fresh meat in order to live," said the hawk. "Could you really kill another creature just to feed me? Somehow I don't think so. Come," he said at last, "give me the dove. It's the simplest way."

"It's true!" thought the king, "I couldn't kill some other creature in order to supply him with food. He's right. That would be no solution at all! Yet, I can't let him have the dove. He will kill her. But if I don't let him have her he himself shall die. What right have I to let even a hawk starve in my presence? As a living creature with a place in the scheme of things, he also deserves my help." The king sat silently, tugging at his beard. Then, all at once, he rose to his feet. "I have it!" he announced.

"Fierce hawk," he said, "I have a plan. You shall be fed, the dove shall remain free, and no other creature need be killed."

"What is your plan?" asked the hawk suspiciously.

"It's simple," said the king. "I will give you a piece of my own flesh. As it shall weigh exactly as much as the dove's body, you will lose nothing by the bargain. Will you agree to this?"

"Yes," said the hawk, "I will. As long as the piece you give me weighs exactly as much as the dove, I shall be satisfied."

"Good! You have my word."

A golden scale was brought from the treasury and set before the throne. The little dove was placed in one of the scale's hanging trays. A silver perch was brought for the hawk and a little, smooth golden dish was set before him. Then, the weeping noblewomen were directed to leave the room. The king's physicians and courtiers argued with him. They begged him, in the name of reason, to stop. But the king was resolved. "I will give what I can," he said. "After all, how much can a little bird weigh?"

A sharp knife with an inlaid handle was brought in on an embroidered cushion. The room grew quiet. King Sivi took up the knife. Then, in terrible silence, he sliced a piece of flesh from the muscle of his thigh and placed it on the scale. Bright blood ran down his leg but not a single groan escaped his lips. He watched the pointer. But the scale did not move! The dove's side of the balance did not rise at all! Unflinchingly, the king cut more flesh from his thigh. But again, the golden scale would not rise. Unhesitatingly, he cut and cut and cut. He cut till both thighs were like sticks. Then he cut the flesh from his left arm. But still the scale would not rise. Too weak to cut any more, he dropped the knife and had his whole body placed in the now bloody scale.

"Enough!" cried the hawk and dove together with a single voice. The chamber was lit with a golden light. Both birds were gone! In the center of the room hovered Shakra, king of the shining gods. And beside him, standing firmly on the polished floor, stood King Sivi, whole and completely unharmed.

"Noble King," said the god, "you have been tested as few have ever been tested. And you have passed nobly. For this, you shall live for many years and your kingdom shall be at peace. Later, you shall reside near me, in the highest heavens, for many thousands of years before returning to this earth. Be well, O King, for today you have done well, indeed." And Shakra, as is his way, vanished, leaving not a trace.

Then the people of the kingdom came running to the king. They embraced him, crying with joy. And everything came to pass as Shakra had announced. There was peace and harmony for many, many years.

Eventually, King Sivi did go to live among the gods. But often, seated in splendor at the window of his shining palace, he would look with love out over the earth and all its creatures. He would think, too, with joy of the day to come when he would be back on the earth again.

What contentment, after all, can a kindly heart have in heaven?

So, in time, King Sivi returned.

Traditional Buddhist

WHEN I LOST MY VISION, I HAD BEEN VERY SELF-sufficient and together. I was raising five children. I was working. I was volunteering in my community. I was independent enough to be contemplating a divorce from a bad marriage—I'd even given an attorney five hundred dollars. Just before I had to go into the hospital.

I'd begun to find myself knocking things over and stumbling around. I went to an ophthalmologist, then a neurologist, then a radiologist, then a neurosurgeon. And finally a doctor said, "You have a growth in your brain. If you don't have surgery it will continue to grow and it will take your life." Just like that.

The operation took seven and a half hours. The doctor said he almost lost me twice. He'd removed a tumor the size of a hen's egg. All I could see was the faintest bit of light.

It didn't hit me until I got home. I didn't recognize myself. I went into the hospital with long hair; I came out with short. I went in at 145 pounds; I came out at 175, wearing my mother's dress. I went in and could see; I left and couldn't. It wasn't me. And things were bad at home. I couldn't get a divorce now; I was too dependent. I tried to do things for myself, but it often just created more trouble. My youngest daughter didn't want to be seen on the street with me. She was ashamed. I felt so bitter. But I kept pushing my feelings away. What had happened? Why me? I just wanted out of there.

One nice fall day, I told my husband I was going out. I went down the elevator and out of the house. I got to the corner and just stopped. I stood there, expecting any minute he'd come down and join me. He never came. I just stood there on the corner.

A lot happened on that corner. I saw my past life. I recalled how lonely and helpless I'd felt as a little girl. And there I was now, just like a child again, only with five of my own. I stayed there a long time. Finally, I said to myself, "Well, here you are and there's no place to go. It's time you brought a little help into your life."

So I went into rehabilitation. And I told them everything I felt. I gave them everything. I gave them my shame and my anger and my fear. I felt it was the truth. And if it was the truth, then how could I be helpless? You don't suffer from truth. The truth sets you free.

Of course it was hard work, coming to terms with change. But after a while you have nothing left to hide. You want to bring it all out. You want to make room to receive help. And when you're with a lot of people who are also trying to do that, you get a lot of support. Us blind folks, working together: the more I felt that, the more I found myself beginning to offer help as much as ask for it.

I met a young man there who was blind from birth. He'd never had a birthday party. So I baked him a cake and organized a party. He blew out the candles he couldn't see. He was delirious. It was grand. I felt so happy. I had come from that lost blind person on the corner to someone who had seen a need and done something about it.

I've told people something that sounds a little cruel. Everyone should experience temporary blindness, to see how our vision can give us such hangups, how we judge and condemn, and what that does to us all. Like that boy with the birthday cake. There was a blind girl he had fallen for. Then someone said she was unattractive. He stopped seeing her. It brought tears to my eyes. He'd been seeing fine.

But when you begin to see with that inner eye, that inner eye everyone has, it all changes. Everyone is human, everyone is God's child. Everyone is helpless, one way or another, and everyone is helpful, too. We're all here for each other . . . that's how it is. And we all have something to give, no matter our condition.

There are ups and downs, of course. You start blind and reach out. Sometimes there's nothing to hold on to, but you still reach. Then you learn to hold on to whatever you get. Then you find someone's hand and you take it. Then you see you can reach and hold someone else. Once you start, it all follows. I've seen that.

So now, when I work with handicapped people, or anyone really, I find I have a special understanding to share. That's really all I have to offer. It's hard to put it into words. It's just "I understand," that's all.

And yet, as sure or secure as that may sound, I don't think you're ever really secure. What is security? You can lose it in a flash. I know. And I still get shaky. So I have a little prayer: that the Lord will send me someone to help me along the way on my subway journey every day . . . and that He'll send someone I can share my faith and strength with too. Both things. That's how I set off to work. And it usually happens.

Christian Contemporary

❧

THE DEVIL AND DANIEL WEBSTER

IT'S A STORY THEY TELL IN THE BORDER COUNTRY, where Massachusetts joins Vermont and New Hampshire.

Yes, Dan'l Webster's dead—or, at least, they buried him. But every time there's a thunderstorm around Marshfield, they say you can hear his rolling voice in the hollows of the sky. And they say that if you go to his grave and speak loud and clear, "Dan'l Webster—Dan'l Webster!" the ground 'll begin to shiver and the trees begin to shake. And after a while you'll hear a deep voice saying, "Neighbor, how stands the Union?" Then you better answer the Union stands as she stood, rock bottomed and copper sheathed, one and indivisible, or he's liable to rear right out of the ground. At least, that's what I was told when I was a youngster.

You see, for a while, he was the biggest man in the country. He never got to be President, but he was the biggest man. There were thousands that trusted in him right next to God Almighty, and they told stories about him and all the things that belonged to him that were like the stories of patriarchs and such. They said, when he stood up to speak, stars and stripes came right out in the sky, and once he spoke against a river and made it sink into the ground. They said, when he walked the woods with his fishing rod, Killall, the trout would jump out of the streams right into his pockets, for they knew it was no use putting up a fight against him; and, when he argued a case, he could turn on the harps of the blessed and the shaking of the earth underground. That was the kind of man he was, and his big farm up at Marshfield was suitable to him. The chickens he raised were all white meat down through the drumsticks, the cows were tended like children, and the big ram he called Goliath had horns with a curl like a morning-glory vine and could butt through an iron door. But Dan'l wasn't one of your gentlemen farmers; he knew all the ways of the land, and he'd be up by candlelight to see that the chores got done. A man with a mouth like a mastiff, a brow like a mountain and eyes like burning anthracite—that was Dan'l Webster in his prime. And the biggest case he argued never got written down in the books, for he argued it against the devil, nip and tuck and no holds barred. And this is the way I used to hear it told.

There was a man named Jabez Stone, lived at Cross Corners, New Hampshire. He wasn't a bad man to start with, but he was an unlucky man. If he planted corn, he got borers; if he planted potatoes, he got blight. He had good-enough land, but it didn't prosper him; he had a decent wife and children, but the more children he had, the less there was to feed them. If stones cropped up in his neighbor's field, boulders boiled up in his; if he had a horse with the spavins, he'd trade it for one with the staggers and give something extra. There's some folks bound to be like that, apparently. But one day Jabez Stone got sick of the whole business.

He'd been plowing that morning and he'd just broke the plowshare on a rock that he could have sworn hadn't been there yesterday. And, as he stood looking at the plowshare, the off horse began to cough—that ropy kind of cough that means sickness and horse doctors. There were two children down with the measles, his wife was ailing, and he had a whitlow on his thumb. It was about the last straw for Jabez Stone. "I vow," he said, and he looked around him kind of desperate, "I vow it's enough to make a man want to sell his soul to the devil! And I would, too, for two cents!"

Then he felt a kind of queerness come over him at having said what he'd said; though, naturally, being a New Hampshireman, he wouldn't take it back. But, all the same, when it got to be evening and, as far as he could see, no notice had been taken, he felt relieved in his mind, for he was a religious man. But notice is always taken, sooner or later, just like the Good Book says. And, sure enough, next day, about suppertime, a soft-spoken, dark-dressed stranger drove up in a handsome buggy and asked for Jabez Stone.

Well, Jabez told his family it was a lawyer, come to see him about a legacy. But he knew who it was. He didn't like the looks of the stranger, nor the way he smiled with his teeth. They were white teeth, and plentiful—some say they were filed to a point, but I wouldn't vouch for that. And he didn't like it when the dog took one look at the stranger and ran away howling, with his tail between his legs. But having passed his word, more or less, he stuck to it, and they went out behind the barn and made their bargain. Jabez Stone had to prick his finger to sign, and the stranger lent him a silver pin. The wound healed clean, but it left a little white scar.

After that, all of a sudden, things began to pick up and prosper for Jabez Stone. His cows got fat and his horses sleek, his crops were the envy of the neighborhood, and lightning might strike all over the valley, but it wouldn't strike his barn. Pretty soon he was one of the prosperous people of the county; they asked him to stand for selectman, and he stood for it; there began to be talk of running him for state senate. All in all, you might say the Stone family was as happy and contented as cats in a dairy. And so they were, except for Jabez Stone.

He'd been contented enough the first few years. It's a great thing when bad luck turns; it drives most other things out of your head. True, every now and then, especially in rainy weather, the little white scar on his finger would give him a twinge. And once a year, punctual as clockwork, the stranger with the handsome buggy would come driving by. But the sixth year the stranger lighted, and, after that, his peace was over for Jabez Stone.

The stranger came up through the lower field, switching his boots with a cane—they were handsome black boots, but Jabez Stone never liked the look of them, particularly the toes. And, after he'd passed the time of day, he said, "Well, Mr. Stone, you're a hummer! It's a very pretty property you've got here, Mr. Stone."

"Well, some might favor it and others might not," said Jabez Stone, for he was a New Hampshireman.

"Oh, no need to decry your industry!" said the stranger, very easy, showing his teeth in a smile. "After all, we know what's been done, and it's been according to contract and specifications. So when—ahem—the mortgage falls due next year, you shouldn't have any regrets."

"Speaking of that mortgage, mister," said Jabez Stone, and he looked around for help to the earth and the sky. "I'm beginning to have one or two doubts about it."

"Doubts?" said the stranger not quite so pleasantly.

"Why, yes," said Jabez Stone. "This being the U.S.A. and me always having been a religious man." He cleared his throat and got bolder. "Yes sir," he said, "I'm beginning to have considerable doubts as to that mortgage holding in court."

"There's courts and courts," said the stranger, clicking his teeth. "Still, we might as well have a look at the original document." And he hauled out a big black pocketbook, full of papers. "Sherwin, Slater, Stevens, Stone," he muttered. "'I, Jabez Stone, for a term of seven years—' Oh, it's quite in order, I think."

But Jabez Stone wasn't listening, for he saw something else flutter out of the black pocketbook. It was something that looked like a moth, but it wasn't a moth. And as Jabez Stone stared at it, it seemed to speak to him in a small sort of piping voice, terrible small and thin, but terrible human. "Neighbor Stone!" it squeaked. "Neighbor Stone! Help me! For God's sake, help me!"

But before Jabez Stone could stir hand or foot, the stranger whipped out a big bandanna handkerchief, caught the creature in it, just like a butterfly, and started tying up the ends of the bandanna.

"Sorry for the interruption," he said. "As I was say-ing—"

But Jabez Stone was shaking all over like a scared horse.

"That's Miser Stevens' voice!" he said in a croak. "And you've got him in your handkerchief!"

The stranger looked a little embarrassed.

"Yes, I really should have transferred him to the col-lecting box," he said with a simper, "but there were some rather unusual specimens there and I didn't want them crowded. Well, well, these little contretemps will occur."

"I don't know what you mean by contertan," said Jabez Stone, "but that was Miser Stevens' voice! And he ain't dead! You can't tell me he is! He was just as spry and mean as a woodchuck Tuesday!"

"In the midst of life . . ." said the stranger, kind of pious. "Listen!" Then a bell began to toll in the valley and Jabez Stone listened, with the sweat running down his face. For he knew it was tolled for Miser Stevens and that he was dead.

"These long-standing accounts," said the stranger with a sigh, "one really hates to close them. But business is busi-ness."

He still had the bandanna in his hand, and Jabez Stone felt sick as he saw the cloth struggle and flutter.

"Are they all as small as that?" he asked hoarsely.

"Small?" said the stranger. "Oh, I see what you mean. Why, they vary." He measured Jabez Stone with his eyes, and his teeth showed. "Don't worry, Mr. Stone," he said. "You'll go with a very good grade. I wouldn't trust you outside the collecting box. Now, a man like Dan'l Web-ster, of course—well, we'd have to build a special box for him, and even at that, I imagine the wing spread would astonish you. He'd certainly be a prize. I wish we could see our way clear to him. But, in your case, as I was saying—"

"Put that handkerchief away!" said Jabez Stone, and he began to beg and to pray. But the best he could get at the end was a three years' extension, with conditions.

But till you make a bargain like that, you've got no idea of how fast four years can run. By the last months of those years Jabez Stone's known all over the state and there's talk of running him for governor—and it's dust and ashes in his mouth. For every day, when he gets up, he thinks, "There's one more night gone," and every night, when he lies down, he thinks of the black pocketbook and the soul of Miser Stevens, and it makes him sick at heart. Till, finally, he can't bear it any longer, and, in the last days of the last year, he hitches up his horse and drives off to seek Dan'l Webster. For Dan'l was born in New Hampshire, only a few miles from Cross Corners, and it's well known that he has a particular soft spot for old neighbors.

It was early in the morning when he got to Marshfield, but Dan'l was up already, talking Latin to the farm hands and wrestling with the ram, Goliath, and trying out a new trotter and working up speeches to make against John C. Calhoun. But when he heard a New Hampshireman had come to see him, he dropped everything else he was doing, for that was Dan'l's way. He gave Jabez Stone a breakfast that five men couldn't eat, went into the living history of every man and woman in Cross Corners, and finally asked him how he could serve him.

Jabez Stone allowed that it was a kind of mortgage case.

"Well, I haven't pleaded a mortgage case in a long time, and I don't generally plead now, except before the Supreme Court," said Dan'l, "but if I can, I'll help you."

"Then I've got hope for the first time in ten years," said Jabez Stone and told him the details.

Dan'l walked up and down as he listened, hands behind his back, now and then asking a question, now and then plunging his eyes at the floor, as if they'd bore through it like gimlets. When Jabez Stone had finished, Dan'l puffed out his cheeks and blew. Then he turned to Jabez Stone and a smile broke over his face like the sunrise over Monadnock.

"You've certainly given yourself the devil's own row to hoe, Neighbor Stone," he said, "but I'll take your case."

"You'll take it?" said Jabez Stone, hardly daring to believe.

"Yes," said Dan'l Webster. "I've got about seventy-five other things to do and the Missouri Compromise to straighten out, but I'll take your case. For if two New Hampshiremen aren't a match for the devil, we might as well give the country back to the Indians."

Then he shook Jabez Stone by the hand and said, "Did you come down here in a hurry?"

"Well, I admit I made time," said Jabez Stone.

"You'll go back faster," said Dan'l Webster, and he told 'em to hitch up Constitution and Constellation to the carriage. They were matched grays with one white forefoot, and they stepped like greased lightning.

Well, I won't describe how excited and pleased the whole Stone family was to have the great Dan'l Webster for a guest, when they finally got there. Jabez Stone had lost his hat on the way, blown off when they overtook a wind, but he didn't take much account of that. But after supper he sent the family off to bed, for he had most particular business with Mr. Webster. Mrs. Stone wanted them to sit in the front parlor, but Dan'l Webster knew front parlors and said he preferred the kitchen. So it was there they sat, waiting for the stranger, with a jug on the table between them and a bright fire on the hearth—the stranger being scheduled to show up on the stroke of midnight, according to specification.

Well, most men wouldn't have asked for better company than Dan'l Webster and a jug. But with every tick of the clock Jabez Stone got sadder and sadder. His eyes roved round, and though he sampled the jug you could see he couldn't taste it. Finally, on the stroke of 11:30 he reached over and grabbed Dan'l Webster by the arm.

"Mr. Webster, Mr. Webster!" he said, and his voice was shaking with fear and a desperate courage. "For God's sake, Mr. Webster, harness your horses and get away from this place while you can!"

"You've brought me a long way, neighbor, to tell me you don't like my company," said Dan'l Webster, quite peaceable, pulling at the jug.

"Miserable wretch that I am!" groaned Jabez Stone. "I've brought you a devilish way, and now I see my folly. Let him take me if he wills. I don't hanker after it, I must say, but I can stand it. But you're the Union's stay and New Hampshire's pride! He mustn't get you, Mr. Webster! He mustn't get you!"

Dan'l Webster looked at the distracted man, all gray and shaking in the firelight, and laid a hand on his shoulder.

"I'm obliged to you, Neighbor Stone," he said gently. "It's kindly thought of. But there's a jug on the table and a case in hand. And I never left a jug or a case half finished in my life."

And just at that moment there was a sharp rap on the door.

"Ah," said Dan'l Webster very coolly, "I thought your clock was a trifle slow, Neighbor Stone." He stepped to the door and opened it. "Come in!" he said.

The stranger came in—very dark and tall he looked in the firelight. He was carrying a box under his arm—a black japanned box with little air holes in the lid. At the sight of the box Jabez Stone gave a low cry and shrank into a corner of the room.

"Mr. Webster, I presume," said the stranger, very polite, but with his eyes glowing like a fox's deep in the woods.

"Attorney of record for Jabez Stone," said Dan'l Webster, but his eyes were glowing too. "Might I ask your name?"

"I've gone by a good many," said the stranger carelessly. "Perhaps Scratch will do for the evening. I'm often called that in these regions."

Then he sat down at the table and poured himself a drink from the jug. The liquor was cold in the jug, but it came steaming into the glass.

"And now," said the stranger, smiling and showing his teeth, "I shall call upon you, as a law-abiding citizen, to assist me in taking possession of my property."

Well, with that the argument began—and it went hot and heavy. At first Jabez Stone had a flicker of hope, but when he saw Dan'l Webster being forced back at point after point, he just sat scrunched in his corner, with his eyes on that japanned box. For there wasn't any doubt as to the deed or the signature—that was the worst of it. Dan'l Webster twisted and turned and thumped his fist on the table, but he couldn't get away from that. He offered to compromise the case; the stranger wouldn't hear of it. He pointed out the property had increased in value, and state senators ought to be worth more; the stranger stuck to the letter of the law. He was a great lawyer, Dan'l Webster, but we know who's the King of Lawyers, as the Good Book tells us, and it seemed as if, for the first time, Dan'l Webster had met his match.

Finally, the stranger yawned a little. "Your spirited efforts on behalf of your client do you credit, Mr. Webster," he said, "but if you have no more arguments to adduce,

I'm rather pressed for time . . ." and Jabez Stone shuddered.

Dan'l Webster's brow looked dark as a thundercloud.

"Pressed or not, you shall not have this man!" he thundered. "Mr. Stone is an American citizen, and no American citizen may be forced into the service of a foreign prince. We fought England for that in '12 and we'll fight all hell for it again!"

"Foreign?" said the stranger. "And who calls me a foreigner?"

"Well, I never yet heard of the dev—of your claiming American citizenship," said Dan'l Webster with surprise.

"And who with better right?" said the stranger with one of his terrible smiles. "When the first wrong was done to the first Indian, I was there. When the first slaver put out for the Congo, I stood on her deck. Am I not in your books and stories and beliefs, from the first settlements on? Am I not spoken of still in every church in New England? 'Tis true the North claims me for a Southerner and the South for a Northerner, but I am neither. I am merely an honest American like yourself—and of the best descent—for, to tell the truth, Mr. Webster, though I don't like to boast of it, my name is older in this country than yours."

"Aha!" said Dan'l Webster with the veins standing out in his forehead. "Then I stand on the Constitution! I demand a trial for my client!"

"The case is hardly one for an ordinary court," said the stranger, his eyes flickering. "And, indeed, the lateness of the hour—"

"Let it be any court you choose, so it is an American judge and an American jury!" said Dan'l Webster in his pride. "Let it be the quick or the dead; I'll abide the issue!"

"You have said it," said the stranger, and pointed his finger at the door. And with that, and all of a sudden, there was a rushing of wind outside and a noise of foot-steps. They came, clear and distinct, through the night. And yet they were not like the footsteps of living men.

"In God's name, who comes by so late?" cried Jabez Stone in an ague of fear.

"The jury Mr. Webster demands," said the stranger, sipping at his boiling glass. "You must pardon the rough appearance of one or two; they will have come a long way."

And with that the fire burned blue and the door blew open and twelve men entered, one by one.

If Jabez Stone had been sick with terror before, he was blind with terror now. For there was Walter Butler, the loyalist, who spread fire and horror through the Mohawk Valley in the times of the Revolution; and there was Simon Girty, the renegade, who saw white men burned at the stake and whooped with the Indians to see them burn. His eyes were green, like a catamount's, and the stains on his hunting shirt did not come from the blood of the deer. King Philip was there, wild and proud as he had been in life, with the great gash in his head that gave him his death wound, and cruel Governor Dale, who broke men on the wheel. There was Morton of Merry Mount, who so vexed the Plymouth Colony, with his flushed, loose, hand-some face and his hate of the godly. There was Teach, the bloody pirate, with his black beard curling on his breast. The Reverend John Smeet, with his strangler's hands and his Geneva gown, walked as daintily as he had to the gal-lows. The red print of the rope was still around his neck, but he carried a perfumed handkerchief in one hand. One and all, they came into the room with the fires of hell still upon them, and the stranger named their names and their deeds as they came, till the tale of twelve was told. Yet the stranger had told the truth—they had all played a part in America.

"Are you satisfied with the jury, Mr. Webster?" said the stranger mockingly, when they had taken their places.

The sweat stood upon Dan'l Webster's brow, but his voice was clear.

"Quite satisfied," he said. "Though I miss General Arnold from the company."

"Benedict Arnold is engaged upon other business," said the stranger with a glower. "Ah, you asked for a justice, I believe."

He pointed his finger once more, and a tall man, soberly clad in Puritan garb, with the burning gaze of the fanatic, stalked into the room and took his judge's place.

"Justice Hathorne is a jurist of experience," said the stranger. "He presided at certain witch trials once held in Salem. There were others who repented of the business later, but not he."

"Repent of such notable wonders and undertakings?" said the stern old justice. "Nay, hang them—hang them all!" And he muttered to himself in a way that struck ice into the soul of Jabez Stone.

Then the trial began, and, as you might expect, it didn't look anyways good for the defense. And Jabez Stone didn't make much of a witness in his own behalf. He took one look at Simon Girty and screeched, and they had to put him back in his corner in a kind of swoon.

It didn't halt the trial though; the trial went on, as trials do. Dan'l Webster had faced some hard juries and hanging judges in his time, but this was the hardest he'd ever faced, and he knew it. They sat there with a kind of glitter in their eyes, and the stranger's smooth voice went on and on. Every time he'd raise an objection, it'd be "Objection sustained," but whenever Dan'l objected, it'd be "Objection denied." Well, you couldn't expect fair play from a fellow like this Mr. Scratch.

It got to Dan'l in the end, and he began to heat, like iron in the forge. When he got up to speak he was going to flay that stranger with every trick known to the law, and the judge and jury too. He didn't care if it was contempt of court or what would happen to him for it. He didn't care any more what happened to Jabez Stone. He just got madder and madder, thinking of what he'd say. And yet, curiously enough, the more he thought about it, the less he was able to arrange his speech in his mind.

Till, finally, it was time for him to get up on his feet, and he did so, all ready to bust out with lightnings and denunciations. But before he started he looked over the judge and jury for a moment, such being his custom. And he noticed the glitter in their eyes was twice as strong as before, and they all leaned forward. Like hounds just before they get the fox, they looked, and the blue mist of evil in the room thickened as he watched them. Then he saw what he'd been about to do, and he wiped his forehead, as a man might who's just escaped falling into a pit in the dark.

For it was him they'd come for, not only Jabez Stone. He read it in the glitter of their eyes and in the way the stranger hid his mouth with one hand. And if he fought them with their own weapons, he'd fall into their power; he knew that, though he couldn't have told you how. It was his own anger and horror that burned in their eyes; and he'd have to wipe that out or the case was lost. He stood there for a moment, his black eyes burning like anthracite. And then he began to speak.

He started off in a low voice, though you could hear every word. They say he could call on the harps of the blessed when he chose. And this was just as simple and easy as a man could talk. But he didn't start out by condemning or reviling. He was talking about the things that make a country a country and a man a man.

And he began with the simple things that everybody's known and felt—the freshness of a fine morning when you're young, and the taste of food when you're hungry, and the new day that's every day when you're a child. He took them up and he turned them in his hands. They were good things for any man. But without freedom they sickened. And when he talked of those enslaved, and the sorrows of slavery, his voice got like a big bell. He talked of the early days of America and the men who had made those days. It wasn't a spread-eagle speech, but he made you see it. He admitted all the wrong that had ever been done. But he showed how, out of the wrong and the right, the suffering and the starvations, something new had come. And everybody had played a part in it, even the traitors.

Then he turned to Jabez Stone and showed him as he was—an ordinary man who'd had hard luck and wanted to change it. And, because he'd wanted to change it, now he was going to be punished for all eternity. And yet there was good in Jabez Stone, and he showed that good. He was hard and mean, in some ways, but he was a man. There was sadness in being a man, but it was a proud thing too. And he showed what the pride of it was till you couldn't help feeling it. Yes, even in hell, if a man was a man, you'd know it. And he wasn't pleading for any one person any more, though his voice rang like an organ. He was telling the story and the failures and the endless journey of mankind. They got tricked and trapped and bamboozled, but it was a great journey. And no demon that was ever foaled could know the inwardness of it—it took a man to do that.

The fire began to die on the hearth and the wind before morning to blow. The light was getting gray in the room when Dan'l Webster finished. And his words came back at the end to New Hampshire ground, and the one spot of land that each man loves and clings to. He painted a picture of that, and to each one of that jury he spoke of things long forgotten. For his voice could search the heart, and that was his gift and his strength. And to one his voice was like the forest and its secrecy, and to another like the sea and the storms of the sea; and one heard the cry of his lost nation in it, and another saw a little harmless scene he hadn't remembered for years. But each saw something. And when Dan'l Webster finished he didn't know whether or not he'd saved Jabez Stone. But he knew he'd done a miracle. For the glitter was gone from the eyes of the judge and jury, and, for the moment, they were men again, and knew they were men.

"The defense rests," said Dan'l Webster and stood there like a mountain. His ears were still ringing with his speech, and he didn't hear anything else till he heard Judge Hathorne say, "The jury will retire to consider its verdict."

Walter Butler rose in his place and his face had a dark, gay pride on it.

"The jury has considered its verdict," he said and looked the stranger full in the eye. "We find for the defendant, Jabez Stone."

With that, the smile left the stranger's face, but Walter Butler did not flinch.

"Perhaps 'tis not strictly in accordance with the evidence," he said, "but even the damned may salute the eloquence of Mr. Webster."

With that, the long crow of a rooster split the gray morning sky, and judge and jury were gone from the room like a puff of smoke and as if they had never been there. The stranger returned to Dan'l Webster, smiling wryly.

"Major Butler was always a bold man," he said. "I had not thought him quite so bold. Nevertheless, my congratulations, as between two gentlemen."

"I'll have that paper first, if you please," said Dan'l Webster, and he took it and tore it into four pieces. It was queerly warm to the touch. "And now," he said, "I'll have you!" and his hand came down like a bear trap on the stranger's arm. For he knew that once you bested anybody like Mr. Scratch in fair fight, his power on you was gone. And he could see that Mr. Scratch knew it too.

The stranger twisted and wriggled, but he couldn't get out of that grip. "Come, come, Mr. Webster," he said, smiling palely. "This sort of thing is ridic—ouch!—is ridiculous. If you're worried about the costs of the case, naturally, I'd be glad to pay—"

"And so you shall!" said Dan'l Webster, shaking him till his teeth rattled. "For you'll sit right down at that table and draw up a document, promising never to bother Jabez Stone nor his heirs or assigns nor any other New Hampshireman till doomsday! For any hades we want to raise in this state, we can raise ourselves, without assistance from strangers."

"Ouch!" said the stranger. "Ouch! Well, they never did run very big to the barrel, but—ouch!—I agree!"

So he sat down and drew up the document. But Dan'l Webster kept his hand on his coat collar all the time.

"And now may I go?" said the stranger, quite humble, when Dan'l 'd seen the document's proper and legal form.

"Go?" said Dan'l, giving him another shake. "I'm still trying to figure out what I'll do with you. For you've settled the costs of the case, but you haven't settled with me. I think I'll take you back to Marshfield," he said, kind of reflective. "I've got a ram there named Goliath that can butt through an iron door. I'd kind of like to turn you loose in his field and see what he'd do."

Well, with that the stranger began to beg and plead. And he begged and he pled so humble that finally Dan'l, who was naturally kindhearted, agreed to let him go. The stranger seemed terrible grateful for that and said, just to show they were friends, he'd tell Dan'l's fortune before leaving. So Dan'l agreed to that, though he didn't take much stock in fortune-tellers ordinarily. But, naturally, the stranger was a little different.

Well, he pried and he peered at the lines in Dan'l's hands. And he told him one thing and another that was quite remarkable. But they were all in the past.

"Yes, all that's true, and it happened," said Dan'l Webster. "But what's to come in the future?"

The stranger grinned, kind of happily, and shook his head.

"The future's not as you think it," he said. "It's dark. You have a great ambition, Mr. Webster."

"I have," said Dan'l firmly, for everybody knew he wanted to be President.

"It seems almost within your grasp," said the stranger, "but you will not attain it. Lesser men will be made President and you will be passed over."

"And, if I am, I'll still be Daniel Webster," said Dan'l. "Say on."

"You have two strong sons," said the stranger, shaking his head. "You look to found a line. But each will die in war and neither reach greatness."

"Live or die, they are still my sons," said Dan'l Webster. "Say on."

"You have made great speeches," said the stranger. "You will make more."

"Ah," said Dan'l Webster.

"But the last great speech you make will turn many of your own against you," said the stranger. "They will call you Ichabod; they will call you by other names. Even in New England some will say you have turned your coat and sold your country, and their voices will be loud against you till you die."

"So it is an honest speech, it does not matter what men say," said Dan'l Webster. Then he looked at the stranger and their glances locked.

"One question," he said. "I have fought for the Union all my life. Will I see that fight won against those who would tear it apart?"

"Not while you live," said the stranger grimly, "but it will be won. And after you are dead, there are thousands who will fight for your cause, because of words that you spoke."

"Why, then, you long-barreled, slab-sided, lantern-jawed, fortune-telling note shaver," said Dan'l Webster with a great roar of laughter, "be off with you to your own place before I put my mark on you! For, by the thirteen original colonies, I'd go to the Pit itself to save the Union!"

And with that he drew back his foot for a kick that would have stunned a horse. It was only the tip of his shoe that caught the stranger, but he went flying out of the door with his collecting box under his arm.

"And now," said Dan'l Webster, seeing Jabez Stone beginning to rouse from his swoon, "let's see what's left in the jug, for it's dry work talking all night. I hope there's pie for breakfast, Neighbor Stone."

But they say that whenever the devil comes near Marshfield, even now, he gives it a wide berth. And he hasn't been seen in the state of New Hampshire from that day to this. I'm not talking about Massachusetts or Vermont.

Stephen Vincent Benet

II

Finding the Way

INDING THE WAY TO AUTHENTIC AWAKENING presents us with an immense challenge. Naturally enough we first listen to the voices of external authorities who seem to hold the answers to our questions. It becomes more confusing as we soon discover that the world abounds in a multitude of authorities who gladly and willingly offer us advice, solutions, and formulas. Our bookstores overflow with prescriptions on how to be happy, fulfilled, and liberated. In the beginning we may listen and learn from the wisdom of other people's experience. We can be inspired by the example of teachers and sages of past and present.

At some point in the midst of our listening a number of insights dawn upon us. We see that no single authority holds the hot line to truth nor is there just one way to awakening. It may also become clear to us that what we hear are simply the different melodies through which the great spiritual traditions have expressed one essential harmony. It is this harmony that is significant and not the manner of its expression. The common elements of all who become wise are that they have learned to listen to this wisdom in their own hearts, to hear the underlying harmony, and to travel their own path.

No one can travel our path for us; no one can substitute for us in our quest for awakening. In trusting that wisdom, joy, and awakening are our spiritual heritage, we must discover what awakens them in us. No one else can free us from the confusion, fear, and attachment that cast shadows of pain on our lives. In accepting this aloneness we find it is not an aloneness of alienation or withdrawal. We are supported in our spiritual quest by all those of past generations, of all cultures, who applaud and inspire our exploration. Our quest connects us with millions of contemporary companions who seek inner peace and freedom. In the willingness to know our own aloneness we begin to discover a wisdom and compassion that connects us to all others.

There will be moments when we encounter feelings of despair, doubt, and inadequacy. We may wonder how to bridge the apparently uncrossable gap between confusion and clarity, holding and opening, limitation and freedom. In all moments of darkness we need to remember that we are blessed with humanity's most precious gift—the capacity to be aware. It is a gift to rejoice in; the capacity to be aware is the power to be conscious, to be awake, and to transform. It is an immense power, enabling us to penetrate the veils of confusion that limit us, enabling us to connect with and use the inner resources of energy, focus, and love that lie dormant.

Exploring what it means to be aware, we learn how to be wholeheartedly present in each moment, present with ourselves, present with all that each moment brings to us. Connecting with the present moment we are able to set aside our anxiety about the future and with what we might gain or lose, have or become. We are able to free ourselves from our preoccupations with the past, our histories, and the burden of our regrets. Our awareness illuminates what is actually here, one moment at a time. And it is in this moment that we are able to learn and to open.

The present moment is the most profound and challenging teacher we will ever meet in our lives. It is a compassionate teacher, it extends to us no judgment, no censure, no measurement of success and failure. The present moment is a mirror, and in its reflection we learn how to see. Learning how to look into this mirror without deluding ourselves is the source of all wisdom. In this mirror we see what contributes to the confusion and discord in our lives and what contributes to harmony and understanding. We see the relationship between pain and its cause on a moment-to-moment level; we see the bond between love and its source. We see what it is that connects us and what it is that alienates us.

In this seeing we begin to learn from our own stories, what delights us and what saddens us. Listening inwardly and learning from our own stories, we see that we are in need not so much of experts to define our way as of our own clear and direct inner attunement. Our stories reveal our path. In our listening we can understand what we need to let go of and what we need to develop if we are to live in the spirit of peace and freedom.

Our own stories differ only in superficial form and detail from the stories of all beings. There is no living being that does not share our yearning for liberation, to be free from fear and pain. Grief is grief, no matter the heart that endures it. Peace is peace, regardless of the heart that rejoices in it.

The following stories describe the pains and joys involved in discovering the way. In opening our hearts to them we will be able to empathize with the mountains these travelers have had to climb, the valleys they have found themselves in, the peaks they have reached. They help us to reflect once more upon the learning that is coming alive in our own stories each day.

SEVEN

Here and Now:
Simplicity with
What Is

T O LIVE FULLY, TO LOVE WELL, TO FIND A WISE
and timeless understanding—all of these grow out
of our capacity to experience and know what is
present. The heart of the spiritual life is to live in the
ever-changing reality of the present. A sign in a Las
Vegas casino puts it this way: You Must Be Present to
Win. The Chassidic story in this chapter shows us that
the simplicity of our presence is what really matters, not
the outer trappings.

When we see with the eyes of simplicity, everything
reveals itself to us. The bamboo of China and the trees of
New England teach us about the rhythms and mystery
of life. What more need we ask for—more sights, more
sounds, more smells, more thoughts? Lord knows, we've
had enough already. What we seek is not to be found in
more sights or sounds or tastes or thoughts but in the living reality of any moment that we touch with wisdom
and understanding. Some spiritual teachers speak of it as
putting one foot in front of another or living one day at a
time. Imagine being separated for a long time from home,
from beloved friends, perhaps even from the planet.

How extraordinary it would be simply to return and breathe the fresh spring air, to feel our feet on the earth, to witness the birth of a child or the passing on of someone's spirit at death. The more intimately we touch what is present, the deeper our hearts will open and the more our creativity and freedom will flourish.

The clutter of our lives blinds us to the precious simplicity that surrounds us and is within us. Too often we become possessed and imprisoned by the chains of our own accumulations. We live in fear of their loss; we evolve complex strategies to protect ourselves from failure and deprivation. This burden inhibits our ability to walk with lightness of heart. The noise created through our own busyness deafens us to the wonder of silence.

Modern culture has wrongly learned to equate simplicity with deprivation, silence with absence, and strives to fill our lives and minds with objects, information, and distraction. We have become uncomfortable with quietude. Caught in the web of this complexity, we grow increasingly poor in spirit. To know how much clutter you carry in your life simply ask yourself what you would truly miss if you were suddenly transported to another time and place. It would not be the many things we could have filled our suitcases with; it would be the simple delights of shared laughter and shared sorrow, the simple love of those close to us.

We do not need to retreat to the nearest monastery, renouncing all of our possessions and engagements, in order to discover the wonder of silence and spaciousness. Indeed, confusion and preoccupation can be the companion of the ascetic as well as the commuter. We do not need to withdraw from the world in order to discover true simplicity of heart. Dramatic gestures are not called for. "If one is to do good," says William Blake, "good must be done in the minute particulars. General good is the plea of the hypocrite, the flatterer, and the scoundrel." Simplicity is related not to how much we have but to how

much we hold on to. This simplicity is without preten-
sion. It is like the water that simply runs downhill. There
are no priests in this simplicity nor outcasts. In Zen Bud-
dhism it is called resuming our true nature.

Simplicity and renunciation are acts of compassion—
for ourselves, for the world around us. Gandhi once
stated, "There is enough in this world for everyone's
need, but not enough for everyone's greed." Simplicity in
our lifestyles expresses a care and compassion for the
world. Simplicity in our hearts, letting go of opinions
and craving, is an act of compassion for ourselves. When
we let go of yearning for the future, preoccupation with
the past, and strategies to protect the present, there is
nowhere left to go but where we are. To connect with
the present moment is to begin to appreciate the beauty
of true simplicity.

Every moment is unique and therefore precious. The
sunset on this day will never be duplicated. The caress of
a friend, the laugh of a child will never be precisely repeated or felt again. The moment we are experiencing
can never be recaptured. To be present is the only way
we can appreciate life to the fullest and be touched by the
wonder of each moment.

The stories in this chapter speak to us of the wonder
of simplicity, the revelations discovered when we are
truly present. As you read these stories about simplicity,
think of your own life. In what ways is it cluttered, over-
full, confused, or rushed? What would it be like to live
more simply? What would you have to let go of? What
would you have to change? What assumptions and values that you hold would need to be abandoned? As you
picture yourself living more simply, try to sense how that
would feel. We have within us the capacity to shape our
lives. We can create complexity or simplicity, just as we
can create hatred or love and harmony. What would it
take to create a breath of simplicity and bring the spirit
of directness and presence alive in our own time?

IN THE COURSE OF THEIR LONG WANDERINGS, THE two brothers, Rabbi Zusya and Rabbi Elimelekh, often came to the city of Ludmir. There they always slept in the house of a poor, devout man. Years later, when their reputation had spread all over the country, they came to Ludmir again, not on foot as before, but in a carriage. The wealthiest man in that little town, who had never wanted to have anything to do with them, came to meet them, the moment he heard they had arrived, and begged them to lodge in his house. But they said: "Nothing has changed in us to make you respect us more than before. What is new is just the horses and the carriage. Take them for your guests, but let us stop with our old host, as usual."

Chassid

NASRUDIN WAS NOW AN OLD MAN LOOKING BACK on his life. He sat with his friends in the tea shop telling his story.

"When I was young I was fiery—I wanted to awaken everyone. I prayed to Allah to give me the strength to change the world.

"In mid-life I awoke one day and realized my life was half over and I had changed no one. So I prayed to Allah to give me the strength to change those close around me who so much needed it.

"Alas, now I am old and my prayer is simpler. 'Allah,' I ask, 'please give me the strength to at least change myself.'"

Sufi

IN THE AGE WHEN LIFE ON EARTH WAS FULL NO ONE paid any special attention to worthy men, nor did they single out the man of ability. Rulers were simply the highest branches on the trees and the people were like deer in the woods. They were honest and righteous without realizing that they were "doing their duty." They loved each other and did not know this was "love of neighbor." They deceived no one yet did not know they were "men to be trusted." They were reliable and did not know that this was "good faith." They lived freely together giving and taking and did not know they were generous. For this reason their deeds have not been narrated. They made no history.

Chuang-tzu

❧❧

THE VENERABLE ANANDA, THE MONK WHO WAS the attendant and closest disciple to the Buddha, was passing through a rural village one day. As he was thirsty he neared the village well, and seeing there a young girl, he requested of her a cup of water to drink. The girl said to him, "Oh, great monk, I'm unworthy to give water to you. Please do not ask this of me for I would only cause you impurity. I am a child of the lowest caste in this village." The great monk Ananda looked at her with eyes of compassion and said, "I did not ask you for your caste, but for a drink of water."

Early Buddhist

❧❧

THERE WAS A MAN WHO WAS LEADING AN ASCETIC life and not eating bread. He went to visit an old man. It happened that pilgrims also dropped by, and the old man fixed a modest meal for them. When they sat together to eat, the brother who was fasting picked up a single soaked pea and chewed it. When they arose from the table, the old man took the brother aside and said: Brother, when you go to visit somewhere, do not display your way of life, but if you want to keep to it, stay in your cell and never come out. He accepted what the old man said, and after that behaved like the others whenever he met with them.

Desert Fathers

ONE OF THE DEVOTEES IN THE TEMPLE WAS WELL known for his zealousness and effort. Day and night he would sit in meditation, not stopping even to eat or sleep. As time passed he grew thinner and more exhausted. The master of the temple advised him to slow down, to take more care of himself. But the devotee refused to heed his advice.

"Why are you rushing so, what is your hurry?" asked the master.

"I am after enlightenment," replied the devotee, "there is no time to waste."

"And how do you know," asked the master, "that enlightenment is running on before you, so that you have to rush after it? Perhaps it is behind you, and all you need to encounter it is to stand still—but you are running away from it!"

Zen

I CALL HIM LO BECAUSE HE TOLD ME THE STORY OF Lo, the poor Indian. It was a typically blustery February Boston morning. Traffic was tied up and drivers were glaring at one another. Everyone was unhappy—everyone, that is, except Lo, my cabdriver.

"You don't seem to be upset that we're not moving," I said.

"Nope," he said, very calmly. He gestured at the lines of traffic in every direction. "We can't go anyplace. What's the use of getting excited?" He lit a cigarette, took a deep puff, and turned around to face me. "You play golf?"

I nodded. "When I can, but I'm not very good."

"Ever get to the tee and find two foursomes along the fairway waiting for a foursome on the green? And another foursome waiting on the next tee?"

"Lots of times," I said, somewhat mystified as to what he was getting at.

"No place to go," he said. Then he pointed to the surrounding traffic. "Same thing here." He took another drag on the cigarette. "What's the sense of getting excited? Or mad?" He shrugged. "Nothing anyone can do about it. Yet they all get mad and get ulcers."

"I suppose they all have to get someplace," I said, looking at my watch to notify him that I, too, was going to be late for an appointment. "Business meetings or planes or something."

"Oh, sure," he agreed. "That's why they're in cabs. Everybody's got to be someplace except the cabdriver—he's already there. Now look at that guy," he said, pointing to a well-dressed man who had gotten out of his automobile and was talking to a police officer standing helplessly in the midst of the traffic. "That guy is practically having a stroke."

"He's probably late for work."

"I'm never late for work. I'm on time as soon as I get in my cab."

We sat watching the traffic cop trying to untangle the vehicles for a while and then we were on our way.

"You seem to like being a cabdriver," I remarked.

"Wouldn't be anything else," he said.

"Have you tried anything else?" I asked.

He nodded. "Lots of things. I was a yeoman in the navy, then I did office work, and for a while I was a runner for a stockbrokerage firm. But no more of that stuff for me."

"Wouldn't you make more money doing something else?" I asked.

"Oh, sure," he agreed. "If I stayed with that stockbroker I might have even become a millionaire. Who knows? But I've got no ambition."

"Everyone should have ambition," I told him.

"Why?" he asked.

No one had ever asked me that before. Everyone seems to accept the need for ambition the way they accept other self-evident truths.

"Why?" I repeated. "Well, everyone should have ambition or they won't get ahead."

"So?" he asked.

"So? Well, so they can have a nice home, good clothes, do things for their family. You know, get ahead in life."

"I'm not married and I don't have any family," he told me.

"Even so," I said, "you should still want to get ahead."

And then he said it: "It's just like the Indian," he remarked.

I was nonplussed. "The Indian? What's just like the Indian? What Indian?"

"Lo, the poor Indian," he answered. "I'll tell you the story." He settled back behind the wheel and began. "There was this Indian who was sitting by a river fishing. This white guy used to see him there every day, and whoever he was with, he would point over to the Indian and say to his friend, 'Lo, the poor Indian.' So one day when he was alone, he went over to the Indian and talked to him. 'What are you doing?' he asked. 'Fishing,' the Indian grunted. 'That's all you ever do,' the white guy said. And the Indian just grunted. So the white guy said, 'You ought to get a job and work.' The Indian asked, 'Why?' The white guy said, 'You'll make a lot of money.' The Indian said, 'So?' The white guy said, 'You can invest it and make yourself a lot more money.' What do you think the Indian said to that? He just said, 'So?' Well, the white guy blew his stack. 'So,' he told him, 'if you're rich you can do anything you want to.' The Indian looked at the white man, then turned back to his fishing. 'I'm doing that now,' he said."

The cabdriver laughed. "Lo, the poor Indian." He puffed on his cigarette, then threw it out. "That's me."

I thought about it for a minute. "You're doing what you want?" I said.

"Right."

"And you're satisfied?"

"Right," he said. "Take all that traffic back there. Everybody's unhappy but me. Why? Because they're not at work; they're not where they're going; they're losing time, or money, or something. But not me. I'm not going any-place; I'm already there. I'm not losing time, or money, or anything. They got to get out in the cold and walk through snow, or slush, or rain, or whatever. Me, I'm in a nice, warm, dry cab. Do you know when I get out of this cab?"

"No. When do you get out?"

"When I *feel* like it. When I want coffee or a bite, or I feel like going in someplace and talking to the guys. I get out when I want to, not when I get to someplace where I've got to get out because I've arrived. That *got to* stuff's for the passengers, not for me."

"You've got it made," I said.

"You said it, brother. Now take the good weather," he said. "Summer and spring, or even fall, when the leaves are out and turning. What do you hear people say they want to do on a nice Sunday afternoon? They all want to take a ride, right?"

"A ride through the country," I agreed. "My aunts used to do it every Sunday."

"See the foliage, go by the water, go through the park, ride around someplace," he said. "And not just older people. How about the kids? Do you ever watch the teenagers and the kids in their twenties? What do they want to do except ride around and see the sights?" He pointed toward the Charles. "In the summer you'll see me driving by that river with my windows down. And I'm getting paid for it."

When I got out at my destination, he spoke again. "I don't know what you do for a living, Mister, but whatever it is, I hope you like it. If you don't, I hope you get to be a millionaire so you can do whatever you like. Me, I'm not a millionaire, but I don't have to be one to do whatever I like. I'm doing it now."

As he drove off, I looked after him a long time. Here I was, where I didn't want to be, going into a building to see a man I didn't want to see, and doing some work I didn't want to do.

Lo, the poor cabdriver, I said to myself. And I went about my business.

Governor Foster Furcolo

❧❧

THE POOR MAN HAD COME TO THE END OF HIS ROPE. So he went to his rabbi for advice.

"Holy Rabbi!" he cried. "Things are in a bad way with me, and are getting worse all the time! We are poor, so poor, that my wife, my six children, my in-laws, and I have to live in a one-room hut. We get in each other's way all the time. Our nerves are frayed, and, because we have plenty of troubles, we quarrel. Believe me—my home is a hell and I'd sooner die than continue living this way!"

The rabbi pondered the matter gravely. "My son," he said, "promise to do as I tell you and your condition will improve."

"I promise, Rabbi," answered the troubled man. "I'll do anything you say."

"Tell me—what animals do you own?"

"I have a cow, a goat, and some chickens."

"Very well! Go home now and take all these animals into your house to live with you."

The poor man was dumbfounded, but since he had promised the rabbi, he went home and brought all the animals into his house.

The following day the poor man returned to the rabbi and cried, "Rabbi, what a misfortune have you brought upon me! I did as you told me and brought the animals into the house. And now what have I got? Things are worse than ever! My life is a perfect hell—the house is turned into a barn! Save me, Rabbi—help me!"

"My son," replied the rabbi serenely, "go home and take the chickens out of your house. God will help you!"

So the poor man went home and took the chickens out of his house. But it was not long before he again came running to the rabbi.

"Holy Rabbi!" he wailed. "Help me, save me! The goat is smashing everything in the house—she's turning my life into a nightmare."

"Go home," said the rabbi gently, "and take the goat out of the house. God will help you!"

The poor man returned to his house and removed the goat. But it wasn't long before he again came running to the rabbi, lamenting loudly, "What a misfortune you've brought upon my head, Rabbi! The cow has turned my house into a stable! How can you expect a human being to live side by side with an animal?"

"You're right—a hundred times right!" agreed the rabbi. "Go straight home and take the cow out of your house!"

And the poor unfortunate hastened home and took the cow out of his house.

Not a day had passed before he came running again to the rabbi.

"Rabbi!" cried the poor man, his face beaming. "You've made life sweet again for me. With all the animals out, the house is so quiet, so roomy, and so clean! What a pleasure!"

Chassid

━━

A YOUNG ZEN MONK AND HIS MASTER WERE strolling through the gardens of the monastery. Though he had practiced ardently, the young man still had not come to any deep understanding of Zen. Finally he turned to the master and asked, "Please, master, tell me something of this enlightenment."

The master pointed, "See that bamboo over there? See how short it is?" The monk replied, "Yes." "See that bamboo over there? See how tall it is?" And the monk replied, "Yes." And the master said, "Just that is enlightenment."

Zen

━━

R ABBI ELIMELEKH ONCE SET OUT FOR HOME FROM A city he had visited and all the Hasidim accompanied him for a long stretch of the way. When his carriage drove through the gate, he got out, told the coachman to drive on, and walked behind the carriage in the midst of the throng. The astonished Hasidim asked him why he had done this. He answered: "When I saw the great devotion with which you were performing the good work of accompanying me, I could not bear to be excluded from it!"

Chassid

❦❦

SHAH ABBAS OF PERSIA WAS A MAN OF WIT WHO liked to converse in parables. Among his ministers was Merza Zaki, who understood his parables well.

One day the shah was holding court with his ministers, discussing the ways of this world. Thereon he asked his ministers, "What is the sweetest melody?"

One answered, "The melody of the flute."

"No," answered another minister. "The melody of the harp is the most pleasant to the ear."

The third remarked, "Neither one nor the other! The violin has the finest tone."

Thus a bitter dispute arose.

Merza Zaki was silent and did not say anything. Days passed. Then Merza Zaki invited the shah and the rulers of the state to a banquet arranged in their honor. Musicians entertained the honored guests on all kinds of instruments. But how strange, the table bore no refreshments. The guests were without food and drink. You must know that in the East the tables are always laden with delicacies at a banquet, and when the guests have eaten and drunk their fill, there is still more food, and copper vessels of meat and rice are brought to the loaded tables. Now where was the food? It was embarrassing to ask, so the guests just went on sitting till midnight. Then Merza Zaki beckoned to the headwaiter, and he brought a vessel of cooked food into the room and beat the lid of the pot with a big spoon. *Clink! Clink!*

All the guests breathed a sigh of relief. Indeed it was time. Then Shah Abbas said, "The clink of dishes in the ears of a hungry man—this is the sweetest melody."

Sufi

A CENTURY AGO, A YOUNG STUDENT AT THE GREAT Oxford University in England was taking an important examination in religious studies. The examination question for this day was to write about the religious and spiritual meaning in the miracle of Christ turning water into wine. For two hours he sat in the crowded classroom while other students filled their pages with long essays, to show their understanding. The exam time was almost over and this one student had not written a single word. The proctor came over to him and insisted that he commit something to the paper before turning it in. The young Lord Byron simply picked up his hand and penned the following line: "The water met its Master, and blushed."

Christian

EIGHT

Who Shall
Judge?

I MAGINE A WORLD WITHOUT JUDGMENT. IT WOULD
be a world without hatred and division, without alienation and violence. Acceptance, forgiveness, and understanding would be the pillars of our relationships. No
enemies or opponents would be created, no rejection or
belittlement would be extended on the basis of color,
gender, religion, or race. Imagine your personal world
without judgment.

We all have within us the great voice of the critic or
the judge. It is directed inwardly and outwardly, to com-
pare, discriminate, and censure. Often this inner judge
simply replays the words of a figure who judged us in
the past. Yet we believe it, carry it, pass it along, day after
day and generation after generation. In many of us the
inner judge or critic is so harsh and strident it would find
employment impossible anywhere except in the cruelest
and most punitive of regimes, such as under Stalin or Idi
Amin. We can be so hard on ourselves and others.

Judgment is the refuge and the weapon of self-righteousness and fear. We bolster a sense of superiority by
dwelling upon the weaknesses of others. We defend our
own sense of right through highlighting the imperfections

of others. Our judgments are the visible expression of our disconnection and separation from others, from our own hearts. They are a breeding ground of pain, alienation, and division.

To understand judgment we have to see that it arises from fear, religious, economic, racial fear—all the insecurities we carry that tell us that either we or another are simply not good enough. In the spiritual life we are taught to transform judgment to love and wisdom. Before we judge, consider, as Jesus says, "Who amongst us has not sinned? Are we not to cast the beam out of our own eye before pointing out the mote in others'?"

In one story in this chapter the master of a monastery refuses to evict a pupil who has stolen, even though all the others threaten to leave if the pupil stays, saying to them, "Who will teach him if I do not?" In overcoming the smallness of the judging mind, we are asked to care for those who are confused, in pain, in fear or anger, who then act in ways that harm others. We are asked to touch the same confusion and pain in ourselves and to see all of it with wisdom and compassion.

Our judgments inevitably find their way into action. When we deem someone to be inferior or unworthy, we turn away from them. When we deem another to be attractive or worthy, we admire and pursue them. On the basis of our dislike, we dismiss one person, while personal preference and past experience becomes the basis for relating to another. Often our judgments have their source in superficial impressions or in things long past. The power of our judgments creates an inner environment that can be sorely lacking in kindness and love.

We might believe that it is necessary to judge, that without our judgments we would be unable to distinguish between right and wrong, good and bad, worthy and unworthy. We might believe that without judgment we would suffer paralysis, having no basis upon which to make choices, decisions, and progress in our lives. We might feel that the absence of judgment would deprive us of values and ethics. They are important questions to explore. What would happen if we did not judge?

Is it not true that if we were able to restrain ourselves from judgment we would have no alternative but to call upon great inner depths of clarity and understanding to discern the truth of each moment? Is it not true that if we set aside our judgments of the present, which are so often just leftovers from the past, we would have to connect with each moment fully and freshly? If we set aside the superficiality of so many of our judgments, would we not see with great depth and understanding? It is also true that in this depth and understanding we would discover new dimensions of humility, forgiveness, and tolerance.

The energy employed in the judging mind is sufficient to transform the world. It is an energy we need to rechannel. Forgiveness, tolerance, patience, and love bring us humility. They remind us that the person we see before us is simply ourselves in another form, someone who yearns for the same love, acceptance, and open-heartedness that we yearn for, is capable of suffering the same pain of rejection, judgment, and hatred that we are capable of suffering.

One of the great rules of the heart, one of the great laws of spiritual life, is that no matter what else happens never put anyone out of your heart. Take whatever action is necessary to protect yourself and others from someone acting dangerously, put people in jail if you must, but don't put them out of your heart. There are times when we have all acted out of tremendous confusion, pain, and fear and have thereby created further confusion and pain. Is it our role to judge others in the world? Perhaps a wiser role is to bring the spirit of love, peace, and understanding into the very midst of confusion and pain.

As you read, reflect on the feelings of judgment and self-righteousness that arise in you, as in all of us. How do they feel, how do we actually experience them? Are they pleasant? Do they have a quality of wisdom or truth to them? Or is fear associated with them? Do they leave us more separate, more isolated or frightened? Reflect on their opposite. Remember the moments of forgiveness or understanding, the empathy with another's confusion and struggle that is so much like our own. How do you wish to be treated when you have made a mistake? How then would you wish to treat another? What are the judgments we can let go of even now? What opportunities do we have to set aside the past and see things anew? What immediate relationships would be healed by letting go of our judgments? What level of forgiveness can we extend—to others, to ourselves?

THERE IS A STORY ABOUT BUDDHA AND MARA, who represents the forces of evil. One day the Buddha was in his cave, and Ananda, who was the Buddha's assistant, was standing outside near the door. Suddenly Ananda saw Mara coming. He was surprised. He didn't want that, and he wished Mara would get lost. But Mara walked straight to Ananda and asked him to announce his visit to the Buddha.

Ananda said, "Why have you come here? Don't you remember that in olden times you were defeated by the Buddha under the Bodhi tree? Aren't you ashamed to come here? Go away! The Buddha will not see you. You are evil. You are his enemy." When Mara heard this he began to laugh and laugh. "Did you say that your teacher told you that he has enemies?" That made Ananda very embarrassed. He knew that his teacher had not said that he had enemies. So Ananda was defeated and had to go in and announce the visit of Mara, hoping that the Buddha would say, "Go and tell him that I am not here. Tell him that I am in a meeting."

But the Buddha was very excited when he heard that Mara, such a very old friend, had come to visit him. "Is that true? Is he really here?" the Buddha said, and he went out in person to greet Mara. Ananda was very distressed. The Buddha went right up to Mara, bowed to him, and took his hands in his in the warmest way. The Buddha said, "Hello! How are you? How have you been? Is everything all right?"

Mara didn't say anything. So the Buddha brought him into the cave, prepared a seat for him to sit down, and told Ananda to go and make herb tea for both of them. "I can make tea for my master one hundred times a day, but making tea for Mara is not a joy," Ananda thought to himself. But since this was the order of his master, how could he refuse? So Ananda went to prepare some herb tea for the Buddha and his so-called guest, but while doing this he tried to listen to their conversation.

The Buddha repeated very warmly, "How have you been? How are things with you?" Mara said, "Things are not going well at all. I am tired of being a Mara. I want to be something else."

Ananda became very frightened. Mara said, "You know, being a Mara is not a very easy thing to do. If you talk, you have to talk in riddles. If you do anything, you have to be tricky and look evil. I am very tired of all that. But what I cannot bear is my disciples. They are now talking about social justice, peace, equality, liberation, nonduality, nonviolence, all of that. I have had enough of it! I think that it would be better if I hand them all over to you. I want to be something else."

Ananda began to shudder because he was afraid that the master would decide to take the other role. Mara would become the Buddha, and the Buddha would become Mara. It made him very sad.

The Buddha listened attentively, and was filled with compassion. Finally, he said in a quiet voice, "Do you think it's fun being a Buddha? You don't know what my disciples have done to me! They put words into my mouth that I never said. They build garish temples and put statues of me on altars in order to attract bananas and oranges and sweet rice, just for themselves. And they package me and make my teaching into an item of commerce. Mara, if you knew what it is really like to be a Buddha, I am sure you wouldn't want to be one." And, thereupon, the Buddha recited a long verse summarizing the conversation.

Thich Nhat Hanh

WHEN BANKEI HELD HIS SECLUSION WEEKS OF MED-
itation, pupils from many parts of Japan came to
attend. During one of these gatherings a pupil was caught
stealing. The matter was reported to Bankei with the re-
quest that the culprit be expelled. Bankei ignored the case.

Later the pupil was caught in a similar act, and again
Bankei disregarded the matter. This angered the other
pupils, who drew up a petition asking for the dismissal of
the thief, stating that otherwise they would leave in a
body.

When Bankei had read the petition he called everyone
before him. "You are wise brothers," he told them. "You
know what is right and what is wrong. You may go somewhere else to study if you wish, but this poor brother does
not even know right from wrong. Who will teach him if I
do not? I am going to keep him here even if all the rest of
you leave."

A torrent of tears cleansed the face of the brother who
had stolen. All desire to steal had vanished.

Zen

WHEN THE SON OF GOD WAS NAILED TO THE CROSS
and died, he went straight down to hell from the
cross and set free all the sinners who were there in torment.

And the devil wept and mourned, for he thought he
would get no more sinners for hell.

Then God said to him, "Do not weep, for I shall send
you all those who are self-righteous in their condemnation
of sinners and hell shall be filled up once more until I return."

Traditional Christian

ONCE TWO TIBETAN MONKS TRAVELING ON PIL-
grimage came to a rushing river. There they saw an
ugly old leper woman sitting on the bank, begging alms.

When the monks approached, she begged the priestly
pair to assist her in crossing the river. One monk instinctively felt revulsion; disgusted, he gathered his long, flow-
ing monastic robes about himself, and waded into the
river on his own, soon to reach the other side. There he
wondered if he would even bother to wait for his tardy
friend, being unsure as to whether or not the other monk
would abandon the leper or wish to continue traveling on
with her alongside.

But the second monk felt sorry for the decrepit old hag,
and compassion naturally blossomed in his heart. He
picked up the leprous creature, hoisted her onto his back,
and struggled down the riverbank and into the swirling
current.

Naturally enough, his brother monk had safely
reached the far side long before the heavily laden lama,
bearing his dirty bundle of rags and bones, even reached
midstream.

Then an amazing thing happened. At midstream, just
where the going seemed to be becoming most difficult,
with the muddy water boiling about his thighs and his
water-logged woolen robes billowing out like sails, the
kindly monk suddenly—miraculously, it seemed—felt the
burden lifted from his back. Looking up, he saw the female Buddha Vajra Yogini herself soaring gracefully overhead, reaching down to draw him up to Paradise with her.

The first monk, greatly chastened—having been so
directly instructed in the nature of both compassion and
illusory form—had to continue alone on his solitary,
pedestrian pilgrimage.

Tibetan Buddhist

A MAN WHOSE AXE WAS MISSING SUSPECTED HIS neighbor's son. The boy walked like a thief, looked like a thief, and spoke like a thief. But the man found his axe while he was digging in the valley, and the next time he saw his neighbor's son, the boy walked, looked, and spoke like any other child.

Traditional German

A BUSINESSMAN NEEDING TO ATTEND A CONFERENCE in a faraway city decided to travel on country roads rather than the freeways so he could enjoy a relaxing journey. After some hours of traveling he realized he was hopelessly lost. Seeing a farmer tending his field on the side of the road, he stopped to ask for directions. "Can you tell me how far it is to Chicago?" he asked the farmer. "Well, I don't rightly know," the farmer replied. "Well, can you tell me how far I am from New York?" the businessman questioned again. "Well, I don't rightly know," the farmer again replied. "Can you at least tell me the quickest way to the main road?" the exasperated businessman asked. "No, I don't rightly know," the farmer again answered.

"You really don't know very much at all, do you?" blurted the impatient businessman. "Nope, but I ain't lost," the farmer calmly answered.

Contemporary Folktale

THERE WAS A MAN WHO CAME TO THE LORD Shantih beseeching him to cure his ills. "And what ills do you have?" Lord Shantih asked. "My stomach pains me when I eat too much," the man said. "My throat is parched when I grow thirsty, and my back aches when I spend the day working in the fields." "These are the complaints of life," Lord Shantih told him. "Only death can cure you." The man cursed Lord Shantih and left in an angry mood, grumbling to his companions. "That man," Lord Shantih said, "will find his tomb a trifle too cold for his taste."

Thomas Wiloch

A S FAR AS BUDDHA NATURE IS CONCERNED, THERE is no difference between sinner and sage. . . . One enlightened thought and one is a Buddha, one foolish thought and one is an ordinary person.

Zen Master Hui Neng

A FARMER REQUESTED A TENDAI PRIEST TO RECITE sutras for his wife, who had died. After the recitation was over the farmer asked: "Do you think my wife will gain merit from this?"

"Not only your wife, but all sentient beings will benefit from the recitation of sutras," answered the priest.

"If you say all sentient beings will benefit," said the farmer, "my wife may be very weak and others will take advantage of her, getting the benefit she should have. So please recite sutras just for her."

The priest explained that it was the desire of a Buddhist to offer blessings and wish merit for every living being.

"That is a fine teaching," concluded the farmer, "but please make one exception. I have a neighbor who is rough and mean to me. Just exclude him from all those sentient beings."

Buddhist

In the neighborhood where Mulla Nasrudin lived was a man named Azis, who was known to all as a great gossip. Azis could be found day or night in the market or tea shops telling the latest, often untrue, stories of who did what in every part of town. He spread rumors, passed judgment, told tales, and sowed seeds of disharmony. Some days when his stories came back to him, even he knew it was too much, but what could he do?

Finally his friends decided to send him to Nasrudin, the local wise man. Nasrudin wasn't very helpful at first, having a similar problem himself. But finally he thought of a plan. "Bring me a chicken from the market," he told Azis, "and hurry quickly. And you must make sure it is cleanly plucked, with not a feather remaining on it."

Azis went off to the market and purchased the chicken, after which the seller began the laborious job of plucking. Then Azis became impatient. He took the chicken and immediately returned to Nasrudin, pulling out the remaining feathers as he walked back.

He entered Nasrudin's doorway and handed him the chicken. Nasrudin put it down and demanded that Azis go back and bring him all the chicken's feathers. "Impossible," cried Azis. "By now the feathers are scattered halfway across town."

"It is like this with your words, too, Azis. As soon as you open your mouth to sow a tale it flies out like the wind carries these feathers. It spreads across town and nothing can retrieve it. You must beware the feathers that fly from your tongue and not fill the air with them."

Azis returned home chastened by this. Apologetic to his friends and community, he took more care when plucking his words.

Sufi

Sᴀ'ᴅɪ ᴏꜰ Sʜɪʀᴀᴢ ᴛᴇʟʟꜱ ᴛʜɪꜱ ꜱᴛᴏʀʏ ᴀʙᴏᴜᴛ ʜɪᴍꜱᴇʟꜰ:
When I was a child I was a pious boy, fervent in prayer and devotion. One night I was keeping vigil with my father, the Holy Koran on my lap.

Everyone else in the room began to slumber and soon was sound asleep, so I said to my father, "None of these sleepers opens his eyes or raises his head to say his prayers. You would think that they were all dead."

My father replied, "My beloved son, I would rather you too were asleep like them than slandering."

Sufi

NINE

Faith or
Foolishness?

W E INITIATE NEW BEGINNINGS AND NEW
directions because they promise greater freedom, happiness, and fulfillment. These changes
and aspirations require great faith if they are to be realized—faith in their reality, faith in ourselves. This is our
birthright, our inner potential, our spiritual heritage.
Our faith gives us the courage to go from the familiarity
of the known to the unknown. Faith enables us to for-
sake the sanctuaries of our security and boundaries and
to reach for new and unfamiliar horizons. We need
faith, too, to reach toward and understand that which is
greater than ourselves: faith in the universal law that
governs the seasons and creates the forms of life and
brings us to consciousness; faith that there is an underlying oneness in the multiplicity we perceive; faith that
there is a universal truth and freedom that is the territory of no one person.

When all else seems to fall away or is taken away
from us, we fall back upon this faith to take us through
the dark, confused, or difficult places in our life. Faith
brings us the energy, trust, and inspiration to face those
places and to awaken to their truths rather than running

from them. This faith can be inspired by great books, by great teachers of the past, or by great deeds, but in the end this faith is found primarily in ourselves. Here is where our wisdom grows, where the truth reveals itself. As Rumi puts it in his story of the bird, "Do not believe an absurdity." Faith and belief bring us to see what is true, strengthening our capacity to open.

Faith does not always come easily. Our scientific, analytical culture encourages us to doubt, to have faith only in that which can be proven. Our own disillusionments and disappointments lead us to cynicism and suspicion. We have learned to rely more upon analysis and evidence rather than intuition and trust. Yet both our dissatisfaction and our intuition lead us to search for new horizons, to search within ourselves to realize our potential.

Faith is a powerful double-edged sword. It has the potential to open our eyes or to blind us. Through wise faith we can surmount the greatest obstacle; through foolish faith we sentence ourselves to blind obedience. Faith can bring greater tolerance and humility or narrowness and bigotry. Faith can delude us into believing we are the custodians of truth; it can also instruct us to remain open to the challenges and mysteries of life.

In making new beginnings and traveling new paths, we need to be acutely watchful of our insecurities and self-doubt. These feelings can lead us to settle for boundaries rather than to expand our horizons. If we fear aloneness and seek reassurance, sanction, and identity through belonging, we will be led to blind belief rather than wise faith. It is insecure faith that is then translated into bigoted faith. Foolishness is the offspring of this insecure faith, sentencing us to being perpetual followers, listening to others rather than to ourselves.

Wise faith opens us rather than narrows us. It encourages us to question, to explore, to inquire. It encourages us to discover our own answers and to trust in our own experience. Wise faith enables us to listen to and learn from the guidance and experience of others while knowing that the power of transformation lies within. The greatest faith is the faith that we have in ourselves to live as fully compassionate and loving human beings.

As it matures, true faith, combined with wisdom, brings with it great humor and delight. Faith does not wear a frown, despairing of the frailties of human life. Instead faith points to a perspective of love and awareness so great that it can encompass the pain, the absurdities, the ironies, and the complexities of humanity.

In this chapter we have stories of faith and of foolishness. They lead us to ask ourselves, What do we have faith in? Do we deeply trust in our own potential for inner transformation and to touch the world with our love and wisdom? When has our belief been foolish, and what did that lead to? Where would true faith give us the courage to inquire, open, and grow, to bring freedom to our life? What difference does faith make in our life?

ONCE A MAN WAS ABOUT TO CROSS THE SEA. BIB-hishana, a saint, wrote the name of God on a leaf, tied it in a corner of the man's wearing-cloth, and said to him: "Don't be afraid. Have faith and walk on the water. But look here, the moment you lose faith you will be drowned." The man was walking easily on the water. Suddenly he had an intense desire to see what was tied in his cloth. He opened it and found only a leaf with Rama, the Hindu name for God, written on it. "What is this?" he thought. "Just the name of God!" As soon as doubt entered his mind he sank under the water.

Sri Ramakrishna

Four Indians enter a mosque and begin the
    prostrations.
Deep, sincere praying. But a priest walks by,
and one of the Indians, without thinking,
    says
"Oh, are you going to give the call to prayers
    now?
Is it time?"

The second Indian, under his breath,
"You spoke. Now your prayers are invalid."

The third, "Uncle, don't scold *him!*
You've done the same thing. Correct your-
    self."

The fourth, also out loud, "Praise to God,
I haven't made the mistake of these three."

So all four prayers are interrupted,
with the three fault-finders more at fault
than the original speaker!

Blessed is one who sees his weakness,
and blessed is one who, when he sees a flaw
in someone else, takes responsibility for it.

Because, half of any person is wrong and
    weak and off the path.
Half! The other half is dancing and swim-
    ming and flying
in the Invisible Joy.

Rumi

THERE IS A TALE OF A MAN WHO FELL GRAVELY ILL and then appeared to have died. His body was gathered up, washed, and placed in a coffin, all the funeral preparations were made, and the priest invited. The coffin was being carried to the graveyard when there came a knocking from inside. It was put on the ground, the lid was opened. As people stood around he spoke up, "I am not dead, I have not died—you must take me out of here." But the priest in charge of carrying the coffin said, "I'm sorry sir, you can't be alive. The doctor has certified your death and the priest has also agreed upon it." Whereupon the lid was closed back down and the man was buried as planned.

Sufi

A CHRISTIAN SCHOLAR WHO HELD THE BIBLE TO BE literally true was once accosted by a scientist who said, "According to the Bible the earth was created some five thousand years ago. But we have discovered bones that point to life on earth a million years ago."

Pat came the answer: "When God created earth five thousand years ago he deliberately put those bones in to test our faith and see if we would believe the Word rather than scientific evidence."

Christian

❧❧

ONCE THERE WAS A MONKEY KING WHO LOOKED down the walls of a canyon and saw the bright moon reflected on the water. "Oh, what a beautiful jewel—I must have it," he thought. When he told this to the other monkeys, they all said it would be very hard to obtain, but the monkey king said, "I have an idea. One monkey will hold on to a tree and everyone else will form a line, each one holding tightly to the tail of the monkey in front. Then we can lower our monkey chain down to the water and the last one will be able to reach the jewel." So five hundred monkeys dangled one by one down to the water, but the weight of all the monkeys was too much for the one holding on to the tree and all five hundred monkeys fell into the water and drowned.

Buddhist

❧❧

A RABBI WAS ALWAYS TEACHING HIS FOLLOWERS TO seek the answers in themselves. But the followers always came back expecting more answers from him.

Finally he set up a booth with a sign: "Any Two Questions Answered for $100."

After some deliberation, one of his richest followers decided to ask and brought two important questions. He paid the money and said as he did, "Isn't $100 rather costly for just two questions?" "Yes," said the rabbi, "and what is your second question?"

Chassid

❧

A CERTAIN MAN CAUGHT A BIRD IN A TRAP. THE BIRD says, "Sir, you have eaten many cows and sheep in your life, and you're still hungry. The little bit of meat on my bones won't satisfy you either. If you let me go, I'll give you three pieces of wisdom. One I'll say standing on your hand. One on your roof. And one I'll speak from the limb of that tree."

The man was interested. He freed the bird and let it stand on his hand.

"Number One: Do not believe an absurdity, no matter who says it."

The bird flew and lit on the man's roof. "Number Two: Do not grieve over what is past. It's over. Never regret what has happened."

"By the way," the bird continued, "in my body there's a huge pearl weighing as much as ten copper coins. It was meant to be the inheritance of you and your children, but now you've lost it. You could have owned the largest pearl in existence, but evidently, it was not meant to be."

The man started wailing like a woman in childbirth. The bird, "Didn't I just say, *Don't grieve for what's in the past?* And also, *Don't believe an absurdity?* My entire body doesn't weigh as much as ten copper coins. How could I have a pearl that heavy inside me?"

The man came to his senses. "All right. Tell me Number Three."

"Yes. You've made such good use of the first two!"

Don't give advice to someone who's groggy and falling asleep. Don't throw seeds on the sand. Some torn places cannot be patched.

Rumi

✨

"GOD HAS MANY NAMES," A GURU TOLD HIS DIS-ciple, "and one of these is Rama. If you see God in everything, then you will be safe wherever you go." So the disciple traveled, and everywhere he went he recited "Ram, Ram" to keep himself safe.

One day he came to a village that was being terrorized by a mad elephant who would rampage through the streets regularly. When the villagers warned the disciple that the elephant had been heard nearby, the disciple was not concerned. "My guru told me only to recognize God in everything and I will be safe," he answered. But the villagers persisted, insisting that it was very dangerous to go out when the elephant was around.

"This elephant is God, and I am God, so why should I be afraid?" thought the disciple, and he went right out into the street. The elephant, seeing a man in the middle of the street, charged right at him. "Watch out!" the villagers cried. And even as the disciple thought "I am God and you are God," the mad elephant picked him up and dashed him to the side of the road, nearly killing the poor man.

After a long convalescence the disciple returned to his guru to tell the story and complain. "You told me to see Rama in everything and I would be safe, and now look at me."

"Oh, my disciple," replied the guru, "you were right to see God in yourself and in the elephant. But why," he went on, "did you fail to recognize God warning you in the voice of the villagers?"

Hindu

❧

GESHÉ BEN ONCE LIVED IN RETREAT IN A MOUN-tain cave that generations of hermit yogis had furnished with a door, rock altar, fireplace, and all the other amenities of civilized life. Still, it remained a simple cave in the mountainside, where the Geshé practiced in solitude.

One day at the end of a long period of total solitude, Ben received word that his patrons would be coming on the following day to bring supplies, make offerings, and receive his blessings. Therefore, Geshé Ben cleaned everything, put things in place, and prepared for the visit. He arranged beautiful offerings on his altar and dusted and polished everything, so much of which had been sorely neglected for months. Then he stepped back and surveyed his realm, such as it was, with pride.

"Ah-yii!" Ben suddenly exclaimed, in a pained voice, having observed his own handiwork. "What demonic force has entered here, into this hypocrite's haven?!" And reaching into a dark corner, he grabbed up a double handful of dust and dirt and threw it on the altar.

"Let them see this mountain hermitage and its occupant as it is!" he shouted exultantly. "Better no offerings at all than offerings to the mere facade of virtue." For he had realized that all the offerings he had so generously and artfully arranged on the newly cleaned shrine in the freshly scrubbed hermitage were not at all offerings to the enlightened Buddha, but had been for himself.

"Let them come and visit now," he thought with satisfaction. And so they did.

When Padampa Sangyay, the saint who came from India, heard the tale some years later, he exclaimed with approbation, "That handful of dirt was the best offering made in Tibet."

Tibetan Buddhist

ABBA OR SAID: EITHER FLEE FROM PEOPLE, OR LAUGH at the world and the people in it, and make a fool of yourself in many things.

Desert Fathers

MULLA NASRUDIN IS BOTH A FOOL AND A WISE MAN. He was out one day in his garden sprinkling bread crumbs around the flowerbeds. A neighbor came by and asked, "Mulla, why are you doing that?"

Nasrudin answered, "Oh, I do it to keep the tigers away."

The neighbor said, "But there aren't any tigers within thousands of miles of here."

Nasrudin replied, "Effective, isn't it?"

Sufi

MULLA NASRUDIN WAS SITTING IN A TEA SHOP when a friend came excitedly to speak with him. "I'm about to get married, Mulla," his friend stated, "and I'm very excited. Mulla, have you ever thought of marriage yourself?" Nasrudin replied, "I did think of getting married. In my youth in fact I very much wanted to do so. I waited to find for myself the perfect wife. I traveled looking for her, first to Damascus. There I met a beautiful woman who was gracious, kind, and deeply spiritual, but she had no worldly knowledge. I traveled further and went to Isphahan. There I met a woman who was both spiritual and worldly, beautiful in many ways, but we did not communicate well. Finally I went to Cairo and there after much searching I found her. She was spiritually deep, graceful, and beautiful in every respect, at home in the world and at home in the realms beyond it. I felt I had found the perfect wife." His friend questioned further, "Then did you not marry her, Mulla?" "Alas," said Nasrudin as he shook his head, "She was, unfortunately, waiting for the perfect husband."

Sufi

❧❧

TWO BROTHERS WERE TRAVELING TOGETHER: ONE WAS poor and the other was rich, and each had a horse, the poor one a mare, and the rich one a gelding. They stopped for the night, one beside the other. The poor man's mare bore a foal during the night, and the foal rolled under the rich man's cart.

In the morning the rich man roused his poor brother, saying, "Get up, brother. During the night my cart bore a foal."

The brother rose and said, "How is it possible for a cart to give birth to a foal? It was my mare who bore the foal!"

The rich brother said, "If your mare were his mother, he would have been found lying beside her."

To settle their quarrel they went to the authorities. The rich man gave the judges money and the poor man presented his case in words.

Finally word of this affair reached the tsar himself. He summoned both brothers before him and proposed for them four riddles: "What is the strongest and swiftest thing in the world? What is the fattest thing in the world? What is the softest thing? And what is the loveliest thing?" He gave them three days' time and said, "On the fourth day come back with your answers."

The rich man thought and thought, remembered his godmother, and went to ask her advice. She bade him sit down to table, treated him to food and drink, and then asked, "Why are you so sad, my godson?"

"The sovereign has proposed four riddles to me, and given me only three days to solve them."

"What are the riddles? Tell me."

"Well, godmother, this is the first riddle: 'What is the strongest and swiftest thing in the world?'"

"That's not difficult! My husband has a bare mare; nothing in the world is swifter than she is; if you lash her with a whip she will overtake a hare."

"The second riddle is: 'What is the fattest thing in the world?'"

"We have been feeding a spotted boar for the last two years; he has become so fat that he can barely stand on his legs."

"The third riddle is: 'What is the softest thing in the world?'"

"That's well known. Eider down—you cannot think of anything softer."

"The fourth riddle is: 'What is the loveliest thing in the world?'"

"The loveliest thing in the world is my grandson Ivanushka."

"Thank you, godmother, you have advised me well. I shall be grateful to you for the rest of my life."

As for the poor brother, he shed bitter tears and went home. He was met by his seven-year-old daughter—she was his only child—who said, "Why are you sighing and shedding tears, Father?"

"How can I help sighing and shedding tears? The tsar has proposed four riddles to me, and I shall never be able to solve them."

"Tell me, what are these riddles?"

"Here they are, my little daughter: 'What is the strongest and swiftest thing in the world? What is the fattest thing, what is the softest thing, and what is the loveliest thing?'"

"Father, go to the tsar and tell him that the strongest and fastest thing in the world is the wind; the fattest is the earth, for she feeds everything that grows and lives; the softest of all is the hand, for whatever a man may lie on, he puts his hand under his head; and there is nothing lovelier in the world than sleep."

The two brothers, the poor one and the rich one, came to the tsar. The tsar heard their answers to the riddles, and asked the poor man, "Did you solve these riddles yourself, or did someone solve them for you?"

The poor man answered, "Your Majesty, I have a seven-year-old daughter, and she gave me the answers."

"If your daughter is so wise, here is a silken thread for her: let her weave an embroidered towel for me by tomorrow morning."

The peasant took the silken thread and came home sad and grieving. "We are in trouble," he said to his daughter. "The tsar has ordered you to weave a towel from this thread."

"Grieve not, Father," said the little girl. She broke off a twig from a broom, gave it to her father, and told him, "Go to the tsar and ask him to find a master who can make a loom from this twig; on it I will weave his towel."

The peasant did as his daughter told him. The tsar listened to him and gave him 150 eggs, saying, "Give these eggs to your daughter; let her hatch 150 chicks by tomorrow."

The peasant returned home, even more sad and grieving than the first time. "Ah, my daughter," he said, "you are barely out of one trouble before another is upon you."

"Grieve not, Father," answered the seven-year-old girl. She baked the eggs for dinner and for supper and sent her father to the king. "Tell him," she said to her father, "that one-day grain is needed to feed the chicks. In one day let a field be plowed and the millet sown, harvested, and threshed; our chickens refuse to peck any other grain."

The tsar listened to this and said, "Since your daughter is so wise, let her appear before me tomorrow morning—and I want her to come neither on foot nor on horseback, neither naked nor dressed, neither with a present nor without a gift."

"Now," thought the peasant, "even my daughter cannot solve such a difficult riddle; we are lost."

"Grieve not," his seven-year-old daughter said to him. "Go to the hunters and buy me a live hare and a live quail." The father bought her a hare and a quail.

Next morning the seven-year-old girl took off her clothes, donned a net, took the quail in her hand, sat upon the hare, and went to the palace. The tsar met her at the gate. She bowed to him, saying, "Here is a little gift for you, Your Majesty," and handed him the quail. The tsar stretched out his hand, but the quail shook her wings and—flap, flap—was gone.

"Very well," said the tsar, "you have done as I ordered you to do. Now tell me—since your father is so poor, what do you live on?"

"My father catches fish on the shore, and he never puts bait in the water; and I make fish soup in my skirt."

"You are stupid! Fish never live on the shore, fish live in the water."

"And you—are you wise? Who ever saw a cart bear foals? Not a cart but a mare bears foals."

The tsar awarded the foal to the poor peasant and took the daughter into his own palace; when she grew up he married her and she became the tsarina.

Russian

ONCE THERE WAS A DISCIPLE OF A GREEK PHILOSOpher who was commanded by his Master for three years to give money to everyone who insulted him. When this period of trial was over, the Master said to him: Now you can go to Athens and learn wisdom. When the disciple was entering Athens he met a certain wise man who sat at the gate insulting everybody who came and went. He also insulted the disciple who immediately burst out laughing. Why do you laugh when I insult you? said the wise man. Because, said the disciple, for three years I have been paying for this kind of thing and now you give it to me for nothing. Enter the city, said the wise man, it is all yours.

Desert Fathers

TEN

Ideas or
Wisdom?

IN OUR QUEST TO LIVE LIFE FULLY AND DEEPLY WE are engaged in understanding what it means to see with eyes of innocence, what it means to see anew in each moment. Our eyes of innocence are opened through the sensitivity and loving attention we bring to the moment we find ourselves in. The immediacy of our connection with each moment and all it brings acquaints us with a universe of unfolding enchantment and mystery. When we learn to see with freshness, free of the filters of our judgments and labels, there emerges within us a place of profound stillness and receptivity. In the grace of this stillness we discover the source of all spontaneity, creativity, and wisdom.

Modern culture would have us worship before the altar of the thinking mind, with its endless capacity to produce ideas, fantasies, and formulas. We are taught that the thinking mind is the possessor of all wisdom, and we dedicate much of our lives to the pursuit of knowledge and information. Seeing the world and ourselves through the filter of all the information we have accumulated, we can become imprisoned by the very ideas and images we have so ardently pursued. Often we think that we know ourselves, when what we know is only what we think about ourselves. When we think we know the world around us, our static images bar us from seeing the mystery held within each changing moment.

What is an image if not just a description of the world that is bound to the past? What is a belief if not just an insecure faith that has found sanctuary in a system? The spiritual path asks not a dismissal of the creative capacity of our mind to inquire, question, and analyze but an opening to another way of seeing that is not bound by the limitations of conditioning and second-hand information.

It is especially easy for the mind to get caught in or blinded by religious ideals, by images or beliefs about how things should be. There are so many authorities and opinions dispensing models and images of who we should become and what we should aspire to, so many teachings about what is holy and what is not. We hear so many opinions defining what is "sinful" and what is "righteous," what is "divine" and what is "mundane."

All of the Scriptures and guidance we listen to can at best point to a possibility, to the presence of great mystery that is just here before us.

The stories in this chapter are simple stories, as most great spiritual stories are. They connect wisdom and common sense. Teachings that are bereft of common sense are usually equally bereft of spirituality. The simplicity of these stories tells us of the magic of innocence and freshness. We, too, can set aside the burden of our conditioning and images. We, too, can know an immediacy and vitality in every relationship, in every moment. The enchantment of the universe surrounds us; all we need do is open our eyes.

We might reflect on what religious or spiritual ideas we may be holding on to that keep us from seeing what is true, that keep us from seeing directly our authentic path, guides, and teachers. What is present now in our own lives that is truly our spiritual teaching and practice, in that it offers us the opportunity to deepen our understanding? What would our lives be like if we carried no burden of "should"? What difference would it make in our lives if we set aside our images and connected directly with each moment with innocence and freshness?

WHEN THE GURU SAT DOWN TO WORSHIP EACH evening, the ashram cat would get in the way and distract the worshipers. So he ordered that the cat be tied during evening worship.

After the guru died the cat continued to be tied during evening worship. And when the cat expired, another cat was brought to the ashram so that it could be duly tied during evening worship.

Centuries later learned treatises were written by the guru's scholarly disciples on the liturgical significance of tying up a cat while worship is performed.

Hindu

ONCE UPON A TIME, ANANSI THOUGHT TO HIMSELF that if he could collect all the common sense in the world and keep it for himself, then he was bound to get plenty of money and plenty of power, for everybody would have to come to him with their worries, and he would charge them a whole lot when he advised them.

Anansi started to collect up and collect up all the common sense he could find and put it all into one huge calabash. When he searched and searched and couldn't find any more common sense, Anansi decided to hide his calabash on the top of a very tall tree so that nobody else could reach it.

So Anansi tied a rope around the neck of the calabash and tied the two ends of the rope together and hung the rope around his neck so that the calabash was on his belly. He started up the tall tree, but he couldn't climb very well or very fast because the calabash kept getting in his way. He was trying and trying so hard when all of a sudden he heard a voice burst out laughing in back of him. And when he looked he saw a little boy standing on the tree's root. "What a foolish man! If you want to climb the tree frontways, why don't you put the calabash behind you?"

Well, Anansi was so angry to hear that big piece of common sense coming out of the mouth of such a little boy after he had thought he had collected all the common sense in the world that Anansi took off the calabash, broke it into pieces, and the common sense scattered out in the breeze all over the world. Everybody got a little bit of it, but no one got it all. It was Anansi who made it happen that way.

Jamaican

❧❧

ONE DAY MARA, THE BUDDHIST GOD OF IGNORANCE and evil, was traveling through the villages of India with his attendants. He saw a man doing walking meditation whose face was lit up in wonder. The man had just discovered something on the ground in front of him. Mara's attendants asked what that was and Mara replied, "A piece of truth." "Doesn't this bother you when someone finds a piece of the truth, O evil one?" his attendants asked. "No," Mara replied. "Right after this they usually make a belief out of it."

Buddhist

❧❧

OUTSIDE THE VILLAGE LIVED A LARGE AND DANGER-ous snake, who had killed a man and wounded others with his poisonous bite. A wandering saint, famous for his kind heart, came to stay nearby for some days. The villagers complained loudly about their snake and indeed were intent on hunting and killing it if they could.

"Where will I find him?" asked the saint, who immediately set out down the feared path where the snake lived. With his great loving heart the saint called the snake to him and chastised him for so much destruction. "And now, as a result of this harm you have caused, many people wish to kill you. But if you promise me to not bite anymore, I will get the villagers to call off their snake hunt."

Some months later a battered and bruised snake crawled into the hut of the saint as he paid the village another visit. "After I stopped biting, the villagers began to tease me. Then, since I did not respond, the children started throwing sticks and rocks at me as well. Look at me. This is all because you told me not to bite."

"My friend," said the saint wisely, "I told you not to bite, but I didn't tell you not to hiss!"

Hindu

ONE DAY A RABBI, IN A FRENZY OF RELIGIOUS PASsion, rushed in before the ark, fell to his knees, and started beating his breast, crying, "I'm nobody! I'm nobody!"

The cantor of the synagogue, impressed by this example of spiritual humility, joined the rabbi on his knees. "I'm nobody! I'm nobody!"

The "shamus" (custodian), watching from the corner, couldn't restrain himself, either. He joined the other two on his knees, calling out, "I'm nobody! I'm nobody!"

At which point the rabbi, nudging the cantor with his elbow, pointed at the custodian and said, "Look who thinks he's nobody!"

Chassid

A LEARNED SCHOLAR SET FORTH ON A LONG AND difficult sea journey. Desiring to impress the crew with the depth of his learning, he would stop and question the simple sailors as they went about their duties. "Tell me my good man," he would ask a sailor, "have you studied philosophy?" The sailor would answer, "Oh no, I'm just a simple sailor. I only know how to sail this ship from one shore to the other." The scholar would reply, "You poor man, you have wasted half your life." The following day he would again question the sailor. "Have you studied geometry, my good man?" The sailor would reply again, "No, I'm sorry, sir. I just rig the sails and steer the ship." The scholar again would shake his head in despair and say only, "You poor fellow, dwelling in ignorance, you are wasting much of your life." Day after day the questions would go on, "Have you studied geometry, anthropology, zoology, psychology?" The sailor could only shake his head in denial.

One night the ship foundered in a storm. The scholar anxiously watched the crashing waves and held tightly to the mast. The sailor approached the scholar and asked him, "Have you, my good man, by any chance studied swimology?" In puzzlement the scholar could only shake his head. "That really is too bad," said the sailor. "You have wasted your whole life, for the ship is sinking."

Buddhist

A CERTAIN CONQUEROR SAID TO NASRUDIN: "MULLA, all the great rulers of the past had honorific titles with the name of God in them: there was, for instance, God-Gifted, and God-Accepted, and so on. How about some such name for me?"

"God Forbid," said Nasrudin.

Sufi

TIBETAN BUDDHISTS USE VARIOUS KINDS OF *visualizations in the practice of meditation. Superior practitioners are reputed to manifest what they visualize as realistically as we perceive our ordinary reality.*

One day, a great lama was bestowing teachings on a large gathering, and an old lady came to receive the empowerment. In Tibet it is customary to present a goodwill offering at the end of such an empowerment as a token of gratitude, often accompanied by a white silk scarf, symbolic of inner purity.

This old woman had a kilo of fresh yak butter to offer, one of the principal mediums of exchange in Tibet. It was in a satchel under her cloak, and she intended to offer it to the master after receiving his blessing.

However, this day, there were a great many recipients gathered, so when the lama reached the portion of the empowerment during which he would ordinarily touch each disciple on the head with a sacred vessel filled with nectar, he simply instructed them all to *visualize* the vase he was holding on his head and to imagine him placing it atop each of their heads.

The faithful old lady, needless to say, did exactly as instructed and received the initiation in its entirety. But when the rite was completed, and it was time to offer her precious butter to the venerable master, she merely stood up and uttered—in a stentorian voice reminiscent of the lama's and echoing his very own words—"Now simply visualize, venerable lama, that you are receiving as an offering this kilo of fine butter that you see in my hand!"

And then, chuckling to herself, she made her happy way homeward, a wiser and wealthier woman indeed, with her butter tucked safely away in her arm.

Buddhist

Mulla Nasrudin's students complained to him one day, "You give us teachings with words about truth and falsehood, about ignorance and perfection. Can you not demonstrate it in some other way?" Nasrudin reached in his bag and pulled out an apple. "Here," he said, "This is the perfect apple, the apple from the Garden of Eden." His students looked at it and noticed that it had a rotten spot. "How could this apple be an image of perfection?" they asked. "It takes one to know one," Nasrudin replied.

Sufi

Hogen, a Chinese Zen teacher, lived alone in a small temple in the country. One day four traveling monks appeared and asked if they might make a fire in his yard to warm themselves.

While they were building the fire, Hogen heard them arguing about subjectivity and objectivity. He joined them and said: "There is a big stone. Do you consider it to be inside or outside your mind?"

One of the monks replied: "From the Buddhist viewpoint everything is an objectification of mind, so I would say that the stone is inside my mind."

"Your head must feel very heavy," observed Hogen, "if you are carrying around a stone like that in your mind."

Zen

A great rabbi spent years in solitude meditating on the mystery of the divine in all things. When he finally returned to live among men and women his eyes shone with the beauty of what he had discovered. Many seekers came to him to ask for his truth, yet he was always reluctant to answer them, to put it into words. Pressed for years he finally relented and with eloquent words gave a feeble approximation of what he had discovered.

The seekers took these words with them everywhere. They spoke them, wrote them, created sacred texts about them, and religious societies were formed of those who repeated them, until no one remembered that the words were really about an experience. As his words spread, the rabbi became disheartened. "I had hoped to help but perhaps I should not have spoken at all."

Jewish

A LOVER PRESSED HIS SUIT WITH A WOMAN UNSUC-cessfully for many months, suffering the atrocious pains of rejection. Finally his sweetheart yielded. "Come to such and such a place, at such and such an hour," she said to him.

At that time and place the lover finally found himself seated beside his beloved. He then reached into his pocket and pulled out a sheaf of love letters that he had written to her over the past months.

They were passionate letters, expressing the pain he felt and his burning desire to experience the delights of love and union. He began to read them to his beloved. The hours passed by but still he read on and on.

Finally the woman said, "What kind of a fool are you? These letters are all about me and your longing for me. Well, here I am sitting with you at last and you are lost in your stupid letters."

Traditional

T HERE IS A STORY OF THE GREAT TIBETAN TEACHER Marpa, who lived on a farm with his family a thousand years ago in Tibet. On the farm, there also lived many monks who came to study with this great teacher. One day Marpa's oldest son was killed. Marpa was grieving deeply when one of the monks came to him and said, "I don't understand. You teach us that all is an illusion. Yet you are crying. If all is an illusion, then why do you grieve so deeply?" Marpa replied, "Indeed, everything is an illusion. And the death of a child is the greatest of these illusions."

Buddhist

T HE ZEN MASTER MU-NAN SENT FOR HIS DISCIPLE Shoju one day and said, "I am an old man now, Shoju, and it is you who will carry on this teaching. Here is a book that has been handed down for seven generations from master to master. I have myself added some notes to it that you will find valuable. Here, keep it with you as a sign that I have made you my successor." Shoju burned it immediately!

Zen

A BLACKBIRD FOUND A LARGE PIECE OF FOOD IN THE village and lit out into the sky with the food in its beak. A flock of his brothers chased after him and raucously attacked the food, pulling it from his beak. The blackbird finally let go of the last piece and the frenzied flock left him alone. The bird swooped and dived and thought, "I have lost the food but I have regained the peaceful sky."

Sufi

ELEVEN

Cause

and Effect

W<small>E SEEM TO LIVE IN A RANDOM UNIVERSE</small> composed of accidental and haphazard events and experiences. Our movement from heaven to hell, from the heights of elation to the depths of despair, appear intractable and unpredictable. We use words like *luck, fate, destiny,* and *jinx* to make sense of the variety of experiences that seem to "just happen" to us. Lost in either despair or exhilaration, we do not see the threads of cause and effect that weave the tapestry of our lives.

This tapestry of cause and effect is also called karma, which does not mean belief in reincarnation and past lives. Karma is simply this law of cause and effect. If you plant an apple seed, you don't get a mango tree. If we practice hatred or greed, it becomes our way and the world responds accordingly. If we practice awareness or loving-kindness, it becomes our way and the world responds accordingly.

Like an artist before an easel, we paint the landscape of our life with the colors of our thoughts, values, actions, and feelings. The quality of our life is flavored by the quality of each feeling and gesture. We are heirs to the results of our actions, to the intentions we bring to every movement we initiate. We make ripples upon the ocean of the universe through our very presence.

To understand the cycles of life is to understand that we are no different from anyone else. There is not one mistake we have made that has not been made before by another, not one delight we have experienced that has not been felt before by another. We see ourselves in others and they in us. We are not called upon to judge but to respond with kindness and understanding. How can we know amid the ten thousand joys and sorrows possible in the changing circumstances of our lives what is truly good or bad or what lessons we need? What matters is how we respond. What we create, how we act and respond, embodies itself not only in our own lives but in the lives of our communities, our children, our world. How we hold the world in our eye and heart is what we and the world will become.

Understanding the implications of our presence in the universe need not lead us into self-consciousness, blame, or judgment. Rather this understanding encourages us to see the importance of being awake and aware in each moment in our lives. As a conscious participant in the creation of each moment, of the world we live in, we have the power to heal, to love, to care, and to make our compassion visible.

The path of awakening and loving is a path without end. We cannot measure the worth of a single loving action or the impact of a single caring gesture. We cannot know the results of a single meditation or evaluate the learning we will derive by meeting a single difficulty with openheartedness. When we connect with the precious richness of loving, caring, and connectedness, results fade in importance. We can only trust that the landscape we paint will be colored by our love and care.

Can we observe how our own responses, our care or lack of it, bring parallel or identical responses from the world? If we sense how our actions and responses create our world, how might we wish to change these actions and responses? How would we treat people close to us if we held the power of life and the world in our hands? How would we act if all our acts truly mattered? Suppose we deeply believed that we had the power of healing and transformation in our hands and hearts. How would that affect the way that we live?

WHEN KHRUSHCHEV PRONOUNCED HIS FAMOUS denunciation of Stalin, someone in the Congress Hall is reported to have said, "Where were you, Comrade Khrushchev, when all these innocent people were being slaughtered?"

Khrushchev paused, looked around the hall, and said, "Will the man who said that kindly stand up!"

Tension mounted in the hall. No one moved.

Then Khrushchev said, "Well, whoever you are, you have your answer now. I was in exactly the same position then as you are now."

Russian

A MAN WHO LIVED IN THE SAME TOWN AS RABBI Zusya saw that he was very poor. So each day he put twenty pennies into a little bag in which Zusya kept his phylacteries, so that he and his family might buy the necessaries of life. From that time on, the man grew richer and richer. The more he had, the more he gave Zusya, and the more he gave Zusya, the more he had.

But once he recalled that Zusya was the disciple of a great master, and it occurred to him that if what he gave the disciple was so lavishly rewarded, he might become even more prosperous if he made presents to the master himself. So he traveled to Mezritch and induced Rabbi Baer to accept a substantial gift from him. From this time on, his means shrank until he had lost all the profits he had made during the more fortunate period. He took his trouble to Rabbi Zusya, told him the whole story, and asked him what his present predicament was due to. For had not the rabbi himself told him that his master was immeasurably greater than he?

Zusya replied: "Look! As long as you gave and did not

bother to whom, whether to Zusya or another, God gave to you and did not bother to whom. But when you began to seek out especially noble and distinguished recipients, God did exactly the same."

Chassid

❦

TWENTY MONKS AND ONE NUN, WHO WAS NAMED Eshun, were practicing meditation with a certain Zen master.

Eshun was very pretty even though her head was shaved and her dress was plain. Several monks secretly fell in love with her. One of them wrote her a love letter, insisting upon a private meeting.

Eshun did not reply. The following day the master gave a lecture to the group, and when it was over, Eshun arose. Addressing the one who had written her she said: "If you really love me so much, come and embrace me now."

Zen

❦

ONCE, WHEN RABBI PINCHAS ENTERED THE HOUSE of Study, he saw that his disciples, who had been talking busily, stopped and started at his coming. He asked them: "What were you talking about?"

"Rabbi," they said, "we were saying how afraid we are that the Evil Urge will pursue us."

"Don't worry," he replied. "You have not gotten high enough for it to pursue you. For the time being, you are still pursuing it."

Chassid

❦

"IF YOU WANT YOUR DONKEY TO MOVE FASTER, Nasrudin," said a neighbor, "get some ammonia and rub it on his rump."

Nasrudin found that this worked.

One day, feeling a little listless, he tried the same remedy on himself.

The ammonia burned him so much that he started to run round and round his room.

"What's the matter?" shouted his wife, unable to get hold of him.

"If you want to understand me, use the contents of that bottle over there," panted Mulla Nasrudin.

Sufi

A PHILOSOPHER, HAVING MADE AN APPOINTMENT TO dispute with Nasrudin, called and found him away from home.

Infuriated, he picked up a piece of chalk and wrote "Stupid Oaf" on Nasrudin's gate.

As soon as he got home and saw this, Mulla rushed to the philosopher's house.

"I had forgotten," he said, "that you were to call. And I apologize for not having been at home. Of course, I remembered the appointment as soon as I saw that you had left your name on my door."

Sufi

A MAN WHO LIVED ON THE NORTHERN FRONTIER of China was skilled in interpreting events. One day for no reason, his horse ran away to the nomads across the border. Everyone tried to console him, but his father said,

"What makes you so sure this isn't a blessing?" Some months later his horse returned, bringing a splendid nomad stallion. Everyone congratulated him, but his father said, "What makes you so sure this isn't a disaster?" Their household was richer by a fine horse, which the son loved to ride. One day he fell and broke his hip. Everyone tried to console him, but his father said, "What makes you so sure this isn't a blessing?"

A year later the nomads came in force across the border, and every able-bodied man took his bow and went into battle. The Chinese frontiersmen lost nine of every ten men. Only because the son was lame did father and son survive to take care of each other. Truly, blessing turns to disaster, and disaster to blessing: the changes have no end, nor can the mystery be fathomed.

Taoist

THE BUDDHA IN HIS TRAVELS ENCOUNTERED A JAIN, whose practice consisted of standing still on one leg. The Buddha asked him, "Would you tell me why you are doing this. What will this practice of standing on one leg do for you?"

The Jain replied, "Through this practice I am working out my karma, it will free me of all past karma."

The Buddha asked him, "How much have you worked out so far?" The Jain replied, "I could not say." The Buddha then asked, "How much karma do you still have left to work out?" The Jain again replied, "I do not know." Lastly the Buddha asked him, "But how will you know when you have finished working out your karma?" The Jain could only answer again, "This I do not know."

At this reply the Buddha spoke to him, saying, "It is time for you to set aside this practice and to understand the path to the end of suffering. It lies within the truth of each moment, here and now."

Traditional Buddhist

THERE IS A STORY OF A FELLOW WHO DIES AND finds himself in a shimmering realm. He thinks to himself, "I guess I was better than I thought I was." He is approached by a glistening being who ushers him into a regal banquet hall in which an immense table is laid out with unimaginable delicacies. He is seated at the banquet table with many others, and a choice selection of food is served to him. As he picks up his fork, someone approaches from behind and straps a thin board to the back of his arms so he cannot bend his elbows. Trying to pick up the food, he sees that he can't get it to his mouth because he cannot maneuver his stiff arms to feed himself.

Looking about, he notices that all the other people around the table have their arms bound straight so they cannot bend them. All are grunting and groaning as they attempt to stuff the food into their mouths but they cannot reach and there is a great wailing and moaning at their predicament.

Going to the being who had shown him to this place, he says, "This must be hell. But then what is heaven?"

The glistening being shows him through the archway into another huge banquet hall in which there sits another great table, filled with the same array of foods. "Ah, this is more like it," he thinks. And sitting down at the dinner table he is about to dig in when someone comes and ties a board to the back of his arms so, once again, he cannot bend his elbows to feed himself. Lamenting that this is the same unworkable situation as hell, he looks about in dismay to notice that, at this table, there is something different occurring. Instead of people trying to force the food into their mouths, straining against the rigidity of their arms, each being is holding his arm out straight to feed the person on either side of him. Each person is feeding the person next to him.

Traditional Japanese

A MAN FOUND AN EAGLE'S EGG AND PUT IT IN THE nest of a backyard hen. The eaglet hatched with the brood of chicks and grew up with them.

All his life the eagle did what the backyard chickens did, thinking he was a backyard chicken. He scratched the earth for worms and insects. He clucked and cackled. And he would thrash his wings and fly a few feet into the air.

Years passed and the eagle grew very old. One day he saw a magnificent bird far above him in the cloudless sky. It glided in graceful majesty among the powerful wind currents, with scarcely a beat of its strong golden wings.

The old eagle looked up in awe. "Who's that?" he asked.

"That's the eagle, the king of the birds," said his neighbor. "He belongs to the sky. We belong to the earth—we're chickens."

So the eagle lived and died a chicken, for that's what he thought he was.

Traditional

A FAMOUS MONGOL GENERAL AND HIS TROOPS HAD captured a large part of Central Asia. By now his troops were tired and far from home. He wanted to press on to capture the great city of Samarkhan which was defended by five times as many soldiers as his own. He felt certain they could win but the soldiers were reluctant.

Calling them together they set up a sacred altar and prayed for advice from their gods. At the end of the ceremony, the general took out a large gold coin and said he would now toss it to see what the gods directed. If it came up heads the soldiers would win a great victory.

The toss was indeed heads, and inspired by the gods the soldiers went on to easily overrun the city.

Afterwards a soldier said to the general, "When we have been shown that the gods are with us, nothing can challenge our destiny."

The general laughingly agreed and then showed him the coin, which had a head on both sides.

Chinese

＊＊

THERE IS A STORY ABOUT AN OLD FELLOW WHO HAD worked his whole life to develop a farm that would support his family. The old man, having worked many years tilling the land and fighting the elements to feed and shelter his family, came to a time when he felt it was appropriate to retire, to sit on the porch and contemplate the universe. His son was strong and able, and having a family of his own, it seemed time for him to take over. So the old man handed the farm over to his son and settled into a comfortable chair on the porch to enjoy his remaining years after a life of backbreaking toil.

His son was, at first, proud that finally he was master of his own farm. But as the months went by, working in the fields, he began to resent his father's inactivity. His father sat on the porch, bouncing his grandchildren on his knee, while he had to work all day. Resentment began to arise in the son's mind and he began to look at his father as just another mouth to feed. He thought to himself, "I have my wife and children to take care of now. The old man doesn't understand. He just sits there. It doesn't matter what came before. This is hard work and I wish I didn't have to take care of him, too." So his son went on hoeing and planting, getting angrier and angrier, until at harvest time he began to think that he didn't want to share his food with "that useless old man on the porch." He wanted it all for himself and his family and thought, "His time is over. He doesn't need to be around anymore."

So the son built a great wooden box of heavy teak, and when it was complete, he put the box on a wheelbarrow and wheeled it over to the porch and said firmly to his father, "Dad, I want you to get in this box. Do it now." His father bowed and, without a word, climbed off the porch and into the box. The son closed the heavy lid over his father and snapped the great brass hinge. Wheeling the box to a cliff, he was just about to tip it in the chasm below when he heard a knocking from within.

"What do you want?" he said gruffly. From within the box came his father's soft voice, "You know, I understand. If you want to get rid of me, that's okay. You think I'm just a useless old man. But if you want to throw me over the cliff, what I would do is take me out of the box and just throw my body over. I would save this box if I were you. I think your children may have use for it someday!"

Traditional

❦

LORD KRISHNA WANTED TO TEST THE WISDOM OF HIS kings. One day he summoned a king called Duryodana. Duryodana was well known throughout his kingdom for his cruelty and miserliness, and his subjects lived in terror. Lord Krishna said to King Duryodana, "I want you to go and travel the world over and find for me one truly good man." Duryodana replied, "Yes, Lord," and obediently began his search. He met and spoke with many people, and after much time had passed he returned to Lord Krishna saying, "Lord, I have done as you have asked and searched the world over for one truly good man. He is not to be found. All of them are selfish and wicked. Nowhere is there to be found this good man you seek!"

Lord Krishna sent him away and called another king called Dhammaraja. He was a king well known for his generosity and benevolence and well loved by all his people. Krishna said to him, "King Dhammaraja, I wish for you to travel the world over and bring to me one truly wicked man." Dhammaraja also obeyed, and on his travels met and spoke with many people. After much time had passed he returned to Krishna saying, "Lord, I have failed you. There are people who are misguided, people who are misled, people who act in blindness but nowhere could I find one truly evil man. They are all good at heart despite their failings!"

Hindu

TWELVE

Wisdom
Brings
Balance

THE GREATEST ART IN SPIRITUAL LIFE IS ONE OF
finding balance. The entire teachings of the Buddha are summed up in his encouragement to find
and travel the middle path—to seek neither the extremes of mortification and aversion for life nor the
extreme of indulgence, losing ourselves in pleasure-
seeking. The balance between these two is the path of
awakening and freedom. The path of balance is to be
with what is true in life and to love that, to be committed
to the truth on every level of our being.

The deepest joy we can find in life comes from
within our own being and not from the circumstances
around us. To find deep joy, which is radically different
from being busy, distracted, or entertained, always takes
a balance of heart. As one meditation teacher put it,
"You can't stop the waves, but you can learn to surf." We
cannot control or stop the changing circumstances in our
lives, but we can learn to balance amid them and to bring
balance to them. Learning that poise and balance is the
greatest skill in spiritual life: knowing when energy and
resolution is needed and when it is time to soften and

surrender; knowing when we need greater faith or greater inquiry; listening to the rhythms of our own heart as it tells us it is a time to seek greater solitude and simplicity or a time for service, to make our care and love visible. There is no formula for this responsiveness. We must simply learn to listen with an open heart to what is ever in this moment, this day, this life.

A great mystic once said, "Of what avail is the open eye if the heart is blind?" True wisdom never divorces us from the travails and sorrows of the world but teaches us to live with greater integrity and compassion in the midst of them. Wisdom reveals to us that serenity is not some lofty peak we inhabit after transcending the world but is in learning how to respond to the challenges of this very life with great love. Wisdom is not an attainment but a way of being, a way of responding in which we neither resist the challenges life brings to us nor are overwhelmed by them. It is a question of balance. The visible expression of wisdom lies in the skillful means through which we manifest it. Integrity, forgiveness, and honesty are the responses of a living wisdom. They are the qualities that enable us to walk in the spirit of freedom and to learn the lessons of life.

We are witnesses to an age of endless conflict and destruction. Our planet suffers, human relationships break down, and individuals live in alienation. The wealth of ideas and formulas that have been produced have yet to bring about any meaningful shift in this cycle of pain. The pain of our world will not be changed by yet more ideas. What is needed is a profound change in the human heart. Let us not respond to the pain that surrounds us with righteousness, pious formulas, or withdrawal; let us learn how to respond with love and integrity. Let us not allow our lives to become a record of all the things we wish we had done, might have done, or should have done.

As you read the stories in this chapter, close your eyes and reflect for a moment. Sense in yourself what is out of balance in your body, your life, your relationships. When have you been lost in extremes of fear, indulgence, or avoidance? How does this affect you? What needs greater balance in your life right now? What is needed to heal the imbalances you sense—what energy, attention, surrender is being called for? Where will you find these?

A WESTERN MONK AT A BUDDHIST MONASTERY became frustrated by the difficulties of practice and the detailed and seemingly arbitrary rules of conduct the monks had to follow. He began to criticize other monks for sloppy practice and to doubt the wisdom of the teaching. At one point, he went to Achaan Chah the master and complained, noting that even Achaan Chah himself was inconsistent and seemed often to contradict himself in an unenlightened way.

Achaan Chah just laughed and pointed out how much the monk was suffering by trying to judge others around him. Then he explained that his way of teaching is very simple: "It is as though I see people walking down a road I know well. To them the way may be unclear. I look up and see someone about to fall into a ditch on the right-hand side of the road, so I call out to him, 'Go left, go left!' Similarly, if I see another person about to fall into a ditch on the left, I call out, 'Go right, go right!' That is the extent of my teaching. Whatever extreme you get caught in, whatever you get attached to, I say, 'Let go of that, too.'" Let go on the left, let go on the right. Come back to the center, and you will arrive at the true Way.

Buddhist

"WE MUST NOT MORTIFY OUR FLESH!" THAT IS what the rabbi of Berditchev used to say. "It is nothing but the tempting of the Evil Urge which wants to weaken our spirit, in order to keep us from serving God rightly.

"Once two strong men were wrestling with each other and neither could prevail over his opponent. Then, one of them had an idea. 'I must manage to lessen the power of his mind,' he said to himself. 'With that I shall have conquered his body.' That is just what the Evil Urge wants to do when it tempts us to mortify our flesh."

Chassid

ABOUT A CENTURY AGO, THE ENLIGHTENED VAGA-bond and Tibetan Yogi Paltrul Rinpoche was wandering as an anonymous mendicant, as was his wont, when he heard about a renowned hermit who had long lived in solitary seclusion. Paltrul Rinpoche went to visit him, suddenly entering unannounced into the monk's dim cave, and peered about with a wry grin on his weathered face.

"Where have you come from," asked the hermit, "and where are you going?"

"I came from behind my back, and am going in the direction I am facing," replied Paltrul.

The hermit was nonplussed, but continued, "Where were you born?"

"On earth," was the reply.

By that time the hermit was becoming agitated.

"What is your name?" the hermit demanded.

"Yogi Beyond Action," replied the unexpected guest.

Paltrul Rinpoche then inquired as to why he had come to live in such a wild and remote part of the country. This was the question the hermit was prepared to answer.

"I have been here for twenty years in meditation. At this time I am meditating on the Perfection of Patience." All this was said not without a touch of pride.

"That's a good one!" said the anonymous visitor. Then, leaning forward as if confiding something to him, Paltrul whispered: "A couple of old frauds like us could never manage anything like that!"

The angry hermit rose abruptly from his seat. "You're a liar!" he exploded. "Who do you think you are, disturbing my retreat like this? What made you come here? Why couldn't you leave a humble practitioner like me to meditate in peace?"

"And now, dear friend," said Paltrul Rinpoche calmly, "where is your perfect patience?"

Buddhist

WHEN HE WAS ASKED WHICH WAS THE RIGHT WAY, that of sorrow or that of joy, the rabbi of Berditchev said: "There are two kinds of sorrow and two kinds of joy. When a man broods over the misfortunes that have come upon him, when he cowers in a corner and despairs of help—that is a bad kind of sorrow, concerning which it is said: "The Divine Presence does not dwell in a place of dejection." The other kind is the honest grief of a man who knows what he lacks. The same is true of joy. He who is devoid of inner substance and in the midst of his empty pleasures, does not feel it, nor tries to fill his lack, is a fool. But he who is truly joyful is like a man whose house has burned down, who feels his need deep in his soul and begins to build anew. Over every stone that is laid, his heart rejoices."

Chassid

ONCE ABBOT ANTHONY WAS CONVERSING WITH SOME brethren, and a hunter who was after game in the wilderness came upon them. He saw Abbot Anthony and the brothers enjoying themselves, and disapproved. Abbot Anthony said: Put an arrow in your bow and shoot it. This he did. Now shoot another, said the elder. And another, and another. The hunter said: If I bend my bow all the time it will break. Abbot Anthony replied: So it is also in the work of God. If we push ourselves beyond measure, the brethren will soon collapse. It is right, therefore, from time to time, to relax their efforts.

Desert Fathers

❧❧

IT WAS SAID ABOUT JOHN THE LITTLE THAT ONE DAY he said to his older brother: I want to be free from care and not to work but to worship God without interruption. And he took his robe off, and went into the desert. After staying there one week, he returned to his brother. And when he knocked at the door, his brother asked without opening it: Who is it? He replied: It's John, your brother. The brother said: John has become an angel and is not among people anymore. Then he begged and said: It's me! But his brother did not open the door and left him there in distress until the next morning. And he finally opened the door and said: If you are a human being, you have to work again in order to live. Then John repented, saying: Forgive me, brother, for I was wrong.

Desert Fathers

❧❧

MULLA NASRUDIN USED TO STAND IN THE STREET on market days, to be pointed out as an idiot.

No matter how often people offered him a large and a small coin, he always chose the smaller piece.

One day a kindly man said to him:

"Mulla, you should take the bigger coin. Then you will have more money and people will no longer be able to make a laughing-stock of you."

"That might be true," said Nasrudin, "but if I always take the larger, people will stop offering me money to prove that I am more idiotic than they are. Then I would have no money at all."

Nasrudin, when he was in India, passed near a strange-looking building, at the entrance of which a hermit was sitting. He had an air of abstraction and calm, and Nasrudin thought that he would make some sort of contact with him. "Surely," he thought, "a devout philosopher like me must have something in common with this saintly individual."

"I am a Yogi," said the anchorite, in answer to the Mulla's question, "and I am dedicated to the service of all living things, especially birds and fish."

"Pray allow me to join you," said the Mulla, "for, as I had expected, we have something in common. I am strongly attracted to your sentiments, because a fish once saved my life."

"How pleasurably remarkable!" said the Yogi, "I shall be delighted to admit you to our company. For all my years of devotion to the cause of animals, I have never yet been privileged to attain such intimate communion with them as you. Saved your life! This amply substantiates our doctrine that all the animal kingdom is interlinked."

So Nasrudin sat with the Yogi for some weeks, contemplating his navel and learning various curious gymnastics.

At length the Yogi asked him: "If you feel able, now that we are better acquainted, to communicate to me your supreme experience with the life-saving fish, I would be more than honored."

"I am not sure about that," said the Mulla, "now that I have heard more of your ideas."

But the Yogi pressed him, with tears in his eyes, calling him "Master" and rubbing his forehead in the dust before him.

"Very well, if you insist," said Nasrudin, "though I am not quite sure whether you are ready (to use your parlance) for the revelation I have to make. The fish certainly saved my life. I was on the verge of starvation when I caught it. It provided me with food for three days."

Sufi

A PIOUS MAN WHO TRIED TO LIVE BY GOD'S WILL dwelled in a valley out in the country. One day a great rain came to his valley and the flood waters rose. The man went from the first floor to the second floor as the rains continued. Finally he climbed out onto the roof. A rescue boat came up and offered to row him to safety but this man sent them away saying, "I have full faith in God. I pray and believe and trust he will care for me." So the rowboat left. The storm continued, it rained further, and soon the flood waters were up to his neck. A second rowboat came to rescue him and again was dismissed in the same way. "I have faith and trust in God. I pray and believe," and they were sent away. It continued to rain and the water got so high that the man could barely breathe through his mouth and nose. A helicopter flew over and let down a ladder to rescue him. "Come up," they said, "we will take you to safety." "No," he cried with the same words as before, "I have faith in God. I pray and believe and I trust and I have followed him," and he sent the helicopter away. However, it continued to rain, the waters rose, and finally he was drowned.

He went to heaven and after a short period there was granted an interview with God. He went in and was seated in front of the Almighty and then began to ask, "I had so much faith in you. I believed in you so fully. I prayed and tried to follow your will. I just don't understand." At this point God scratched his head and said, "I don't understand either! I sent you two rowboats and a helicopter."

Contemporary Christian

⌐⌐

THE BUDDHA TELLS THE STORY OF A FAMILY OF ACRO-bats. A grandfather and granddaughter traveled and made their living by performing balancing acts. They came to the Buddha to discuss what was the best way to safeguard and care for each other. The grandfather put forth the idea that each should care for the other, that he should care for his granddaughter in the balancing, and she should take care of him. Thus they would protect each other. The granddaughter asked the Buddha if that was not backward. "Would it not be better for each of us to care for ourselves, and in that way we best safeguard each other, and our acrobatics will prosper?" After listening to the little girl, the Buddha replied, "Though she is young, she is wise. If you as a grandfather guard yourself with care and pay attention to what you do, you will also guard the safety of your grandchild; and if you as a child guard yourself with awareness, with care, with respect, then you guard both yourself and those around you."

Buddhist

⌐⌐

EXCEPT WHEN HE WAS VERY MUCH INTO THE HOLY hum of things so that nothing could knock him off course, the Dalai Lama disliked meeting with foreigners.

They obviously thought that he regarded himself as a holy man, and they insisted on treating him as such. Trying to compensate for this misapprehension on their parts, he would lean over backward to be casual, to make small talk, to show that he could be as common, superficial, and even vulgar as the next fellow. Since he was none of these any more than he was a holy man, he would chastise himself for putting on a phony hail-fellow-well-met act during visits, especially from Europeans.

After a visit with Europeans, the inner soliloquy which every good Buddhist hopes to be rid of once and for all would start up again, generated by the nagging question, Why do I always look for postures with these people?

Because when I start just being myself they start treating me with some kind of phony reverence. When I start being real, they start being phony, so I try to get phony to make them real. It's a lost cause. Why do I bother? They don't think I'm holy any more than I do. In fact, they probably think they're much holier than I am but that if they reveal this they'll be insulting Tibetan customs. So, to hide their self-esteem, they pretend to think me holier than they, confident that I'll go along with the game, since I undoubtedly have the same opinion of myself. In fact, I couldn't possibly have this opinion of myself, could I, since no holy man ever consciously thinks of himself as such. Ah me, it's hard to be myself with foreigners. I must avoid them.

Troubled by such ruminations and by the fact that even a number of people in his own country suffered under the delusion that he was the holiest among them, he went to the roof of the Potala and up the ladder to the highest golden-domed cell, where lived the lama whom he considered the holiest of all. This lama, who was called Great Hum, was no mere official incarnation of God. Tibet would never have wasted him on ceremonial functions.

He was much more than a sacred symbol trying diligently to become its own reality. The Great Hum *was* his own reality. He was neither more nor less than himself, neither happier nor sadder than himself, wiser nor more foolish than himself. He was exactly what he was.

There was no need for the Great Hum to change expressions on his face since a single expression could allow all moods to flow from it. Seriousness and humor, light and darkness, soul and spirit were all united in the evenness of his gaze. He could smile without moving his lips. Just when you thought his eyes were full of amusement, you would realize how utterly sad they were; and when you thought the sadness was on the verge of moving him to tears, you would perceive that he was feeling no deep emotions whatsoever but was only watching you with calm, purely intellectual curiosity; and when you had this perception well in mind so that you felt prepared to provide him with some detached answers to whatever questions he might wish to ask, it would dawn on you that he could not possibly be curious since he was all-knowing and there was nothing left for him to be curious about. Whether such omniscience made him supremely indifferent or passionately concerned was impossible to tell.

Finally you gave up trying to decipher the Great Hum's expression and you began to project your own feelings upon him. He absorbed these in a comforting way, letting his face appear as the image not of what you were but of what you would become if you continued on your present course—a realization that made you change your course with haste until you had given up desiring every stance in life that you could imagine as being desirable. You were left with no feelings for him to reflect, at which time his face would begin to withdraw from you into a kind of shadow until you could only see the vague slit where his mouth had been. The face would stay hidden, causing you to fear that it might disappear altogether without satisfying the absolute necessity you now felt for conversation with it. When you were entirely possessed by this sense of necessity, you would hear him start to hum and you would realize that he had been humming all along. Then he would emerge from his shadow. The hum would break down into words and he would begin speaking to you without ever opening his mouth.

This most holy of the teaching lamas was noted more sensationally for being able to carry on ten conversations at once. In his golden tower, he held audience for an hour every evening. He would sit facing the ten visitors, looking at none of them yet looking at them all by looking inward and finding them there within himself as he saw them struggling with the dilemmas they had brought to him. It was said of him that just as the ocean can dissolve into a drop of water so all men can dissolve into the Great Hum.

The Dalai Lama climbed the ladder and entered the dome of this same Great Hum. Already five others had seated themselves. One of these was a highly developed lama who could sing three notes at once, each note carrying a different conversation. Another could carry on two conversations and the other three could carry on only one. This meant that eight conversations were already taking place. Since the Dalai Lama could carry on two, his arrival completed the number of visitors allowed and he closed the door after him.

The golden dome was like a beehive, for all the conversations consisted of humming. Words were superfluous.

The humming of the Dalai Lama sounded more like a groan. It went something like this: "I accuse myself of being a fakir who tricks people into seeing God with faces that are nothing but grotesque masks. I'm afraid that my father might get drunk one night and give away the trick.

Then all the people of Tibet will know that I'm not God, and the country will fall into despair. I try to let them know that I'm only a boy from the country with a certain amount of religious education and a lucky streak that won him the throne. But they insist on treating my act as a reality. The more I try to act like I'm not holy, the more holy everybody thinks I am."

"The magicians and the storytellers," answered the Great Hum, "open us up to wonder with their tricks. We are lured into the eternal reality by well-timed illusion, for illusions appear as enticing emanations from around that oval into which all faces vanish when ego surrenders to the mystifying Self. Great are those actors who can put people on and take people off. You accuse yourself of being two-faced. Look at me."

The Great Hum was transforming himself into an old woman, a beautiful girl, a fierce warrior, a child . . . yet the voice remained the same as it went on to say, "Once you're free from bondage to your face, you'll be able to take on as many faces as you like—not just two or three but a thousand. The more faces you assume, the more your expression will remain the same. Eventually, when you try to resemble me, as you are doing now, you will find that I have come to resemble you instead. But you have much to learn before then. You are faced with contradictory feelings about your role and will remain so until you can assume any mask the world places upon you and wear it with ease. Only then will your own divine countenance shine through. Are you not a god? Do the gods not wear masks?"

While one of the Dalai Lama's voices was talking to the Great Hum about faces, the other was talking about voices. "My top voice," said the boy king, "is very cultured and polite. It serves to hide the sensitivities that I need to protect. This voice keeps the silence secret, screens my meditating self from the petty and persistent interruptions of curiosity seekers. My lower voice has to do with the powerful bottom desires and the private urges to become a bodhisattva."

"Quite right," said the Great Hum. "Religious ceremonials should be surrounded by clowns. The mask must do parodies of the face beneath it, lest the sacred be profaned and the immortal confound itself with mortality. There's an old saying about the public domain: 'If you're going to do anything serious, make sure you've got the tourists laughing; and when they stop laughing let the humor begin.' Have you heard any good stories lately? The old monk on your left has been telling me two funny stories at once while his middle voice whispers about God."

The Dalai Lama was embarrassed. He could not think of a single funny story to tell the Great Hum. "Wisest of Us All," he murmured, "forgive me, for I can think of nothing that would make you laugh."

"I'm laughing already," said the Great Hum, "so relax. I've been laughing ever since you came in. So much of what you talk about is pure clowning. I know that one of your voices is down in the chapel talking to God, but the louder one is up here on the roof playing games with virtuoso religious ideas and amusing itself with psychological analyses of its ambiguous self. I know that your voice of voices cares only to keep the seasons changing and the world from blowing up. It cares nothing for how many faces or voices it has but only for the continuing beauty of the cosmos. Unless you perfect your style, few people will hear this voice. Try on all the masks you like, speak in as many voices as you can. Someday you'll be able to carry on ten conversations at once just as I do. Then you can come up here all alone and we can talk face to face, voice to voice, one to one, a single presence with nothing to hide."

It came to the Dalai Lama as he climbed back down the ladder that a single voice can be heard in ten different ways when it responds to ten different conditions, and he remembered once when the spirit of a famous guru appeared to heal a small, discordant community of monks. All the monks had seen the spirit come out of the wall long enough to utter just one word. But each monk had heard a different word. The event is immortalized in this poem:

> The one who wanted to die heard *live*.
> The one who wanted to live heard *die*.
> The one who wanted to take heard *give*.
> The one who wanted to give heard *keep*.
> The one who was always alert heard *sleep*.
> The one who was always asleep heard *wake*.
> The one who wanted to leave heard *stay*.
> The one who wanted to stay, *depart*.
> The one who never spoke heard *preach*.
> The one who always preached heard *pray*.
> Each one learned how he had been
> In someone else's way.

Pierre Delattre

III

Living
Our Truth

HOW TO MAKE OUR LIVES AN EMBODIMENT OF wisdom and compassion is the greatest challenge spiritual seekers face. The truths we have come to understand need to find their visible expression in our lives. Our every thought, word, or action holds the possibility of being a living expression of clarity and love. It is not enough to be a possessor of wisdom. To believe ourselves to be custodians of truth is to become its opposite, is a direct path to becoming stale, self-righteous, or rigid. Ideas and memories do not hold liberating or healing power.

There is no such state as enlightened retirement, where we can live on the bounty of past attainments. Wisdom is alive only as long as it is lived, understanding is liberating only as long as it is applied. A bulging portfolio of spiritual experiences matters little if it does not have the power to sustain us through the inevitable moments of grief, loss, and change. Knowledge and achievements matter little if we do not yet know how to touch the heart of another and be touched.

We must be wary, however, of being entranced by idealism. Profound love, compassion, sensitivity, and awakening are the possibilities of spirituality that move and attract us. Yet we know that it is easier to love a thousand people in our thoughts than to fully love one person in actuality. It is not difficult to extend boundless acceptance and compassion to those who do not actively challenge us. We acknowledge that it is easy to be arm-chair philosophers, but then what do we do? Only in the midst of our concrete relationships and day-to-day living can we actually express our wisdom and demonstrate compassion.

We live in undeniable connectedness with all life. Every word we speak, every action we initiate creates a ripple upon this relationship. Understanding this con-nectedness brings a sacredness to each moment. There is no contact, no perception, no engagement that is incon-sequential or insignificant. Each contact is an opportu-nity for deepening sensitivity and understanding. Our spirituality must touch every area of our lives. We live within our bodies, therefore we are sexual beings, and our sexuality is a vehicle for honoring and respecting the life of all beings. We live in relationship with one an-other, therefore we are social beings, and every relation-ship offers us the opportunity to learn how to give and receive with an open heart. We participate consciously or unconsciously in the structures that govern us, and we are political beings by virtue of this participation. Our wisdom empowers us to contribute to the creation of structures that respect the dignity and spirit of all beings. Our spirituality is visible and vital when it embraces every facet of our lives.

THIRTEEN

The Nothing
That Contains
Everything

THERE ARE MOMENTS WHEN WE STAND IN AWE before the mystery of our unfolding universe and ask ourselves, Where does it all come from? What does it all mean? The planets, the creatures, the stars, the seasons are born and they disappear. Every ending is the parent of a new beginning, every death gives birth to a new form of life. As we experience how transitory and frail is each new birth, we can be profoundly touched by the tremendous, timeless silence and wholeness that contains and embraces each birth and passing. To realize and awaken to this timeless space brings a peace with all things.

In the great spiritual traditions of the East, the understanding of emptiness is considered to be an important part of seeing the fullness and essential harmony of all life. The depth of this understanding is born of pure silence. When our interpretation about the universe is still, when we no longer locate ourselves in past or future or yearn to become someone or something, a profound silence is revealed. This silence embraces all time and place, all change. It is not the opposite of movement but is the essential background that holds and embraces all movement.

As we deepen in silence, learning to listen to the rhythms of our breath and body, we discover we are listening to the rhythms of the seasons, the expansion and contraction of all things. We discover that all things inner and outer are connected in the fabric of our consciousness. The changing rhythms and seasons of the universe mirror the perpetual motion within us. As the samurai story in this chapter tells us, within each moment we can find heaven and hell. To learn this is to make ourselves empty; it's to discover how to swim in that emptiness, to love silence and to come to peace in the space that contains all things.

All things—we, too—arise for a time and then disappear back into emptiness. Our infancy and our youth feel like fleeting moments that have vanished. They, too, have completely disappeared to join the dinosaurs, the pharaohs, the ice caps that once made such an impact upon our world. Each day and each moment appears and then strides offstage to make space for the next. In moments of despair this endless arising and dissolution gives rise to a feeling of meaninglessness, of nothingness. Yet when we are silent, we are astonished to see how life renews itself in form after form, moment after moment. All these changing moments and forms are bound together by an abiding silence.

Emptiness reveals the greatest paradox of the spiritual life: just as death is a testimony to birth, just as endings signal beginnings, so emptiness reveals itself in fullness and wholeness. Superficially understanding emptiness, we may dismiss life as a dream, an echo, a phantom, a rainbow. We may tell ourselves that since all life is empty and insubstantial, it doesn't really matter, and we may look upon the world with contempt. In those moments it is wise to reflect upon the teachings of the great Zen masters who greeted students proudly exhibiting their understanding of emptiness with a blow from a stick. They would then be asked to speak of the emptiness of their anger. We may sense the dreamlike nature of life, but we experience its joys and sorrows, its difficulties and successes as profoundly real. To live fully and wisely we need to understand and embrace both of these dimensions of our lives just as the underlying silence of the universe holds us.

In the East the word *akinchina* is used to describe a person who is fully awakened. It is translated to mean one who has nothing, longs for nothing, stands upon nothing, and becomes nothing. We may shudder with horror at the prospect of such a state, equating such emptiness with meaninglessness, annihilation, and nonexistence. Much of our lives have been lived in pursuit of the opposite of this state. We have looked to our identities, possessions, and roles to reassure us that we are indeed someone and something. We rely on the props we gather as evidence of the worth of our existence and fear their loss.

By deepening in silence, we discover that emptiness holds no fear, that it is truly beautiful and joyful. Resting in the space that contains our infinitely changing universe, we live in accord with this actuality and we begin to live in harmony. Silence brings wholeness, peace, and well-being. As a great Tibetan lama once said, "To discover we are nothing is to discover our connection with everything."

The stories in this chapter tell of the pure spontaneity, creativity, and wisdom that are born of silence. They encourage us to discover that place of deep stillness and awareness within ourselves. As you read these stories, you might ask yourself, How often do I give myself periods of silence, meditation, prayer, and openness to nature? What effect would listening more deeply have on me? Can I allow space in my relationships—space for the people around me to change as the seasons do, space for myself to change? Can I rest in something great and still, the simple space between each breath? How might I have to change my life in order to learn to rest in that space, to feel the rhythms of the world, to be more the container of things rather than lost in my reactions?

ONE DAY MULLA NASRUDIN GOT WORD THAT HE HAD received a special message from the Sheik in Basra. When he went to pick it up they told him he must first identify himself.

Nasrudin fished in his trousers and took out a brass mirror. Looking into it he exclaimed, "Yup, that's me all right."

Sufi

I AM A MONK MYSELF, AND THE ONE QUESTION I really wanted to ask was, "What is a monk?" Well, I finally did, but for an answer I got a most peculiar question: "Do you mean in the daytime or at night?" Now what could that mean?

When I didn't answer, he picked it up again, "A monk, like everyone else, is a creature of contraction and expansion. During the day he is contracted—behind his cloister walls, dressed in a habit like all the others, doing the routine things you expect a monk to do. At night he expands. The walls cannot contain him. He moves throughout the world and he touches the stars."

"Ah," I thought, "poetry." To bring him down to earth I began to ask, "Well, during the day, in his REAL body . . . "

"Wait," he said, "that's the difference between us and you. You people regularly assume that the contracted state is the real body. It is real, in a sense. But here we tend to start from the other end, the expanded state. The daytime state we refer to as the 'body of fear.' And whereas you tend to judge a monk by his decorum during the day, we tend to measure a monk by the number of persons he touches at night, and the number of stars."

Father Theophane

THERE WAS A MAN WHO WANDERED THROUGH-out the world seeking his deepest desire. He wandered from one city to another, from one realm to another looking for fulfillment and happiness, but in all his wanderings never came to it. Finally one day, tired from his search, he sat down underneath a great tree at the foot of a mountain. What he did not know is that this was The Great Wish Fulfilling Tree. Whatever one wishes for when seated underneath it immediately becomes true.

As he rested in his weariness he thought to himself, "What a beautiful spot this is. I wish I had a home here," and instantly before his eyes a lovely home appeared. Surprised and delighted he thought further, "Ah, if only I had a partner to be here with me, then my happiness would be complete," and in a moment a beautiful woman appeared calling him "husband" and beckoning to him. "Well, first, I am hungry," he thought. "I wish there was food to eat." Immediately a banquet table appeared covered with every wonderful kind of food and drink, main courses, pastries, sweets of every variety. The man sat down and began to feast himself hungrily, but partway through the meal, still feeling tired he thought, "I wish I had a servant to serve me the rest of this food," and sure enough a manservant appeared.

Finishing the meal the man sat back down to lean against this wonderful tree and began to reflect, "How amazing it is that everything I wish has come true. There is some mysterious force about this tree. I wonder if there is a demon who lives in it," and sure enough no sooner had he thought this than a great demon appeared. "Oh, my," he thought, "this demon will probably eat me up," and that is just what it did.

Hindu

270

"WOULD YOU TEACH ME SILENCE?" I ASKED.

"Ah!"

He seemed to be pleased. "Is it the Great Silence that you want?"

"Yes, the Great Silence."

"Well, where do you think it's to be found?" he asked.

"Deep within me, I suppose. If only I could go deep within, I'm sure I'd escape the noise at last. But it's hard. Will you help me?" I knew he would. I could feel his concern, and his spirit was so silent.

"Well, I've been there," he answered. "I spent years going in. I did taste the silence there. But one day Jesus came—maybe it was my imagination—and said to me simply, 'Come, follow me.' I went out, and I've never gone back."

I was stunned. "But the silence . . . "

"I've found the Great Silence, and I've come to see that the noise was inside."

Father Theophane

A long cry at midnight near the mosque,
                    a dying cry.
The young man sitting there hears
and thinks, "That sound doesn't make me
     afraid.
Why should it?
               It's the drumbeat announcing a
     celebration!
It means,
               we should start cooking the
     joy-soup!"

He hears beyond his death-fear, to the
   Union.
"It's time for that Merging in me now,
or it's time to leave my body."

He jumps up and shouts to God,
If You can be human, come inside me now!

The signal of a death-yell splits him open.
Gold pours down, many kinds, from all directions,
gold coins, liquid gold, gold cloth, gold bars.
They pile up, almost blocking the doors of
   the mosque.

The young man works all night carrying the
   gold away
in sacks and burying it, and coming back for
   more.
The timid church-members sleep through
   it all.
If you think I'm talking about actual gold,
you're like those children who pretend that
   pieces
of broken dishes are money, so that anytime
   they see
pottery shards, they think of money, as when
   you hear
the word *gold* and think "Goody."

This is the other gold
that glows in your chest when you love.

The enchanted mosque is in *there,* and the
   pointed cry is a candleflame on the altar.
                        The young man is a
   moth

who gambles himself and wins. A True
   Human Being
is not human! This candle does not burn.
                           It illuminates.

Some candles burn themselves, and one another, up,
Others taste like a surprise of roses in a room
and you just a stranger who wandered in.

                              Rumi

A BIG, TOUGH SAMURAI ONCE WENT TO SEE A LITTLE
monk. "Monk," he said, in a voice accustomed to instant obedience, "teach me about heaven and hell!"

The monk looked up at this mighty warrior and replied
with utter disdain, "Teach you about heaven and hell? I
couldn't teach you about anything. You're dirty. You smell.
Your blade is rusty. You're a disgrace, an embarrassment to
the samurai class. Get out of my sight. I can't stand you."

The samurai was furious. He shook, got all red in the
face, was speechless with rage. He pulled out his sword
and raised it above him, preparing to slay the monk.

"That's hell," said the monk softly.

The samurai was overwhelmed. The compassion and
surrender of this little man who had offered his life to give
this teaching to show him hell! He slowly put down his
sword, filled with gratitude, and suddenly peaceful.

"And that's heaven," said the monk softly.

                              Zen

N ASRUDIN WAS EATING A POOR MAN'S DIET OF CHICK-
peas and bread. His neighbor, who also claimed to

be a wise man, was living in a grand house and dining on sumptuous meals provided by the emperor himself.

His neighbor told Nasrudin, "if only you would learn to flatter the emperor and be subservient like I do, you would not have to live on chickpeas and bread."

Nasrudin replied, "and if only you would learn to live on chickpeas and bread, like I do, you would not have to flatter and live subservient to the emperor."

Sufi

THE DEVIL APPEARED TO A BROTHER, IN THE DISguise of an angel of light, and said to him: I am the angel Gabriel and I have been sent to you. However, the brother said to him: See if you are not being sent to someone else. I certainly do not deserve to have an angel sent to me. Immediately, the devil disappeared.

Desert Fathers

A YOUNG FEMALE DISCIPLE UNDERTOOK TO DEVELOP the meditation on loving-kindness. Sitting in her small room, she would fill her heart with loving-kindness for all beings, yet each day as she went to the bazaar to gather her food, she would find her loving-kindness sorely tested by one shopkeeper who would daily subject her to unwelcome caresses. One day she could stand no more and began to chase the shopkeeper down the road with her upraised umbrella. To her mortification she passed her meditation master standing on the side of the road observing this spectacle. Shame-faced she went to stand before him expecting to be rebuked for her anger.

"What you should do," her master kindly advised her, "is to fill your heart with loving-kindness, and with as much mindfulness as you can muster, hit this unruly fellow over the head with your umbrella."

Buddhist

❧

Ex-Emperor: Gudo, what happens to the man of enlightenment and the man of illusion after death?
Gudo: How should I know, sir?
Ex-Emperor: Why, because you're the master!
Gudo: Yes, sir, but not a dead one!

Zen

❧

One day Tesshu, the famous swordsman and Zen devotee, went to Dokuon and told him triumphantly he believed all that exists is empty, there is no you or me, and so on. The master, who had listened in silence, suddenly snatched up his long tobacco pipe and struck Tesshu's head.

The infuriated swordsman would have killed the master there and then, but Dokuon said calmly, "Emptiness is quick to show its anger, isn't it?"

Forcing a smile, Tesshu left the room.

Zen

❧

Abba Nisteros the Great was walking through the desert with a brother, and seeing a dragon, they ran away. Then the brother said to him: Are you afraid,

too, Father? The old man replied: I was not afraid, my
son, but it was good for me to run away from the dragon;
otherwise, I would not have escaped from the spirit of
vainglory and pride.

Desert Fathers

I N HIM THERE WAS NO ONE. BEHIND HIS FACE (EVEN
in the poor paintings of the period it is unlike any other)
and his words (which were swarming, fanciful, and excited), there was only a touch of coldness, a dream un-
dreamed by anyone. At first he thought all people were
like him, but when he had tried to explain this inner
emptiness, a schoolmate's blank look showed him his mistake and made him realize from then on that an individual had best not differ from his species. From time to time
he thought books might cure his strange ailment, and in
this way he learned the small Latin and less Greek of
which a contemporary was to remark. Later on he considered that in the practice of one of humanity's age-old
habits he might actually find what he was looking for, and
during the course of a long, lazy June afternoon he let
himself be initiated by Anne Hathaway. In his twenties he
went to London. By instinct, so as to cover up the fact that
he was nobody, he had grown skilled in the trick of making believe he was somebody. There in London he came to
the profession to which he was destined—that of an actor,
who on a stage plays at being someone else before an audience who plays at taking him for that other person. Stage-
craft brought him singular happiness, perhaps the first he
ever knew, but once the last line was spoken and the last
corpse carted off, a hateful taste of the unreal came down
on him. He was no longer Ferrex or Tamburlaine and

went back to being nobody. So driven, he began to imagine other heroes and other tragic tales. And while in London bawdyhouses and taverns his flesh fulfilled its destiny as flesh, the spirit that inhabited him was Caesar, ignoring the augur's prophecy, and Juliet, hating the lark, and Macbeth, speaking on the heath to the witches, who are also the Fates. No one was ever so many men as this man, who, like the Egyptian Proteus, could run through all of life's guises. Occasionally, he left a confession in some nook of his work, sure it would never be deciphered; Richard II says that in one person he plays many people, and with strange words Iago says, "I am not what I am." The underlying sameness of existing, dreaming, and acting inspired him to famous pages.

For twenty years he persisted in this willful hallucination, but one day he was overcome by the surfeit and the horror of being so many kings who die by the sword and so many star-crossed lovers who meet and who part and who at last so melodiously die. That same day he decided to sell his theater. Before a week was over, he had gone back to the village of his birth, where again he discovered the trees and the river of his childhood, never linking them to those other trees and rivers—made illustrious by mythological allusions and Latin words—which his muse had celebrated. He had to be someone; he became a retired stage manager who has made his fortune and to whom loans, lawsuits, and petty usury are amusements. In this personage, he dictated the dry testament that has come down to us, in which he deliberately avoided any trace of the pathetic or the literary. Friends from London used to visit him in his country retreat, and for their sake he again took up the part of poet.

The tale runs that before or after death, when he stood face to face with God, he said to Him, "I, who in vain have been so many men, want to be one man—myself." The voice of the Lord answered him out of the whirlwind, "I too have no self; I dreamed the world as you dreamed your work, my Shakespeare, and among the shapes of my dreams are you, who, like me, are many men and no one."

Jorge Luis Borges

FOURTEEN

*Discovering
One's True
Path*

THE PATHS TO AWAKENING ARE MANY, THE teachings rich and varied; the guides of past and present offer us the richness of their wisdom and experience. Never before has there been an age when the spiritual richness of the centuries has been so accessible. These maps have true meaning for us, but only when we actually undertake the path for ourselves.

We soon find, however, that there is no standard map to enlightenment. Each one of us is unique, with unique gifts and strengths. It is not enough to emulate those who have traveled this path before or to attempt to model ourselves after them, no matter how much we may admire their spiritual greatness. The fundamental message of every great spiritual teacher is that we must learn to see through our own eyes and to travel this path ourselves.

Others teach us the fundamentals needed for beginning any authentic spiritual venture: integrity, compassion, and attention. But we ourselves must discover how to bring these into blossom. The map is not the journey. One Chassidic rabbi named Zusha told his students, "When I die, God will not ask me, was I like Moses or was I like Joshua in my life. He will ask me, was I Zusha." To see with clarity and to respect what is here now in our lives, to fulfill and offer our own inner gifts—this is our spiritual path. To let our lives be a deep expression of heartfelt values, to know what awakens us and to nurture it—this is our way.

This must be done by each of us. No matter how deeply we yearn for it, freedom cannot be delivered to us by another, nor our hearts opened for us by someone else. But we can be inspired and moved by another to make the spiritual journey authentically our own. An authentic spiritual path is one in which we learn to deepen the joy, harmony, and clarity of each day. We will know the genuine path by our own experience, if we are transformed and liberated each day.

The stories in this chapter are about those who have discovered their own true paths in different ways, in different places. They encourage us to question, to see through belief systems and models to the authenticity and simplicity of the spiritual life.

The stories in this chapter also raise the great spiritual question, What do we wish to give back to this earth? How can we enhance the well-being of our world? In discovering a path that awakens us, we also discover tremendous gratitude. We have been cared for in so many ways, large and small. We have been supported, guided, and loved. There rests within the heart of wisdom a longing to give to, to support, and to care for the world that has nourished us. We may offer our gifts through silence or through action; it is the giving that enables us to fulfill our time here with as much love and compassion as possible.

In reading these stories, we might reflect upon our own lives. Have we been guided by our hearts? Have we lived with an integrity and love that fulfills what we know to be true? What is our own true path, and what would it mean to listen to that drummer, to tread that path? What would we have to change in order to do so?

Two DISCIPLES OF AN OLD RABBI WERE ARGUING about the true path to God. One said that the path was built on effort and energy. "You must give yourself totally and fully with all your effort to follow the way of the Law. To pray, to pay attention, to live rightly." The second disciple disagreed. "It is not effort at all. That is only based on ego. It is pure surrender. To follow the way to God, to awaken, is to let go of all things and live the teaching. 'Not my will but thine.'"

As they could not agree on who was right they went to see the master. He listened as the first disciple praised the path of wholehearted effort and when asked by this disciple, "Is this the true path?" the master said, "You're right." The second disciple was quite upset and responded eloquently by describing the path of surrender and letting go. When he had finished he said, "Is this not the true path?" and the master replied, "You're right." A third student who was sitting there said, "But master, they can't both be right," and the master smiled and said, "You're right too!"

Chassid

❧

IN THE CITY OF SĀVATTHI IN NORTHERN INDIA, the Buddha had a large center where people would come to meditate and to listen to his Dharma talks. Every evening one young man used to come to hear his discourses. For years he came to listen to the Buddha but never put any of the teaching into practice.

After a few years, one evening this man came a little early and found the Buddha alone. He approached him and said, "Sir, I have a question that keeps arising in my mind, raising doubts."

"Oh? There should not be any doubts on the path of Dharma; have them clarified. What is your question?"

"Sir, for many years now I have been coming to your meditation center, and I have noticed that there are a large number of recluses around you, monks and nuns, and a still larger number of lay people, both men and women. For years some of them have been coming to you. Some of them, I can see, have certainly reached the final stage; quite obviously they are fully liberated. I can also see that others have experienced some change in their lives. They are partially liberated. But sir, I also notice that a large number of people, including myself, are as they were, or sometimes they are even worse. They have not changed at all, or have not changed for the better.

"Why should this be, sir? People come to you, such a great man, fully enlightened, such a powerful, compassionate person. Why don't you use your power and compassion to liberate them all?"

The Buddha smiled and said, "Young man, where do you live? What is your native place?"

"Sir, I live here in Sāvatthi, this capital city of the state of Kosala."

"Yes, but your facial features show that you are not from this part of the country. Where are you from originally?"

"Sir, I am from the city of Rājagaha, the capital of the state of Magadha. I came and settled here in Sāvatthi a few years ago."

"And have you severed all connections with Rājagaha?"

"No sir. I still have relatives there. I have friends there. I have business there."

"Then certainly you must go from Sāvatthi to Rājagaha quite often?"

"Yes sir. Many times each year I visit Rājagaha and return to Sāvatthi."

"Having traveled and returned so many times on the path from here to Rājagaha, certainly you must know the path very well?"

"Oh yes sir, I know it perfectly. I might almost say that even if I was blindfolded I could find the path to Rājagaha, so many times have I walked it."

"And your friends, those who know you well, certainly they must know that you are from Rājagaha and have settled here? They must know that you often visit Rājagaha and return, and that you know the path from here to Rājagaha perfectly?"

"Oh yes, sir. All those who are close to me know that I often go to Rājagaha and that I know the path perfectly."

"Then it must happen that some of them come to you and ask you to explain to them the path from here to Rājagaha. Do you hide anything or do you explain the path to them clearly?"

"What is there to hide, sir? I explain it to them as clearly as I can: you start walking toward the east and then head toward Banaras, and continue onward until you reach Gaya and then Rājagaha. I explain it very plainly to them, sir."

"And these people to whom you give such clear explanation, do all of them reach Rājagaha?"

"How can that be, sir? Those who walk the entire path to its end, only they will reach Rājagaha."

"This is what I want to explain to you, young man. People keep coming to me knowing that this is someone who has walked the path from here to Nirvana and so knows it perfectly. They come to me and ask, 'What is the path to Nirvana, to liberation?' And what is there to hide? I explain it to them clearly: 'This is the path.' If somebody just nods his head and says, 'Well said, well said, a very good path, but I won't take a step on it; a wonderful path, but I won't take the trouble to walk over it,' then how can such a person reach the final goal?

"I do not carry anyone on my shoulders to take him to the final goal. *Nobody* can carry anyone else on his shoulders to the final goal. At most, with love and compassion one can say, 'Well, this is the path, and this is how I have walked on it. You also work, you also walk, and you will reach the final goal.' But each person has to walk himself, has to take every step on the path himself. He who has taken one step on the path is one step nearer the goal. He who has taken a hundred steps is a hundred steps nearer the goal. He who has taken all the steps on the path has reached the final goal. You have to walk on the path yourself."

Early Buddhist

W E HAVE TO BE AWARE OF HOW PEOPLE TEND TO imitate their teachers. They become copies, prints, castings. It is like the story of the king's horse trainer. The old trainer died, so the king hired a new trainer. Unfortunately, this man limped when he walked. New and beautiful horses were brought to him, and he trained them exquisitely—to run, to canter, to pull carriages. But each of the new stallions developed a limp. Finally, the king summoned the trainer, and seeing him limp as he entered the court, he understood everything and immediately hired a new trainer.

Buddhist

T HE GREAT PERSIAN POET RUMI HAD AN EXTRA-ordinary teacher named Shams. Even as a child Shams seemed different. His own parents struggled with whether to send him to a monastery or the village of fools. They did not know what to do with him.

When he had grown he told them the story of the duck's egg that was found by the hen and hatched. The hen raised the duckling with her other chicks. One day they walked to a lake. The duck went right in the water, swam and dove, and the hen stayed timidly on the shore. Shams said to his parents, "Now, father and mother, I have found my place. I have learned to swim in the ocean, even if you must remain on the shore."

Persian

❧❧

THE RICH INDUSTRIALIST FROM THE NORTH WAS horrified to find the Southern fisherman lying lazily beside his boat, smoking a pipe.

"Why aren't you out fishing?" said the industrialist.

"Because I have caught enough fish for the day," said the fisherman.

"Why don't you catch some more?"

"What would I do with it?"

"You could earn more money" was the reply. "With that you could have a motor fixed to your boat to go into deeper waters and catch more fish.

"Then you would make enough money to buy nylon nets. These would bring you more fish and more money. Soon you would have enough money to own two boats . . . maybe even a fleet of boats. Then you would be a rich man like me."

"What would I do then?"

"Then you could really enjoy life."

"What do you think I am doing right now?"

Contemporary

❧❧

EPILOGUE TO THE ODYSSEY:
THE PLANTING OF THE OAR

ODYSSEUS NOW SET ABOUT ESTABLISHING THE PEACE and goodwill ordained by Zeus, enjoying the longed-for reunion with Penelope, watching the young radiant manhood of his son and the serene old age of his father. But gradually as the years passed the restlessness came upon him and increased. After his father's death he felt freer and began to dream of discovering new lands, of sailing again to the west, even past the pillars of Hercules to the unknown southern seas. [This is the epilogue that Dante imagined as the chosen death of Ulysses.] Athene had befriended him before; might she not do so again? He had defeated the final attacks of his enemy Poseidon and this once offended god would surely have forgotten by now the injury to his son Polyphemos. Slowly and unconsciously the arrogance that had caused his long sufferings returned—working, as it always does, through the best of his human qualities—through his longing to know and to see all the wonders of creation and to understand things as yet hidden for most men. Beloved of his subjects and with his son grown to maturity to hold the country safe, he began to think he could easily take one more voyage over the wine-dark sea in a swift well-built ship with some of his friends and a trusty crew. Penelope would understand and be exposed to no danger now.

One day he sat alone on a high cliff gazing out to sea, plans teeming in his head. He would delay no longer. The sun was hot. He found a tree and lay down in the shade to rest, his decision made; and soon he slept and there came to him a dream.

There was in the dream no warrior goddess to encourage him, but rather a memory. Once more he stood, as long ago, on the borders of the darkness of Hades; once more he slaughtered a black ewe and poured out the blood that the shades might speak to him; and once more he heard the voice of Teiresias the blind seer.

"Odysseus," the old man said, "you sleep indeed—and I do not mean your body but that shrewd mind that has been your great gift from the gods. Often you have misused it and brought great suffering on yourself and others, but you stand on the threshold of old age and the exploits you plan come from your inner blindness and not from the wisdom that is truly yours. I am the voice of reason in you, whose eyes are closed to that outer world but are clear and see far and near into the meanings of life.

"A great poet, blind as I am, will tell the story of your journeyings from Troy through the long years until your return to Ithaca. He is a storyteller who will make you immortal, a hero beyond time. But there shall come another poet as great and likewise unsurpassed in the telling of stories. This poet will tell that he, still living, and led by another great one, met you in the deep pit of hell, enclosed forever in a burning flame among the 'deceivers.' He knew some of your story, and asked to speak with you. This poet will imagine in unforgettable lines your final sailing beyond the pillars of the western world in high hope and with the ever-increasing ambition of your exploring mind towards the southern pole for month after month, five moons in all, until you see ahead of you on the horizon a great mountain rising out of the sea towards heaven. With cries of eagerness you urge your crew towards it, but there comes a huge wave rolling from the mountain, becoming a whirlpool as it sucks your ship, yourself, and all your companions down into the depths to join the shades below. The mountain is for this poet of the future the image of the climb that brings all men who approach it, if they are girdled with humility, to the vision of God in his totality. To this mountain and the glory beyond, this poet would come, knowing perhaps that the fate he imagined had befallen you could also have been his, had his yearning for knowledge possessed him to his undoing.

"I shall say no more except that I already told you many years ago of the alternative journey you are now called to take—a journey which does indeed lie on the slopes of that mountain but holds no fame or glory for you; only loneliness and sadness. The choice is yours. Will you deceive yourself as Dante's Ulysses did in a sin far worse than the deceit of the Trojan horse?"

The voice ceased, the vision faded, and Odysseus woke.

He sat on as the sun sank in the red and golden sky, and he indeed remembered. He was appalled that the words of Teiresias all those years ago had been so completely blotted out from his conscious mind; and he remembered many other things too, every one of his adventures in turn with their moments of courage, skill, faithfulness, pride, cunning, deceit, and folly. Most vividly of all came the memory of that foolish arrogance which had been the beginning of the evils brought upon him by the great god of the sea. He remembered the adolescent stubbornness that had made him close his ears to the pleadings of his crew and recognized with shame that his present intention to show that, even in old age, he could equal the dangerous exploits of youth came from the very same root of pride and disregard of all the values of relatedness. Care for his wife's feelings, for the needs of his people and the lives of his crew—all these had been blotted out again. He saw once more the horror of the closed cave where the giant Cyclops devoured his men two by two, and the thought of his ingenuity in saving some of them and himself by trickery and blinding of Polyphemos no longer brought the old satisfaction. For he also remembered other things he had never before allowed himself to recognize. Polyphemos' life was, until he came, the life of a simple shepherd tending his flocks and he, Odysseus, had thought only to rob him. He had not seen the giant eat or drink anything but milk, whey, and cheese before the invasion of the men whom he must have greatly feared as an unknown threat; and Polyphemos had cared for his sheep and lambs in a way which, in one so crude and ignorant, was gentle and thoughtful of their every need. For the first time Odysseus allowed himself to hear the voice of the Cyclops after his blinding, speaking to the leading ram of his flock, who was leaving the cave weighed down by Odysseus himself clinging to the wool under his belly.

> Sweet cousin ram, why lag behind the rest
> in the night cave? You never linger so,
> but graze before them all, and go afar
> to crop sweet grass, and take your stately
>   way
> leading along the streams, until at evening
> you run to be the first one in the fold.
> Why, now, so far behind? Can you be griev-
>   ing
> over your master's eye? (Robert Fitzgerald
>   translation, Book Nine)

With shame he realized, as he heard it in memory, the feeling in Polyphemos' crude breast for his animals and how he must have mourned their loss—not out of greed but out of love. And a strange new compassion awoke in his heart for one he had always thought of as nothing but a cannibal and a brute. Then he saw himself sailing away, hurling insults back, glorying in his prowess; and he knew he had nearly paid with the loss of the whole crew; indeed he did so pay with the lives of all those others in the years that followed.

After the deadening years of the siege of Troy, and the victory brought about by Odysseus' own great cunning with the deception of the Trojan horse, it was perhaps no great wonder that he had been puffed up with his own cleverness to such an extent that he had fallen into that arrogant folly so many years ago. He had paid through long years of bitter experiences, but he knew there could be no final forgiveness or peace for him if he fell again into that fever to discover the unknown at any cost, to be the unconquered one, dragging down yet again his friends, his wife, his crew into sorrow, despair, or death.

He rose to his feet in the twilight as the sun sank into the western sea. His choice was made. He knew that there was an old legend in the island, which no one took seriously, that somewhere in the interior in valleys among the mountains there were people who never came down to the shore, who indeed had no idea the sea existed. None of the sea-faring islanders were interested in exploring the interior anyway and no one had ever tried to penetrate far. He had been told by the blind seer that he must take a well-cut oar and seek out these people. He did not understand—not yet—but he would obey. One thing was clear—this journey would bring no glory. Most men would deem it a foolish waste of time and think of him perhaps as already somewhat senile. Only Penelope would understand and rejoice. He was certain that she had not forgotten his telling her of Teiresias' prophecy on that night of their reunion, and he suddenly realized that she had spoken recently, once or twice, words which could have reminded him of this unfulfilled task, had he not been blinded by the glittering images of his longing to possess knowledge no other man had found, beyond the boundaries of the world. Never would she try to push him in his choices; but she knew, in her wisdom, of his danger and his need. And now his sense of sterile darkness in the final sacrifice of his heroic image of himself was taken up or down, as it were, into that quiet wisdom—wisdom that had always saved him in these moments of his extreme danger. The darkness would return and he had no illusions about the journey before him. It sounded easy in those few words of Teiresias, but he could not guess its length or the hardships of the way. He knew only that he must go, and go soon, and alone.

So he went quickly home and straight to Penelope's room. She looked at him with a question in her eyes and he knew she had waited once more in silence and fear for his choice. Now one look was enough—there was a surge of joy that has passed beyond desire for both of them. They held each other and Odysseus said quietly, "Forgive me, Penelope, for what I have done to you of late. I will take my finest oar and go forth again, but this time, even if I should die, nothing can threaten the unity between us any more."

Odysseus set out alone. There were no maps to follow once he came to the last known village on the slopes of the hills. He must simply walk on into the unknown, following the tracks of animals in the forests, crossing the deserts on weary feet, climbing beside streams to their source. Beside him a small sturdy donkey carried his stores of food and the minimum of equipment for the way.

Odysseus struggled up a bare hillside track until he came at last to a crossroad where four tracks met and where he found a stranger watching him approach. Now he heard the words for which he had longed but which by now he had almost forgotten, sounding at last like a song of liberation in his heart. "What winnowing fan is that upon your shoulder?" With enormous relief he set down his burden, holding it as it rested on its handle, blade upwards; and, straightening his shoulders, he looked at the stranger and for the first time wondered whatever was the meaning of this question of which Teiresias had warned him. It cannot be, he thought, simply the ignorance of a man who never saw the sea.

The stranger was dressed like a peasant in a rough tunic and held a staff in his hand, but his face was sensitive and intelligence shone in his eyes, and humor showed in the generous mouth. "Why do you speak of a winnowing fan," said Odysseus, "when you must know very well that this is a beautiful oar with which I cleave the great waters of the wine-dark seas around us?" And as he spoke his eyes took on the far-away look of the sailor scanning wide horizons.

The stranger smiled and answered, "You are right, I am not ignorant of the oar—though you see below you here a village, or rather an encampment, where no man will recognize it. But nevertheless I was not pretending by using the words 'winnowing fan.' For I recognize you, Lord Odysseus, and I know your story—and it may be that you will come to recognize me, for you have glimpsed me now and then on your journeying. I ask you now only to think of the meaning of that image." Odysseus looked keenly at the other. "Why, the winnowing fan is something that creates a wind whereby the chaff is separated from the grain at the time of harvest. What has that to do with an oar?"

"Remember only what the oar has meant to you through the many years of your life, Odysseus. You have been brought, by the seer who is blind to outer shapes but who sees the shape of things within and their meaning in each man's life, to make this last journey precisely in order that you may finally recognize your own oar as a true winnowing fan. Do you not know that your travels, your achievements and failures, the gains and losses to which your winged ship carried you were all slowly forging for you a 'winnowing fan'? Now that the harvest is gathered and

you stand in the autumn of your life, your oar is no longer
a driving force carrying you over the oceans of your inner
and outer worlds, but a spirit of discriminating wisdom,
separating moment by moment the wheat of life from the
chaff, so that you may know in both wheat and chaff their
meaning and their value in the pattern of the universe.
This final journey seemed pointless—indeed merely a
kind of 'chaff' blowing in the wind, but you chose it
nonetheless because at last you trusted the blind seer hidden in your heart, as Penelope has trusted him for so
long."

There was silence, and then Odysseus spoke, and his
eyes were smiling. "Yes," he said, "I truly begin to look
now through the blind eyes of the seer. But that being so,
tell me, stranger, why I should plant this well-cut oar here
and leave it where no one will know its uses or its meaning? Why should I not take it home—not for my own use
any more, but maybe for my son's?"

"To leave it is essential, Odysseus. If you were to put it
in your son's hands you would watch his sea journey
through life, transferring to him your yearning for great
deeds; you would never let go of the goals of youth. Mor-
over you might thus prevent your own son from carving
his own oar from the wood, finding his own way. To leave
it here is like a gift of your lifetime's effort to people who
live here in such simplicity. They will see it and begin to
ask questions—and travellers, I for one, will tell them of
the great waters beyond their present horizons—of the
wonders and dangers of the deep, of the beauty of swift
ships, and of the tang of salt to be found there—salt which
will always mean for future men and women the latent
wisdom and humor and savor of the spirit. They will not
understand these tales, but their bolder spirits will grow
restless and curious, and they will leave home to seek for
answers. Torn from their simple natural roots, they will

suffer greatly as all men and women must ultimately suffer. A future legend will tell of this in an image of the first woman giving to the first man the apple of the knowledge of good and evil, and of their expulsion from the paradise of their unconscious unity with nature to begin the long journey over land and sea, through the darkness and danger, through light and happiness, through doubt and faith, conflict and coherence, to the Return. It is a return to the same simplicity and oneness with nature and spirit that these people here have, but they live without understanding, as do beast and flower. In the Return, however, the oneness is known, experienced, through the awakening of the mind of God in each man and woman. That future now becomes possible for you, my friend. Come, I will help you dig a hole. You have a dagger, do you not? There is soft earth here in the center of this crossroad."

They set to work with their hands and knife and, as the hole deepened, the stranger said, almost chanting as minstrels do, "I see your oar standing stark and meaningless in this place, but as the years go by and questions grow and multiply I see roots growing down into the earth and green shoots bearing leaves begin to spring out from the blade; and in the future, when the blind poet Homer has come here with the tale of your life, Odysseus, the blossoms and the fruit will break from the tree of your oar year after year, through aeons of time."

In silence they deepened the hole, set the oar in it, filled it again with earth, and finally collected stones and built a small cairn around the base of the standing oar.

"It is time now to make the sacrifice to your enemy Poseidon, of which Teiresias spoke," said the stranger. "I will go to the people in the valley who will give me a ram and a bull from the flocks, but you yourself must go into the wild country and bring the breeding boar. I cannot help you there; but perhaps you may find him ready to come with you."

Odysseus looked at him in disbelief. "I must bring him alive," he said despairingly, "but that is surely impossible. Bow or knife cannot be used. I will take only a rope with a noose—and pray."

Odysseus took the road that led into the woods. He knew now what this sacrifice meant: three offerings of the driving power of his masculinity, which had carried him through so many trials but had also been given over to pride and ambition and greed of achievement. The ram and the bull were not hard to find and offer—but the breeding boar? That wild and dangerous beast, hidden in the forests of his soul, breeding unseen new and more deadly threats of pride—pride now in his own renunciations—how could he be tamed?

He heard a rustling in the undergrowth and stood still. All his senses, his fears, his doubts and longings, seemed to come together into a point of sheer attention beyond thought. He moved slowly to stand on a flat rock at the side of the path and heard a sound, a kind of humming chant, and he knew in wonder that it was his own voice singing—calling to the huge boar whose head now showed amongst the trees. Gradually the threat in the black angry eyes sank to rest and Odysseus dropped the rope with its noose. The huge creature emerged slowly into sight and approached the stone. Odysseus with a stab of fear stood without moving, then dared to turn, still singing, and walk back along the path. He heard the heavy plodding of the boar behind him and knew with joy, "He comes consenting." The stranger was there as he approached the oar: a white ram and red bull were beside him and the black boar quietly joined them. Together Odysseus and his companion built three fires and, taking the ritual knife,

Odysseus shed the blood of the sacrifice, and as it poured out he knew that the long enmity between him and the great god Poseidon, Earthshaker and Power of the Sea, was at an end, and that he and Polyphemos, son of the god, were one at last in the new life in which he was unique and yet many, nothing and everything. He and the other ate the ritual part of the threefold offering to the god; then Odysseus said, "I leave the meat to the people of this place and I go now, O stranger, no longer strange to me, to make the ceremonial offerings, as Teiresias foretold, at home among my people." He called to his quietly grazing donkey and looked back to say goodbye, but the stranger had disappeared and with him all traces of the sacrifice: the oar stood tall and straight between the earth and sky.

So Odysseus came home, and, day by day, he made offerings to each of the gods in turn, under their Greek names and forms—names which differ in time and space throughout the centuries and in all varying cultures of our world. They carry always for men and women the meanings of life, both human and divine, and in these final rites Odysseus surely affirmed the wholeness of his life's journey, his readiness to die. He made offering to Zeus and Hera, Apollo and Artemis, Dionysus and Aphrodite, Hephaestos, Ares, Hecate, Hades, Demeter-Persephone; then came his particular gratitude to the great powers who had chiefly guided him and brought him and Penelope to their present rich serenity—grey-eyed Athene, who in dreams had given the wisdom and courage to save them both; and Hermes, who long ago had given him the herb "moli" with its black roots and milky flowers, the one protection from Circe who turned men into swine. Hermes was the one also who brought him release from Calypso and who, he now knew, had met him at the crossroads and awakened him on the threshold of old age. Last of all he remembered and gave thanks for Eros and Psyche, united after much suffering and giving birth to "Joy."

In the time that followed I imagine the old Greek living the simple life in the mode of his time, as so many in other times and cultures who have experienced the return to innocence. It is a life, we may imagine, both wholly symbolic and yet wholly natural, empty yet full, spontaneous as a child's, yet constantly chosen. "Love and do as you will," in St. Augustine's words. Thus, as Teiresias saw, he would grow into a rich old age until, weighted with the length of years yet light as a breath of wind, death would come gently to him out of the sea.

Helen Luke

WHY DID I VISIT THE MAGIC MONASTERY? WELL, I'm a monk myself, and the strangest thing happened in my monastery. We had a visit from the Buddha. We prepared for it, and gave him a very warm, though solemn, welcome. He stayed overnight, but he slipped away very early in the morning. When the monks woke up, they found graffiti all over the cloister walls. Imagine! And do you know what he wrote? One word—TRIVIA—TRIVIA—TRIVIA—all over the place.

Well, we were in a rage. But then when I quieted down I looked about and realized, "Yes, it is true." So much of what I saw was trivia, and most of what I heard. But what is worse, when I closed my eyes, all inside was trivia. For several weeks this was my experience, and my very efforts to rectify it just made it worse. I left my monastery and headed for the Magic Monastery.

The Brother showed me around. First, the Hall of Laughter. Everything fed the flame of laughter, big things and small, sacred, solemn, inconsequential. Only laughter there.

Next, the Room of Sorrow. The very essence of bitter tears—those of the bereaved mother, the lonely, depressed. *Only* sorrow here.

Now the Hall of Words. Words upon words, spoken and written. Alone they must have had some sense, but all together—total confusion. I cried out, "Stop! Stop!" but I was only adding words to words.

Next, the great Hall of Silence. Here there is no time.

He took me finally to the Hall of Treasures. "Take anything you want," he whispered. The heart of Jesus, the smile of a Buddha, the wisdom of Solomon, the compassion of Mary. What to take?

I chose the heart of Jesus, and with it I am heading back to my monastery. What would you pick?

Father Theophane

NASRUDIN WAS AT A FOOTBALL GAME. HE HAD BEEN shouting until half-time, and felt thirsty. "I'm going to get a drink of water," he told his friend.

"And one for me," said the friend.

In a few minutes Nasrudin came back.

"I tried to have a drink of water for you, but I found, after I had had my own drink, that you were not thirsty after all."

Sufi

THE HAPPY PRINCE

High above the city, on a tall column, stood the statue of the Happy Prince. He was gilded all over with

thin leaves of fine gold, for eyes he had two bright sapphires, and a large red ruby glowed on his sword-hilt.

He was very much admired indeed. "He is as beautiful
as a weather-cock," remarked one of the Town Councillors
who wished to gain a reputation for having artistic tastes;
"only not quite so useful," he added, fearing lest people
should think him unpractical, which he really was not.

"Why can't you be like the Happy Prince?" asked a
sensible mother of her little boy who was crying for the
moon. "The Happy Prince never dreams of crying for
anything."

"I am glad there is some one in the world who is quite
happy," muttered a disappointed man as he gazed at the
wonderful statue.

"He looks just like an angel," said the Charity Children as they came out of the cathedral in their bright scarlet cloaks and their clean white pinafores.

"How do you know?" said the Mathematical Master,
"you have never seen one."

"Ah, but we have, in our dreams," answered the children; and the Mathematical Master frowned and looked
very severe, for he did not approve of children dreaming.

One night there flew over the city a little Swallow. His
friends had gone away to Egypt six weeks before, but he
had stayed behind, for he was in love with the most beautiful Reed. He had met her early in the spring as he was
flying down the river after a big yellow moth, and had
been so attracted by her slender waist that he had stopped
to talk to her.

"Shall I love you?" said the Swallow, who liked to
come to the point at once, and the Reed made him a low
bow. So he flew round and round her, touching the water
with his wings, and making silver ripples. This was his
courtship, and it lasted all through the summer.

"It is a ridiculous attachment," twittered the other Swallows; "she has no money, and far too many relations"; and

indeed the river was quite full of Reeds. Then, when autumn came, they all flew away.

After they had gone he felt lonely, and began to tire of his lady-love. "She has no conversation," he said, "and I am afraid that she is a coquette, for she is always flirting with the wind." And certainly, whenever the wind blew, the Reed made the most graceful curtseys. "I admit that she is domestic," he continued, "but I love travelling, and my wife, consequently, should love travelling also."

"Will you come away with me?" he said finally to her, but the Reed shook her head, she was so attached to her home.

"You have been trifling with me," he cried. "I am off to the Pyramids. Good-bye!" and he flew away.

All day long he flew, and at night-time he arrived at the city. "Where shall I put up?" he said; "I hope the town has made preparations."

Then he saw the statue on the tall column.

"I will put up there," he cried; "it is a fine position, with plenty of fresh air." So he alighted just between the feet of the Happy Prince.

"I have a golden bedroom," he said softly to himself as he looked round, and he prepared to go to sleep; but just as he was putting his head under his wing a large drop of water fell on him. "What a curious thing!" he cried; "there is not a single cloud in the sky, the stars are quite clear and bright, and yet it is raining. The climate in the north of Europe is really dreadful. The Reed used to like the rain, but that was merely her selfishness."

Then another drop fell.

"What is the use of a statue if it cannot keep the rain off?" he said; "I must look for a good chimney-pot," and he determined to fly away.

But before he had opened his wings, a third drop fell, and he looked up, and saw—Ah! what did he see?

The eyes of the Happy Prince were filled with tears, and tears were running down his golden cheeks. His face was so beautiful in the moonlight that the little Swallow was filled with pity.

"Who are you?" he said.

"I am the Happy Prince."

"Why are you weeping then?" asked the Swallow; "you have quite drenched me."

"When I was alive and had a human heart," answered the statue, "I did not know what tears were, for I lived in the Palace of Sans-Souci, where sorrow is not allowed to enter. In the daytime I played with my companions in the garden, and in the evening I led the dance in the Great Hall. Round the garden ran a very lofty wall, but I never cared to ask what lay beyond it, everything about me was so beautiful. My courtiers called me the Happy Prince, and happy indeed I was, if pleasure be happiness. So I lived, and so I died. And now that I am dead they have set me up here so high that I can see all the ugliness and all the misery of my city, and though my heart is made of lead yet I cannot choose but weep."

"What! is he not solid gold?" said the Swallow to himself. He was too polite to make any personal remarks out loud.

"Far away," continued the statue in a low musical voice, "far away in a little street there is a poor house. One of the windows is open, and through it I can see a woman seated at a table. Her face is thin and worn, and she has coarse, red hands, all pricked by the needle, for she is a seamstress. She is embroidering passion-flowers on a satin gown for the loveliest of the Queen's maids-of-honour to wear at the next Court-ball. In a bed in the corner of the room her little boy is lying ill. He has a fever, and is asking for oranges. His mother has nothing to give him but river water, so he is crying. Swallow, Swallow, little Swallow, will you not bring her the ruby out of my sword-hilt? My feet are fastened to this pedestal and I cannot move."

"I am waited for in Egypt," said the Swallow. "My friends are flying up and down the Nile, and talking to the large lotus-flowers. Soon they will go to sleep in the tomb of the great King. The King is there himself in his painted coffin. He is wrapped in yellow linen, and embalmed with spices. Round his neck is a chain of pale green jade, and his hands are like withered leaves."

"Swallow, Swallow, little Swallow," said the Prince, "will you not stay with me for one night, and be my messenger? The boy is so thirsty, and the mother so sad."

"I don't think I like boys," answered the Swallow. "Last summer, when I was staying on the river, there were two rude boys, the miller's sons, who were always throwing stones at me. They never hit me, of course; we swallows fly far too well for that, and besides, I come of a family famous for its agility; but still, it was a mark of disrespect."

But the Happy Prince looked so sad that the little Swallow was sorry. "It is very cold here," he said; "but I will stay with you for one night, and be your messenger."

"Thank you, little Swallow," said the Prince.

So the Swallow picked out the great ruby from the Prince's sword, and flew away with it in his beak over the roofs of the town.

He passed by the cathedral tower, where the white marble angels were sculptured. He passed by the palace and heard the sound of dancing. A beautiful girl came out on the balcony with her lover. "How wonderful the stars are," he said to her, "and how wonderful is the power of love!"

"I hope my dress will be ready in time for the State-ball," she answered; "I have ordered passion-flowers to be embroidered on it; but the seamstresses are so lazy."

He passed over the river, and saw the lanterns hanging to the masts of the ships. He passed over the Ghetto, and saw the old Jews bargaining with each other, and weighing out money in copper scales. At last he came to the poor house and looked in. The boy was tossing feverishly on his bed, and the mother had fallen asleep, she was so tired. In he hopped, and laid the great ruby on the table beside the woman's thimble. Then he flew gently round the bed, fanning the boy's forehead with his wings. "How cool I feel!" said the boy, "I must be getting better"; and he sank into a delicious slumber.

Then the Swallow flew back to the Happy Prince, and told him what he had done. "It is curious," he remarked, "but I feel quite warm now, although it is so cold."

"That is because you have done a good action," said the Prince. And the little Swallow began to think, and then he fell asleep. Thinking always made him sleepy.

When day broke he flew down to the river and had a bath. "What a remarkable phenomenon!" said the Professor of Ornithology as he was passing over the bridge. "A swallow in winter!" And he wrote a long letter about it to the local newspaper. Every one quoted it, it was full of so many words that they could not understand.

"Tonight I go to Egypt," said the Swallow, and he was in high spirits at the prospect. He visited all the public monuments, and sat a long time on top of the church steeple. Wherever he went the Sparrows chirruped and said to each other, "What a distinguished stranger!" so he enjoyed himself very much.

When the moon rose he flew back to the Happy Prince. "Have you any commissions for Egypt?" he cried; "I am just starting."

"Swallow, Swallow, little Swallow," said the Prince, "will you not stay with me one night longer?"

"I am waited for in Egypt," answered the Swallow. "Tomorrow my friends will fly up to the Second Cataract. The river-horse couches there among the bullrushes, and on a great granite house sits the God Memnon. All night long he watches the stars, and when the morning star shines he utters one cry of joy, and then he is silent. At noon the yellow lions come down to the water's edge to drink. They have eyes like green beryls, and their roar is louder than the roar of the cataract."

"Swallow, Swallow, little Swallow," said the Prince, "far away across the city I see a young man in a garret. He is leaning over a desk covered with papers, and in a tumbler by his side there is a bunch of withered violets. His hair is brown and crisp, and his lips are as a pomegranate, and he has large and dreamy eyes. He is trying to finish a play for the Director of the Theatre, but he is too cold to write any more. There is no fire in the grate, and hunger has made him faint."

"I will wait with you one night longer," said the Swallow, who really had a good heart. "Shall I take him another ruby?"

"Alas! I have no ruby now," said the Prince; "my eyes are all that I have left. They are made of rare sapphires, which were brought out of India a thousand years ago. Pluck out one of them and take it to him. He will sell it to the jeweller, and buy firewood, and finish his play."

"Dear Prince," said the Swallow, "I cannot do that"; and he began to weep.

"Swallow, Swallow, little Swallow," said the Prince, "do as I command you."

So the Swallow plucked out the Prince's eye, and flew away to the student's garret. It was easy enough to get in, as there was a hole in the roof. Through this he darted, and came into the room. The young man had his head buried in his hands, so he did not hear the flutter of the bird's wings, and when he looked up he found the beautiful sapphire lying on the withered violets.

"I am beginning to be appreciated," he cried; "this is from some great admirer. Now I can finish my play," and he looked quite happy.

The next day the Swallow flew down to the harbour. He sat on the mast of a large vessel and watched the sailors hauling big chests out of the hold with ropes. "Heave a-hoy!" they shouted as each chest came up. "I am going to Egypt!" cried the Swallow, but nobody minded, and when the moon rose he flew back to the Happy Prince.

"I am come to bid you good-bye," he cried.

"Swallow, Swallow, little Swallow," said the Prince, "will you not stay with me one night longer?"

"It is winter," answered the Swallow, "and the chill snow will soon be here. In Egypt the sun is warm on the green palm-trees, and the crocodiles lie in the mud and look lazily about them. My companions are building a nest in the Temple of Baalbec, and the pink and white doves are watching them, and cooing to each other. Dear Prince, I must leave you, but I will never forget you, and next spring I will bring you back two beautiful jewels in place of those you have given away. The ruby shall be redder than a red rose, and the sapphire shall be as blue as the great sea."

"In the square below," said the Happy Prince, "there stands a little match-girl. She has let her matches fall in the gutter, and they are all spoiled. Her father will beat her if she does not bring home some money, and she is crying. She has no shoes or stockings, and her little head is bare. Pluck out my other eye, and give it to her, and her father will not beat her."

"I will stay with you one night longer," said the Swallow, "but I cannot pluck out your eye. You would be quite blind then."

"Swallow, Swallow, little Swallow," said the Prince, "do as I command you."

So he plucked out the Prince's other eye, and darted down with it. He swooped past the match-girl and slipped the jewel into the palm of her hand. "What a lovely bit of glass!" cried the little girl; and she ran home, laughing.

Then the Swallow came back to the Prince. "You are blind now," he said, "so I will stay with you always."

"No, little Swallow," said the poor Prince, "you must go away to Egypt."

"I will stay with you always," said the Swallow, and he slept at the Prince's feet.

All the next day he sat on the Prince's shoulder, and told him stories of what he had seen in strange lands. He told him of the red ibises, who stand in long rows on the banks of the Nile, and catch goldfish in their beaks; of the Sphinx, who is as old as the world itself, and lives in the desert, and knows everything; of the merchants, who walk slowly by the side of their camels and carry amber beads in their hands; of the King of the Mountains of the Moon, who is as black as ebony, and worships a large crystal; of the great green snake that sleeps in a palm-tree, and has twenty priests to feed it with honey-cakes; and of the pygmies who sail over a big lake on large flat leaves, and are always at war with the butterflies.

"Dear little Swallow," said the Prince, "you tell me of marvellous things, but more marvellous than anything is the suffering of men and of women. There is no Mystery so great as Misery. Fly over my city, little Swallow, and tell me what you see there."

So the Swallow flew over the great city, and saw the rich making merry in their beautiful homes, while the beggars were sitting at the gates. He flew into dark lanes, and saw the white faces of starving children looking out listlessly at the black streets. Under the archway of a bridge two little boys were lying in one another's arms to try and keep themselves warm. "How hungry we are!" they said. "You must not lie here," shouted the watchman, and they wandered out into the rain.

Then he flew back and told the Prince what he had seen.

"I am covered with fine gold," said the Prince, "you

must take it off, leaf by leaf, and give it to my poor; the living always think that gold can make them happy."

Leaf after leaf of the fine gold the Swallow picked off, till the Happy Prince looked quite dull and grey. Leaf after leaf of the fine gold he brought to the poor, and the children's faces grew rosier, and they laughed and played games in the street. "We have bread now!" they cried.

Then the snow came, and after the snow came the frost. The streets looked as if they were made of silver, they were so bright and glistening; long icicles like crystal daggers hung down from the eaves of the houses, everybody went about in furs, and the little boys wore scarlet caps and skated on the ice.

The poor little Swallow grew colder and colder, but he would not leave the Prince, he loved him too well. He picked up crumbs outside the baker's door when the baker was not looking, and tried to keep himself warm by flapping his wings.

But at last he knew he was going to die. He had just enough strength to fly up to the Prince's shoulder once more. "Good-bye, dear Prince!" he murmured, "will you let me kiss your hand?"

"I am glad that you are going to Egypt at last, little Swallow," said the Prince, "you have stayed too long here; but you must kiss me on the lips, for I love you."

"It is not to Egypt that I am going," said the Swallow. "I am going to the House of Death. Death is the brother of Sleep, is he not?"

And he kissed the Happy Prince on the lips, and fell down dead at his feet.

At that moment a curious crack sounded inside the statue, as if something had broken. The fact is that the leaden heart had snapped right in two. It certainly was a dreadfully hard frost.

Early the next morning the Mayor was walking in the square below in company with the Town Councillors. As they passed the column he looked up at the statue: "Dear me! how shabby the Happy Prince looks!" he said.

"How shabby, indeed!" cried the Town Councillors, who always agreed with the Mayor; and they went up to look at it.

"The ruby has fallen out of his sword, his eyes are gone, and he is golden no longer," said the Mayor; "in fact, he is little better than a beggar!"

"Little better than a beggar," said the Town Councillors.

"And here is actually a dead bird at his feet!" continued the Mayor. "We must really issue a proclamation that birds are not to be allowed to die here." And the Town Clerk made a note of the suggestion.

So they pulled down the statue of the Happy Prince. "As he is no longer beautiful he is no longer useful," said the Art Professor at the University.

Then they melted the statue in a furnace, and the Mayor held a meeting of the Corporation to decide what was to be done with the metal. "We must have another statue, of course," he said, "and it shall be a statue of myself."

"Of myself," said each of the Town Councillors, and they quarrelled. When I last heard of them they were quarrelling still.

"What a strange thing!" said the overseer of the workmen at the foundry. "This broken lead heart will not melt in the furnace. We must throw it away." So they threw it on a dust-heap where the dead Swallow was also lying.

"Bring me the two most precious things in the city," said God to one of His Angels; and the Angel brought him the leaden heart and the dead bird.

"You have rightly chosen," said God, "for in my garden of Paradise this little bird shall sing for evermore, and in my city of gold the Happy Prince shall praise me."

Oscar Wilde

FIFTEEN

*Letting Go
into Our
Freedom*

L ETTING GO IS THE ESSENCE OF THE SPIRITUAL LIFE, the heart of spiritual practice. Beginning to let go brings an immediate and profound revelation. Only when we are no longer full of opinions and expectations are we truly receptive. Only when we are no longer afraid of loss do we begin to open in a wholehearted way to the world around us. In the discovery of aloneness is the discovery of what it means to be truly together with others. Letting go is an expression of compassion for ourselves and of love for the universe we live in.

In traveling this path of inner transformation, we are encouraged to let go of everything, to relinquish every form of clinging. We are encouraged to let go of preoccupations with the past, investment in the future, and clinging in the present. We are encouraged to renounce our images, expectations, fears, and guilt. We are taught that holding is the path to limitation, letting go the direct path to awakening. This letting go is what allows us to be fully present here rather than occupied with what was or what we hope for.

It may feel like a severe and formidable teaching. We may wonder if there will be anything of meaning left to us after this letting go. We may fear that we will be left passionless, empty, and directionless when we have let go of everything that used to define us. We have learned to equate being without with deprivation and being alone with loneliness. If this total letting go is the price of freedom, we may doubt if we are prepared or even able to pay it. Yet our openness repays us at every step.

In spiritual life there is no room for compromise. Awakening is not negotiable; we cannot bargain to hold on to things that please us while relinquishing things that do not matter to us. A lukewarm yearning for awakening is not enough to sustain us through the difficulties involved in letting go. It is important to understand that anything that can be lost was never truly ours, anything that we deeply cling to only imprisons us.

The spiritual life is to learn the joy of letting go, and this great art serves us in any circumstance, so we may meet both the robber in our own cave and the inevitable changes in our life with grace. Letting go allows us to live wisely. Life is inevitably a process of letting go into greater and greater capacities of being, from infant to child, adolescent to adult. Letting go of our fears and habits allows a more spacious wisdom to emerge. Moving through this changing world and letting go of the beliefs, the attachments, the fixed sense of ourselves one day at a time is to travel with a graceful and spacious heart. To release the old is to allow the new to be born. This is freedom.

When we see clearly, we discover that we are never actually the owners, the possessors, of the things in our life. Our homes, the things we call mine, even our children are here with us only for a time. We live in relationship to them either skillfully and wisely or graspingly and unwisely. Even our bodies do not belong to us. They are gifts, which will change and eventually need to be released in their own way. Their changing cycles reflect the very nature of the world. We cannot possess them nor can we stop them. We are asked to relate wisely to them and all things, not by holding and possessing but by loving. To do this is to let go one moment at a time in a spirit of love and respect. When we learn to be truly present, we discover that what we deeply seek has always been with us.

The joy expressed by the stories of this chapter is the same joy we will find as we let go. In reading these stories, we might reflect on what is hardest for us to let go of and why. What do we need to let go of in order to live more freely? Where do we cling to ideas and expectations that keep us from fully loving those around us? What do we possess that keeps us from being free? Can we imagine what changes would occur if we let go?

ONCE SOME ROBBERS CAME INTO THE MONASTERY of the desert fathers and said to one of the elders: We have come to take away everything that is in your cell. And he said: My sons, take all you want. So they took everything they could find in the cell and started off. But they left behind a little bag that was hidden in the cell. The elder picked it up and followed after them, crying out: My sons, take this, you forgot it in the cell! Amazed at the patience of the elder, they brought everything back into his cell and did penance, saying: This one really is a man of God!

Desert Fathers

ON MY WAY UP THERE I MET A BEGGAR AND WENT over to give him some money. (My saintly mother had taught me never to pass a beggar without giving him something.) But he took my quarter and, with a look of disdain, flipped it into the bushes. "I don't need your money," he barked. "Why don't you give me your boredom?"

What could I say? I heard myself saying, "I'll have to ask my wife." And I hurried on before he could devastate me further.

Well, there were other things I had planned to think about on my retreat, but his words kept breaking in. "Why don't you give me your boredom?"

"No, I can't. Not that! I'll have to ask my wife. Can't I give you something else? You don't understand my situation. I won't."

For forty days I resisted.

On the fortieth day I rose up, left the monastery, and dumped my boredom into his lap. Do you know what he said?

Father Theophane

THE ANIMALS MET IN ASSEMBLY AND BEGAN TO COMplain that humans were always taking things away from them.

"They take my milk," said the cow. "They take my eggs," said the hen. "They take my flesh for bacon," said the hog. "They hunt me for my oil," said the whale.

Finally the snail spoke. "I have something they would certainly take away from me if they could. Something they want more than anything else. I have TIME."

Sufi

❧❧

ONCE THERE WAS A MOUSE.

He was a busy mouse, searching everywhere, touching his whiskers to the grass, and looking. He was busy as all mice are, busy with mice things. But once in a while he would hear an odd sound. He would lift his head, squinting hard to see, his whiskers wiggling in the air, and he would wonder. One day he scurried up to a fellow mouse and asked him, "Do you hear a roaring in your ears, my brother?"

"No, no," answered the other mouse, not lifting his busy nose from the ground. "I hear nothing. I am busy now. Talk to me later."

He asked another mouse the same question and the mouse looked at him strangely. "Are you foolish in your head? What sound?" he asked and slipped into a hole in a fallen cottonwood tree.

The little mouse shrugged his whiskers and busied himself again, determined to forget the whole matter. But there was that roaring again. It was faint, very faint, but it was there! One day, he decided to investigate the sound just a little. Leaving the other busy mice, he scurried a little way away and listened again. There it was! He was listening hard when suddenly, someone said hello.

"Hello, little brother," the voice said, and Mouse almost jumped right out of his skin. He arched his back and tail and was about to run.

"Hello," again said the voice. "It is I, Brother Raccoon." And sure enough, it was! "What are you doing here all by yourself, little brother?" asked the raccoon. The mouse blushed, and put his nose almost to the ground. "I hear a roaring in my ears and I am investigating it," he answered timidly.

"A roaring in your ears?" replied the raccoon as he sat down with him. "What you hear, little brother, is the river."

"The river?" Mouse asked curiously. "What is a river?"

"Walk with me and I will show you the river," Raccoon said.

Little Mouse was terribly afraid, but he was determined to find out once and for all about the roaring. "I can return to my work," he thought, "after this thing is settled, and possibly this thing may aid me in all my busy examining and collecting. And my brothers all said it was nothing. I will show them. I will ask Raccoon to return with me and I will have proof."

"All right Raccoon, my brother," said Mouse. "Lead on to the river. I will walk with you."

Little Mouse walked with Raccoon. His little heart was pounding in his breast. The raccoon was taking him upon strange paths and Little Mouse smelled the scent of many things that had gone by this way. Many times he became so frightened he almost turned back. Finally, they came to the river! It was huge and breathtaking, deep and clear in places, and murky in others. Little Mouse was unable to see across it because it was so great. It roared, sang, cried, and thundered on its course. Little Mouse saw great and little pieces of the world carried along on its surface.

"It is powerful!" Little Mouse said, fumbling for words.

"It is a great thing," answered the raccoon, "but here, let me introduce you to a friend."

In a smoother, shallower place was a lily pad, bright and green. Sitting upon it was a frog, almost as green as the pad it sat on. The frog's white belly stood out clearly.

"Hello, little brother," said the frog. "Welcome to the river."

"I must leave you now," cut in Raccoon, "but do not fear, little brother, for Frog will care for you now." And Raccoon left, looking along the river bank for food that he might wash and eat.

Little Mouse approached the water and looked into it. He saw a frightened mouse reflected there.

"Who are you?" Little Mouse asked the reflection. "Are you not afraid being that far out in the great river?"

"No," answered the frog, "I am not afraid. I have been given the gift from birth to live both above and within the river. When winter man comes and freezes this medicine, I cannot be seen. But all the while thunderbird flies, I am here. To visit me, one must come when the world is green. I, my brother, am the Keeper of the Water.

"Amazing!" Little Mouse said at last, again fumbling for words.

"Would you like to have some medicine power?" Frog asked.

"Medicine power? Me?" asked Little Mouse. "Yes, yes! If it is possible."

"Then crouch as low as you can, and then jump as high as you are able! You will have your medicine!" Frog said.

Little Mouse did as he was instructed. He crouched as low as he could and jumped. And when he did, his eyes saw the Sacred Mountains.

Little Mouse could hardly believe his eyes. But there they were! But then he fell back to earth, and he landed in the river!

Little Mouse became frightened and scrambled back to the bank. He was wet and frightened nearly to death.

"You have tricked me," Little Mouse screamed at the frog.

"Wait," said the frog. "You are not harmed. Do not let your fear and anger blind you. What did you see?"

"I," Mouse stammered, "I, I saw the Sacred Mountains!"

"And you have a new name!" Frog said. "It is Jumping Mouse."

"Thank you. Thank you," Jumping Mouse said, and thanked him again. "I want to return to my people and tell them of this thing that has happened to me."

"Go. Go then," Frog said. "Return to your people. It is easy to find them. Keep the sound of the Medicine River to the back of your head. Go opposite to the sound and you will find your brother mice."

Jumping Mouse returned to the world of the mice. But he found disappointment. No one would listen to him. And because he was wet, and had no way of explaining it because there had been no rain, many of the other mice were afraid of him. They believed he had been spat from the mouth of another animal that had tried to eat him. And they all knew that if he had not been food for the one who wanted him, then he must also be poison for them.

Jumping Mouse lived again among his people, but he could not forget his vision of the Sacred Mountains.

The memory burned in the mind and heart of Jumping Mouse, and one day he went to the edge of the river place. . . .

Jumping Mouse went to the edge of the place of mice and looked out onto the prairie. He looked up for eagles. The sky was full of many spots, each one an eagle. But he was determined to go to the Sacred Mountains. He gathered all of his courage and ran just as fast as he could onto the prairie. His little heart pounded with excitement and fear.

He ran until he came to a stand of sage. He was resting and trying to catch his breath when he saw an old mouse. The patch of sage Old Mouse lived in was a haven for mice. Seeds were plentiful and there was nesting material and many things to be busy with.

"Hello," said Old Mouse. "Welcome."

Jumping Mouse was amazed. Such a place and such a mouse. "You are truly a great mouse," Jumping Mouse said with all the respect he could find. "This is truly a wonderful place. And the eagles cannot see you here, either," Jumping Mouse said.

"Yes," said Old Mouse, "and one can see all the beings of the prairie here: the buffalo, antelope, rabbit, and coyote. One can see them all from here and know their names."

"That is marvelous," Jumping Mouse said.

"Can you also see the river and the Great Mountains?"

"Yes and no," Old Mouse said with conviction. "I know there is the Great River, but I am afraid that the Great Mountains are only a myth. Forget your passion to see them and stay here with me. There is everything you want here, and it is a good place to be."

"How can he say such a thing?" thought Jumping Mouse. "The medicine of the Sacred Mountains is nothing one can forget."

"Thank you very much for the meal you have shared with me, Old Mouse, and also for sharing your great home," Jumping Mouse said. "But I must seek the mountains."

"You are a foolish mouse to leave here. There is danger on the prairie! Just look up there!" Old Mouse said, with even more conviction. "See all those spots! They are eagles, and they will catch you!"

317

It was hard for Jumping Mouse to leave, but he gathered his determination and ran hard again. The ground was rough. But he arched his tail and ran with all his might. He could feel the shadows of the spots upon his back as he ran. All those spots! Finally he ran into a stand of chokecherries. Jumping Mouse could hardly believe his eyes. It was cool there and very spacious. There was water, cherries and seeds to eat, grasses to gather for nests, holes to be explored, and many, many other busy things to do. And there were a great many things to gather.

He was investigating his new domain when he heard very heavy breathing. He quickly investigated the sound and discovered its source. It was a great mound of hair with black horns. It was a great buffalo. Jumping Mouse could hardly believe the greatness of the being he saw lying there before him. He was so large that Jumping Mouse could have crawled into one of his great horns. "Such a magnificent being," thought Jumping Mouse, and he crept closer.

"Hello, my brother," said the buffalo. "Thank you for visiting me."

"Hello, great being," said Jumping Mouse. "Why are you lying here?"

"I am sick and I am dying," the buffalo said, "And my medicine has told me that only the eye of a mouse can heal me. But little brother, there is no such thing as a mouse."

Jumping Mouse was shocked. "One of my eyes!" he thought. "One of my tiny eyes." He scurried back into the stand of chokeberries. But the breathing became harder and slower.

"He will die," thought Jumping Mouse, "if I do not give him my eye. He is too great a being to let die."

He went back to where the buffalo lay and spoke. "I am a mouse," he said with a shaky voice. "And you, my brother, are a great being. I cannot let you die. I have two eyes, so you may have one of them."

The minute he had said it, Jumping Mouse's eye flew out of his head and the buffalo was made whole. The buffalo jumped to his feet, shaking Jumping Mouse's whole world.

"Thank you, my little brother," said the buffalo. "I know of your quest for the Sacred Mountains and of your visit to the river. You have given me life so that I may give-away to the people. I will be your brother forever. Run under my belly and I will take you right to the foot of the Sacred Mountains, and you need not fear the spots. The eagles cannot see you while you run under me. All they will see will be the back of a buffalo. I am of the prairie and I will fall on you if I try to go up the mountains."

Little Mouse ran under the buffalo, secure and hidden from the spots, but with only one eye it was frightening. The buffalo's great hooves shook the whole world each time he took a step. Finally they came to a place and Buffalo stopped.

"This is where I must leave you, little brother," said the buffalo.

"Thank you very much," said Jumping Mouse. "But you know, it was very frightening running under you with only one eye. I was constantly in fear of your great earthshaking hooves."

"Your fear was for nothing," said Buffalo. "For my way of walking is the Sun Dance Way, and I always know where my hooves will fall. I now must return to the prairie, my brother. You can always find me there."

Jumping Mouse immediately began to investigate his new surroundings. There were even more things here than in the other places. Busier things, and an abundance of seeds and other things mice like. In his investigation of these things, suddenly he ran upon a gray wolf who was sitting there doing absolutely nothing.

"Hello, Brother Wolf," Jumping Mouse said.

The wolf's ears came alert and his eyes shone. "Wolf! Wolf! Yes, that is what I am. I am a Wolf!" But then his mind dimmed again and it was not long before he sat quietly again, completely without memory as to who he was. Each time Jumping Mouse reminded him who he was, he became excited with the news, but soon would forget again.

"Such a great being," thought Jumping Mouse, "but he has no memory."

Jumping Mouse went to the center of this new place and was quiet. He listened for a very long time to the beating of his heart. Then suddenly he made up his mind. He scurried back to where the wolf sat and he spoke.

"Brother Wolf," Jumping Mouse said.

"Wolf! Wolf," said the wolf.

"Please, Brother Wolf," said Jumping Mouse, "please listen to me. I know what will heal you. It is one of my eyes. And I want to give it to you. You are a greater being than I. I am only a mouse. Please take it."

When Jumping Mouse stopped speaking his eye flew out of his head and the wolf was made whole.

Tears fell down the cheeks of Wolf, but his little brother could not see them, for now he was blind.

"You are a great brother," said the wolf, "for now I have my memory. But now you are blind. I am the guide into the Sacred Mountains. I will take you there. There is a Great Medicine Lake there. The most beautiful lake in the world. All the world is reflected there. The people, the lodges of the people, and all the beings of the prairies and skies."

"Please take me there," Jumping Mouse said.

The wolf guided him through the pines to the Medicine Lake. Jumping Mouse drank the water from the lake. The wolf described the beauty to him.

"I must leave you here," said Wolf, "for I must return so that I may guide others, but I will remain with you as long as you like."

"Thank you, my brother," said Jumping Mouse. "But although I am frightened to be alone, I know you must go so that you may show others the way to this place."

Jumping Mouse sat there trembling in fear. It was no use running, for he was blind, but he knew an eagle would find him here. He felt a shadow on his back and heard the sound that eagles make. He braced himself for the shock. And the eagle hit! Jumping Mouse went to sleep.

Then he woke up. The surprise of being alive was great, but now he could see! Everything was blurry, but the colors were beautiful.

"I can see! I can see!" said Jumping Mouse over again and again.

A blurry shape came toward Jumping Mouse. Jumping Mouse squinted hard but the shape remained a blur.

"Hello, brother," a voice said. "Do you want some medicine?"

"Some medicine for me?" asked Jumping Mouse. "Yes! Yes!"

"Then crouch down as low as you can," the voice said, "and jump as high as you can."

Jumping Mouse did as he was instructed. He crouched as low as he could and jumped! The wind caught him and carried him higher.

"Do not be afraid," the voice called to him. "Hang on to the wind and trust!"

Jumping Mouse did. He closed his eyes and hung on to the wind and it carried him higher and higher. Jumping Mouse opened his eyes and they were clear, and the higher he went the clearer they became. Jumping Mouse saw his old friend upon a lily pad on the beautiful Medicine Lake. It was the frog.

"You have a new name," called the frog. "You are Eagle."

Native American

There were two old men who had lived together for many years, and they never quarreled. Now one of them said: Let us try to quarrel once just like other people do. And the other replied: I don't know how a quarrel happens. Then the first said: Look, I put a brick between us, and I say, This is mine, and you say, No, it's mine, and after that a quarrel begins. So they placed a brick between them, and one of them said: This is mine, and the other said: No, it's mine. And he replied: Indeed, it's all yours, so take it away with you! And they went away unable to fight with each other.

Desert Fathers

If a man is crossing a river
And an empty boat collides with his own
    skiff,
Even though he be a bad-tempered man
He will not become very angry.
But if he sees a man in the boat,
He will shout at him to steer clear.
If the shout is not heard, he will shout again,
And yet again, and begin cursing.
And all because there is somebody in the
    boat.
Yet if the boat were empty,
He would not be shouting, and not angry.

If you can empty your own boat
Crossing the river of the world,
No one will oppose you,
No one will seek to harm you.

Chuang-tzu

WHEN RAMANA MAHARSHI LAY DYING, THE CRIES of his devotees' grief reached his ears. He asked one of his attendants, "Why do they despair so deeply?" His attendant answered, "It is because you are leaving them, master." Ramana turned to his attendant in puzzlement, "But where do they think I could go?"

Hindu

IN INDIA HUNTERS HAD A PROVEN WAY OF CATCHING monkeys. A half coconut would be hollowed out and a hole made that was only large enough to let a monkey's open hand pass through. The coconut was then pinned to the ground and tempting food placed beneath. A monkey would approach, intent on getting hold of the food beneath the coconut, but alas as soon as it grasped the food in its fist it found itself unable to pull its hand and the food free of the coconut. Imprisoned it would stay, caught by its own unwillingness to open its fist.

Hindu

THERE WAS A CHILD MADE ALL OF SALT WHO VERY much wanted to know where he had come from. So he set out on a long journey and traveled to many lands in pursuit of this understanding. Finally he came to the shore of the great ocean. How marvelous, he cried, and stuck one foot in the water. The ocean beckoned him in further saying, "If you wish to know who you are, do not be afraid." The salt child walked further and further into the water dissolving with each step, and at the end exclaimed, "Ah, now I know who I am."

Traditional

WHEN THE MULLA WAS A JUDGE IN HIS VILLAGE, a disheveled figure ran into his courtroom, demanding justice.

"I have been ambushed and robbed," he cried, "just outside this village. Someone from here must have done it. I demand that you find the culprit. He took my robe, sword, even my boots."

"Let me see," said the Mulla, "did he not take your undershirt, which I see you are still wearing?"

"No he did not."

"In that case, he was not from this village. Things are done thoroughly here. I cannot investigate your case."

Sufi

TWO MONKS JOURNEYING HOME CAME TO THE BANKS of a fast-flowing river, where they met a young woman unable to cross the current alone. One of the monks picked her up in his arms and set her safely on her feet on the other side and the two monks continued on their travels. The monk who had crossed the river alone could finally restrain himself no longer and began to rebuke his brother, "Do you not know it is against our rules to touch a young woman? You have broken the holy vows."

The other monk answered, "Brother, I left that young woman on the banks of the river. Are you still carrying her?"

Zen

ONE NIGHT, THIEVES ENTERED RABBI WOLF'S HOUSE and took whatever they happened to find. From his room the zaddik watched them but did not do anything to stop them. When they were through, they took some utensils and among them a jug from which a sick man had drunk that very evening. Rabbi Wolf ran after them. "My good people," he said, "whatever you have found here, I beg you to regard as gifts from me. I do not begrudge these things to you at all. But please be careful about that jug! The breath of a sick man is clinging to it, and you might catch his disease!"

From this time on, he said every evening before going to bed: "All my possessions are common property," so that in case thieves came again they would not be guilty of theft.

Chassid

᪇

IN THE LAST CENTURY, A TOURIST FROM THE STATES visited the famous Polish rabbi Hafez Hayyim.

He was astonished to see that the rabbi's home was only a simple room filled with books. The only furniture was a table and a bench.

"Rabbi, where is your furniture?" asked the tourist.

"Where is yours?" replied Hafez.

"Mine? But I'm only a visitor here."

"So am I," said the rabbi.

Chassid

᪇

RYŌKAN, A ZEN MASTER, LIVED THE SIMPLEST KIND of life in a little hut at the foot of a mountain. One evening a thief visited the hut only to discover there was nothing in it to steal.

Ryōkan returned and caught him. "You may have come a long way to visit me," he told the prowler, "and you should not return empty-handed. Please take my clothes as a gift."

The thief was bewildered. He took the clothes and slunk away.

Ryōkan sat naked, watching the moon. "Poor fellow," he mused, "I wish I could give him this beautiful moon."

Zen

❦

A T THE TIME OF THE BUDDHA A STORY IS TOLD about a young woman named Kisa Gotami who experienced a series of tragedies. First her husband and another close family member died. All that remained for her was her only son. Then he was stricken with illness and died as well. Wailing in grief, she carried the body of her dead child everywhere asking for help, for medicine, to bring him back to life, but of course, no one could help her. Finally someone directed her to the Buddha who was teaching in a nearby forest grove. She approached the Buddha, crying with grief, and said, "Great teacher, master, please bring my boy back to life." The Buddha replied, "I will do so, but first you must do something for me, Kisa Gotami. You must go into the village and get me a handful of mustard seed [the most common Indian spice] and from this I will fashion a medicine for your child. There is one more thing, however," the Buddha said. "The mustard seed must come from a home where no one has died, where no one has lost a child or a parent, a spouse or a friend."

Kisa Gotami ran into the village and ran into the first house begging for mustard seed. "Please, please, may I have some?" And the people seeing her grief responded immediately. But then she asked, "Has anyone in this home died? Has a mother or daughter or father or son?"

They answered, "Yes. We had a death just last year." So Kisa Gotami ran away and ran to the next house. Again they offered her mustard seed and again she asked, "Has anyone here died?" This time it was the maiden aunt. And at the next house it was the young daughter who had died. And so it went house after house in this village. There was no household she could find which had not known death.

Finally Kisa Gotami sat down in her sorrow and realized that what had happened to her and to her child happens to everyone, that all who are born will also die. She carried the body of her dead son back to the Buddha. There he was buried with all proper rites. She then bowed to the Buddha and asked him for teachings that would bring her wisdom and refuge in this realm of birth and death, and she herself took these teachings deeply to heart and became a great yogi and a wise woman.

Early Buddhist

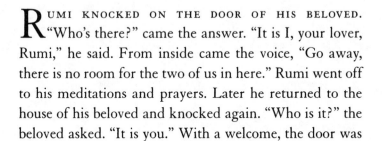

RUMI KNOCKED ON THE DOOR OF HIS BELOVED. "Who's there?" came the answer. "It is I, your lover, Rumi," he said. From inside came the voice, "Go away, there is no room for the two of us in here." Rumi went off to his meditations and prayers. Later he returned to the house of his beloved and knocked again. "Who is it?" the beloved asked. "It is you." With a welcome, the door was thrown wide open.

Rumi

SIXTEEN

*Teaching
Through
Being*

MANY OF THE WISEST HUMANS HAVE NOT BEEN people of great fame and power or leaders of vast numbers of followers. Much of the profound healing and transformation that takes place in any age emanates from people who are not known for great abilities or miraculous deeds. Great compassion and transformation often radiate from the simplest of people, those whose lives embody love and truth.

There is great truth in the statement, "If you want to know a Zen master, you must ask his or her spouse." We are known through our most personal actions, our care, our words, and our feelings. Living in inner harmony and peace means including every thought and action in the organic expression of that harmony and peace. Those rooted in true wisdom and compassion feel no need to proclaim it from a pedestal. They know that the only meaningful way to live is to enact the spirit of wisdom and compassion every day.

We are moved by the stories of great sages and spiritual masters because they are living examples of a profound wisdom that we can also sense in ourself. They have discovered how to find great calm amid chaos, how to greet conflict and derision with forgiveness and acceptance. They live a life of profound trust and faith in the midst of skepticism and cynicism. Their mission is not to change the world or to impose their own truths upon others but to live in accord with the truths they have come to understand and to express that inner harmony in every area of their lives.

The example of the people in these stories is an invitation to us to embody and fulfill this same harmony in our own lives. It is said that the greatest miracle in spiritual life is a change of heart. How we touch others and how we live, how we speak and act are our contributions to the world. Embodying wise and loving being is not accomplished by enacting specific gestures or by allegiance to a particular religion or community. It is much more simple and basic than that. We embody it through the way we treat our neighbors, our families, our communities, our environment, and ourselves. The power of our heart is contagious, the spirit of wakefulness and integrity is contagious. If we wish to have peace, we must be peace; if we wish to have love in this world, we must be love. Our children, friends, and communities will most benefit when we are a brother or sister to them, bringing our bodies and hearts, our integrity and wakefulness to being together.

When Gandhi was asked if he had any message for the world, he said, "My life is my message." What message does our life give? What qualities of our being do we bring into the difficult situations of our life? Without words, in what way do we touch our friends, family, and community? What is the spirit we touch them with and how will they remember us? Where do we live and embody our greatest wisdom, love, and values? Where do we not do so? If we were to live our life with true wakefulness and compassion, how might we live?

A PROPHET ONCE CAME TO A CITY TO CONVERT ITS inhabitants. At first the people listened to his sermons, but they gradually drifted away till there was not a single soul to hear the prophet when he spoke.

One day a traveler said to him, "Why do you go on preaching?"

Said the prophet, "In the beginning I hoped to change these people. If I still shout it is only to prevent them from changing me."

Sufi

I SAW ONE OF THE CLEAREST EXAMPLES OF TEACHING presence demonstrated in the Cambodian refugee camps. I was with Mahaghosananda, an extraordinary Cambodian monk, one of the few to survive, when he opened a Buddhist temple in a barren refugee camp of the Khmer Rouge communists. There were fifty thousand villagers who had become communists at gunpoint and had now fled the destruction to camps on the Thai border. In this camp the underground Khmer Rouge camp leaders threatened to kill any who would go to the temple. Yet on its opening day more than twenty thousand people crowded into the dusty square for the ceremony. These were the sad remnants of families, an uncle with two nieces, a mother with only one of three children. The schools had been burned, the villages destroyed, and in nearly every family, members had been killed or ripped away. I wondered what he could say to people who had suffered so greatly.

Mahaghosananda began the service with the traditional chants that had permeated village life for a thousand years. Though these words had been silenced for eight years of war and the temples destroyed, they still remained in the hearts of these people whose lives had known as much sorrow and injustice as any on earth. Then Mahaghosananda began teaching one of the central verses of the Buddha, first in Pali and then in Cambodian, reciting the words over and over:

> Hatred never ceases by hatred
> but by love alone is healed.
> This is an ancient and eternal law.

As he chanted these verses over and over thousands began to chant with him. They chanted and wept. It was an amazing moment, for it was clear that their hearts longed for this forgiveness like a parched desert. And it was clear that the presence of this monk and the truth he chanted was even greater than the sorrows they had to bear.

Buddhist

THE MASTER SOYEN SHAKU PASSED FROM THIS WORLD when he was sixty-one years of age. Fulfilling his life's work, he left a great teaching, far richer than that of most Zen masters. His pupils used to sleep in the daytime during midsummer, and while he overlooked this he himself never wasted a minute.

When he was but twelve years old he was already studying Tendai philosophical speculation. One summer day the air had been so sultry that little Soyen stretched his legs and went to sleep while his teacher was away.

Three hours passed when, suddenly waking, he heard his master enter, but it was too late. There he lay, sprawled across the doorway.

"I beg your pardon, I beg your pardon," his teacher whispered, stepping carefully over Soyen's body as if it were that of some distinguished guest. After this Soyen never slept again in the afternoon.

Zen

ONCE A POOR BRAHMIN WAS GIVEN AN OX-CALF. He delighted in the tiny creature. He loved its gentle eyes and awkward, frisky ways. He fed the little ox well and lavished affection and care on it. And the ox loved the man, too. And it grew and grew and GREW! until it was a huge, powerful beast. Yet, big as it was, it was gentle, too. Whatever the Brahmin told it to do, it did—even the heaviest tasks. With good will, it pulled stumps from the fields and dragged boulders. When children wanted a ride, it was willing. So pleased was the Brahmin with the ox that he named it "Great Joy."

One day, Great Joy thought to himself, "The Brahmin, my master, is poor. Yet here am I, a great, powerful ox. I should use my strength to help him. I want to repay all the kindness he has shown."

So Great Joy walked over to the open window of the Brahmin's mud house. Carefully, he put his huge, horned head through the weathered window frame. There sat the Brahmin at a crooked wooden table, mending the torn page of a book. Then the good-hearted ox said, "Dear master, I would like to repay you for the years of kindness you have shown me. I have a plan. Please listen."

Amazed, the Brahmin ceased his work and listened.

"Tomorrow, on the market day," said Great Joy, "when you go into the village, seek out a wealthy merchant. Bet him a thousand pieces of silver that you have an ox who can pull a hundred carts loaded to the top with boulders, gravel, and stone."

"What!" exclaimed the Brahmin, finding his tongue, "I have such an ox?"

"Yes," said Great Joy, "you do. I am that ox."

"Wait, my friend," said the Brahmin. "No ox has ever pulled such a load."

"Trust me," said the ox, "have I ever let you down?"

"No," said the Brahmin upon reflection, "you never have."

"Well, then," continued Great Joy, "don't worry. We'll win the bet. You have my word."

So, in the end, the Brahmin agreed.

The next day, when the sun rose, the poor Brahmin tied on his worn sandals and set off for the town. Entering the already crowded market, he moved through the stalls looking for bargains. He found a piece of white cloth and a few sheets of thick paper, which he bought for a small bag of rice. He also got a fistful of sweet corn for Great Joy.

When the sun rose higher and the day grew very hot, he hurried from the noisy bazaar. He entered a little tea shop where the merchants and farmers gathered to refresh themselves during the midday heat.

He seated himself at a table. Then, gathering his courage, he called out to the wealthy merchant coming through the doorway, "My friend, will you join me?"

"Why not?" said the merchant. Sitting down, he joined the Brahmin at his table.

After pleasantries, a few sweets and some tea, the Brahmin drew a deep breath and announced, "I have an ox."

"So?" responded the wealthy merchant, licking a last crumb of pastry from his fingers. "I have many oxen and, let me tell you, they cost me plenty."

"Yes," said the Brahmin, "but you see, my ox is strong!"

"Bah!" said the merchant. "What else is new? Is it not the ox's nature to be strong?"

"Of course," stammered the poor Brahmin, "of course, but . . . but, not so strong as mine."

"Huh!" snorted the merchant, sipping his tea.

The Brahmin continued, "Why, this ox of mine is so strong he can pull a hundred carts loaded to the top with boulders, gravel, and stone!"

"Impossible!" laughed the merchant. "Let me tell you something. No ox, no matter how strong, can pull such a load. After all," he added confidentially, "this world is one of weights and measures. An ox is, after all, just an ox. Like everything else, it has its necessary limits. No, my friend. This cannot be done."

"But it can!" insisted the Brahmin.

"It can't!" persisted the merchant.

"Let us wager," said the Brahmin.

"If you wish," said the merchant.

"One thousand pieces of silver?" suggested the Brahmin.

"Very good!" said the merchant. "One thousand pieces of silver it is! Now, when shall we test this great ox of yours?"

"Tomorrow?" asked the Brahmin.

"Yes, tomorrow, by all means," said the merchant. "Tomorrow, in the square. Let us meet before the sun is above the mango trees. You bring this great ox of yours and I'll see to it that loaded carts are waiting. Until then, my friend, good day." And with that the merchant rose and walked smiling from the shop.

Soon the whole town was alight with the news. "One thousand pieces!" said some. "One hundred carts!" exclaimed others. "One ox!" laughed the rest.

Money changed hands and bets were placed. And then, at last, all waited in expectation for the morning.

That night the Brahmin tossed and turned anxiously. Would he win? Would he lose? Could Great Joy really pull so many loaded carts? The odds, after all, were entirely against it. "Ah," he thought with dismay, "what utter foolishness my life is resting on!"

But in the morning he awoke brightly enough with the rising sun and went out at once to Great Joy's stall.

There stood Great Joy, waiting quietly for him as usual, flicking his long tail in the warm air and contentedly chewing the golden straw. His great dark eyes looked out mildly at the Brahmin, with such good humor in them as if to say, "So, today's the day, eh? Well, don't worry, my friend, all shall be well." But today the Brahmin was preoccupied. He rested his arms on the rough edge of the ox's stall and stared at this great, contented ox. Motes of straw dust danced in the warm sunlit air. Yet it was cool in the stable. Everything there seemed so solid, so ordinary. The thick mud walls, the wooden buckets, the yokes, the worn ropes and brushes—how real, how sturdy they all were today. The Brahmin thought, "Perhaps this bet—perhaps my whole life, who knows, has been just a dream!"

He shook himself. "Dream or no, there's work to be done!" he announced. And picking up a stiff brush, he began to slap and brush the hard muscles of Great Joy's back with all his strength, so that the dust rose up in clouds from the glossy hide.

Then, combed, brushed, and curried, Great Joy and the Brahmin set off together across the fields and down the dirt roads to the town.

They arrived just as the sun was rising to the top of the tallest mango tree. The square was packed with a noisy crowd. And there were the carts, waiting. The Brahmin was shocked! He had never seen so many carts! "What a fool I have been," he suddenly thought, "to have taken the advice of a mere beast. What have I done? I am lost!"

And, with a sinking feeling in the pit of his stomach, he stepped forward.

The crowd parted to let the Brahmin and his Great Joy through. They walked along the row of carts. The merchant was waiting for them. He stood, smiling, alongside the very first cart.

"So are you ready?" he asked.

"Certainly. Of course we are ready!" replied the Brahmin.

The merchant motioned and two men stepped from the crowd. Stooping, they lifted the massive yoke onto Great Joy's shoulders. They knotted the new ropes tightly. In a last rush, final bets were placed (and indeed, a few, seeing Great Joy, now shouted out, "The ox! The ox! My money on the ox!"). Then, complete silence fell.

It was so quiet you could hear the birds singing in the nearby trees. It was so quiet you could hear the sweep of Great Joy's tail. It was so quiet you could hear the buzzing of the glittering flies.

Unconcerned, Great Joy gently eyed the staring crowd and mildly watched the white clouds drifting slowly by. He shook his huge head and exhaled loudly, as if to say, "What's all the fuss?"

Then the Brahmin, feeling all eyes focused on them, stepped closer to Great Joy's side and, raising a whip, struck Great Joy sharply on the shoulder, crying out, "On, you beast! On, you wretch! Do as I say! Pull those carts! Show your strength!"

But when Great Joy felt the bite of the whip and heard the Brahmin's harsh words, his eyes opened wide. "What's this!" he thought to himself. "Blows and curses? Well, not for this ox!" Planting his hooves massively in the earth, he stood rooted like a tree. Despite all the shouts and threats, all the pulls and prods, he would not budge. Not even an inch. He would not even try to pull those carts. He stood unmoved, resolute, beneath all the blows. The crowd laughed and jeered; they threw clods of earth and stones; they shouted and screamed. But Great Joy would not budge.

"Ah, my friend, my friend," spluttered the wealthy merchant, tears of laughter streaming down his cheeks, "you were certainly right. That is some, ha! ha! ha!, ox indeed!"

When the prodding and threats had at last ceased, and the crowd had drifted away, and the merchant, still dabbing his wet eyes, had been paid ("Better luck next time!" he joked), only then did Great Joy, at last, let himself be unhitched and led silently away, home.

Once there, the Brahmin put his head in his arms and sobbed and sobbed with shame and grief. Then once again, Great Joy came to the window and spoke clearly to him, saying, "Why do you weep, my friend?"

Between his broken breaths the Brahmin, in great bitterness, cried out, "How can you ask such a thing, you ungrateful beast? What you told me to do, I have done. But, for all your promises, I have lost everything. And it's all because of you! Not only that, the wealthy merchant and the whole town have laughed at me as well. You alone are responsible!"

But Great Joy said sadly, "Did I let you down? Let me ask you something. Did I ever break any of your fences? Or smash a pot? Or crack a plow?"

"No," said the Brahmin, raising his head. "You never did."

"Did I then, perhaps, ever step on or injure you or hurt any of the children?"

"No," said the Brahmin once again. "Never!"

"Perhaps, then, I may have tracked mud into the clean places of your home or before some sacred shrine?"

"No," repeated the Brahmin a third time. "You never did anything like that either. You have always been a great joy to me."

"Then why," asked Great Joy the ox, "did you strike me and call me 'wretch' and 'beast'? Was this indeed the reward I deserved—I who wanted only to work hard for you?"

The Brahmin wiped his eyes and sat erect. In silence he looked at the ox and, knowing the truth of his words, grew ashamed.

"You are right," he said at last. "It was actually I who let you down. And I am sorry."

"Well," said the Ox, not unkindly, "since you now feel this way, let us try again. But this time you must bet two thousand pieces."

"My friend!" cried the Brahmin, "I shall do my best. It shall be just as you say!"

"And I too shall do my best," said the Ox. "For if you don't let me down, I will certainly not let you down."

The next day the Brahmin ran to the town and entered the tea shop once again. There was the merchant calmly sipping his tea and eating his sweets.

"May I join you?" asked the Brahmin.

"By all means," said the merchant merrily. "Have you not brought me great joy?"

"Let us bet again," said the Brahmin.

"What!" cried the merchant, astonished, "My friend, don't you know when you are beaten?"

"Come," said the Brahmin calmly, "one last wager, on the ox and the carts as before. But this time let us bet two thousand pieces?"

"Well, really," thought the merchant to himself, "fools like this don't grow on every tree." At last he shrugged, "Who am I to say no?"

"So, it's a wager?" asked the Brahmin.

"If you wish," said the merchant, smiling.

"Yes, I do wish," said the Brahmin, delighted. "Tomorrow in the square, at the same time as before. Tomorrow, my friend." And then he departed, wishing the merchant a good day.

The next morning the Brahmin once again curried Great Joy and brushed and cleaned him. Then, once again, he led his mighty ox to the center of town.

Once more the crowd gathered, ready for some fun. But as Great Joy was led up to the carts, spiritedly tossing his great, horned head, sunlight suddenly sparkled like fire upon him and power pulsed from his shining back. His tail seemed to lash the skies like a dragon's tail and his wide, curved horns seemed to tear at the clouds. Each hair on his glossy, red-brown hide bristled and crackled and lifted electrically. The power of a thousand breaths flowed from him and pulsed through the surging crowd, pouring from his heavy hooves into the dark earth and from his curling tail into the bright morning air. The crowd gasped. "What an ox!" they cried. "Perhaps he will be able to do it!"

Once again the heavy yoke was set upon him; once again the thick, new ropes were firmly tied. Then the Brahmin, stepping up to his ox's side, hung a wreath of flowers around Great Joy's massive neck, patted him on a giant shoulder and said quietly, "Now is the time, my mighty friend. This is the moment, my great-hearted ox; so pull, my brother, pull, my Great Joy, and let the whole world see your noble strength."

And with those kind, encouraging words, Great Joy happily planted his hooves firmly in the warm earth and stiffened his legs till they stood as strongly as ancient trees. Then he pulled and pulled and PULLED, straining and struggling with every muscle and every nerve until slowly, steadily, the wheels began to turn. Inch by inch, bit by bit, the carts rolled forward. "They move! They move!" cried the astonished crowd. "The carts begin to move!" Faster and faster and faster rolled the carts as Great Joy pulled and pulled and pulled. The wealthy merchant's eyes opened wide. His jaw dropped in disbelief and the silver coins slipped from between his fingers into the dust. It wasn't possible! It couldn't be! But, "He's done it!" cried the crowd. "The ox has won!"

Still gathering speed, Great Joy pulled the carts right around the square and out through the gates of the town! Rolling, rolling, rolling, he circled the village and pulled all one hundred loaded carts back through the gates and into the square once again.

And all the people followed, laughing wildly, slapping each other on the back and flinging their shirts high up into the air. For never, no never, had they seen or heard of such a wild and marvelous thing. The wealthy merchant, gathering his silver coins once again, ran, too. And so, of course, did the poor Brahmin. Truly, that day, the self-respecting ox, with his dignity and strength, gave them all great joy.

Now some say it must have been a pretty small town to have made such a fuss over an ox and some carts. But others (and I think, wiser) say that it's always important when anyone, man or beast, shows us that there are no limits, when we find our own way, and when our hearts are really in it. What do you think?

Early Buddhist

❧❧

ON A FREEZING COLD DAY, RABBI WOLF DROVE TO the celebration of a circumcision. When he had spent a little time in the room, he felt sorry for the coachman waiting outside, went to him and said: "Come in and get warm."

"I cannot leave my horses alone," the man replied, moved his arms and stamped his feet.

"I'll take care of them until you get warm and can relieve me again," said Rabbi Wolf. At first the coachman refused to consider such a thing, but after a while he allowed the rabbi to persuade him, and went into the house. There everyone who came, regardless of rank or whether or not he was known to the host, got all the food and drink he wanted. After the tenth glass, the coachman had forgotten who was taking his place with the horses, and stayed hour after hour. In the meantime, people had missed the zaddik but told themselves that he had something important to attend to, and would return when he was through. A good deal later, some of the guests left. When they came out on the street, where night was already falling, they saw Rabbi Wolf standing by the carriage, moving his arms and stamping his feet.

Chassid

ONCE TWO BROTHERS WENT TO VISIT AN OLD MAN. It was not the old man's habit, however, to eat every day. When he saw the brothers, he welcomed them with joy and said: Fasting has its own reward, but if you eat for the sake of love you satisfy two commandments, for you give up your own will and also fulfill the commandment to refresh others.

Desert Fathers

IT WAS SAID ABOUT ONE BROTHER THAT WHEN HE HAD woven baskets and put handles on them, he heard a monk next door saying: What shall I do? The trader is coming but I don't have handles to put on my baskets! Then he took the handles off his own baskets and brought them to his neighbor saying: Look, I have these left over. Why don't you put them on your baskets? And he made his brother's work complete, as there was need, leaving his own unfinished.

Desert Fathers

❧❧

IT HAD TAKEN GRANMA, SITTING IN THE ROCKER that creaked with her slight weight as she worked and hummed, while the pine knots spluttered in the fireplace, a week of evenings to make the boot moccasins. With a hook knife, she had cut the deer leather and made the strips that she wove around the edges. When she had finished, she soaked the moccasins in water and I put them on wet and walked them dry, back and forth across the floor, until they fitted soft and giving, light as air.

This morning I slipped the moccasins on last, after I had jumped into my overalls and buttoned my jacket. It was dark and cold—too early even for the morning whisper wind to stir the trees.

Granpa had said I could go with him on the high trail, if I got up, and he had said he would not wake me.

"A man rises of his own will in the morning," he had spoken down to me and he did not smile. But Granpa had made many noises in his rising, bumping the wall of my room and talking uncommonly loud to Granma, and so I had heard, and I was first out, waiting with the hounds in the darkness.

"So. Ye're here," Granpa sounded surprised.

"Yes, sir," I said, and kept the proud out of my voice.

Granpa pointed his finger at the hounds jumping and prancing around us. "Ye'll stay," he ordered, and they tucked in their tails and whined and begged and ol' Maud set up a howl. But they didn't follow us. They stood, all together in a hopeless little bunch, and watched us leave the clearing.

I had been up the low trail that followed the bank of the spring branch, twisting and turning with the hollow until it broke out into a meadow where Granpa had his barn and kept his mule and cow. But this was the high trail that forked off to the right and took to the side of the mountain, sloping always upward as it traveled along the hollow. I trotted behind Granpa and I could feel the upward slant of the trail.

I could feel something more, as Granma said I would. Mon-o-lah, the earth mother, came to me through my moccasins, I could feel her push and swell here, and sway and give there . . . and the roots that veined her body and the life of the water-blood, deep inside her. She was warm and springy and bounced me on her breast, as Granma said she would.

The cold air steamed my breath in clouds and the spring branch fell far below us. Bare tree branches dripped water from ice prongs that teethed their sides, and as we walked higher there was ice on the trail. Gray light eased the darkness away.

Granpa stopped and pointed by the side of the trail. "There she is—turkey run—see?" I dropped to my hands and knees and saw the tracks: little sticklike impressions coming out from a center hub.

"Now," Granpa said, "we'll fix the trap." And he moved off the trail until he found a stump hole.

We cleaned it out, first the leaves, and then Granpa pulled out his long knife and cut into the spongy ground and we scooped up the dirt, scattered it among the leaves. When the hole was deep, so that I couldn't see over the rim, Granpa pulled me out and we dragged tree branches to cover it, and over these, spread armfuls of leaves. Then, with his long knife, Granpa dug a trail sloping downward into the hole and back toward the turkey run. He took the grains of red Indian corn from his pocket and scattered them down the trail, and threw a handful into the hole.

"Now we will go," he said, and set off again up the high trail. Ice, spewed from the earth like frosting, crackled under our feet. The mountain opposite us moved closer as the hollow far below became a narrow slit, showing the spring branch like the edge of a steel knife, sunk in the bottom of its cleavage.

We sat down in the leaves, off the trail, just as the first sun touched the top of the mountain across the hollow. From his pocket, Granpa pulled out a sour biscuit and deer meat for me, and we watched the mountain while we ate.

The sun hit the top like an explosion, sending showers of glitter and sparkle into the air. The sparkling of the icy trees hurt the eyes to look, and it moved down the mountain like a wave as the sun backed the night shadow down and down. A crow scout sent three hard calls through the air, warning we were there.

And now the mountain popped and gave breathing sighs that sent little puffs of steam into the air. She pinged and murmured as the sun released the trees from their death armor of ice.

Granpa watched, same as me, and listened as the sounds grew with the morning wind that set up a low whistle in the trees.

"She's coming alive," he said, soft and low, without taking his eyes from the mountain.

"Yes, sir," I said, "she's coming alive." And I knew right then that me and Granpa had us an understanding that most folks didn't know.

The night shadow backed down and across a little meadow, heavy with grass and shining in the sun bath. The meadow was set into the side of the mountain. Granpa pointed. There was quail fluttering and jumping in the grass, feeding on the seeds. Then he pointed up toward the icy blue sky.

There were no clouds but at first I didn't see the speck that came over the rim. It grew larger. Facing into the sun, so that the shadow did not go before him, the bird sped down the side of the mountain; a skier on the treetops, wings half-folded . . . like a brown bullet . . . faster and faster, toward the quail.

Granpa chuckled. "It's ol' Tal-con, the hawk."

The quail rose in a rush and sped into the trees—but one was slow. The hawk hit. Feathers flew into the air and then the birds were on the ground; the hawk's head rising and falling with the death blows. In a moment he rose with the dead quail clutched in his claws, back up to the side of the mountain and over the rim.

I didn't cry, but I know I looked sad, because Granpa said, "Don't feel sad, Little Tree. It is The Way. Tal-con caught the slow and so the slow will raise no children who are also slow. Tal-con eats a thousand ground rats who eat the eggs of the quail—both the quick and the slow eggs— and so Tal-con lives by The Way. He helps the quail."

Granpa dug a sweet root from the ground with his knife and peeled it so that it dripped with its juicy winter cache of life. He cut it in half and handed me the heavy end.

"It is The Way," he said softly. "Take only what ye need. When ye take the deer, do not take the best. Take the smaller and the slower and then the deer will grow stronger and always give you meat. Pa-koh, the panther, knows and so must ye."

And he laughed, "Only Ti-bi, the bee, stores more than he can use . . . and so he is robbed by the bear, and the 'coon . . . and the Cherokee. It is so with people who store and fat themselves with more than their share. They will have it taken from them. And there will be wars over it . . . and they will make long talks, trying to hold more than their share. They will say a flag stands for their right to do this ... and men will die because of the words and the flag ... but they will not change the rules of The Way."

We went back down the trail, and the sun was high over us when we reached the turkey trap. We could hear them before we saw the trap. They were in there, gobbling and making loud whistles of alarm.

"Ain't no closing over the door, Granpa," I said. "Why don't they just lower their heads and come out?"

Granpa stretched full length into the hole and pulled out a big squawking turkey, tied his legs with a thong and grinned up at me.

"Ol' Tel-qui is like some people. Since he knows everything, he won't never look down to see what's around him. Got his head stuck up in the air too high to learn anything."

... Granpa laid them out on the ground, legs tied. There were six of them, and now he pointed down at them. "They're all about the same age ... ye can tell by the thickness of the combs. We only need three so now ye choose, Little Tree."

I walked around them, flopping on the ground. I squatted and studied them, and walked around them again. I had to be careful. I got down on my hands and knees and crawled among them, until I had pulled out the three smallest I could find.

Granpa said nothing. He pulled the thongs from the legs of the others and they took to wing, beating down the side of the mountain. He slung two of the turkeys over his shoulder.

"Can ye carry the other?" he asked.

"Yes, sir," I said, not sure that I had done right. A slow grin broke Granpa's bony face. "If ye was not Little Tree ... I would call ye Little Hawk."

I followed Granpa down the trail. The turkey was heavy, but it felt good over my shoulder. The sun had tilted toward the farther mountain and drifted through the branches of the trees beside the trail, making burnt gold patterns where we walked. The wind had died in that late afternoon of winter, and I heard Granpa, ahead of me, humming a tune. I would have liked to live that time forever . . . for I knew I had pleased Granpa. I had learned The Way.

Forrest Carter

⋙⋘

MANY PUPILS WERE STUDYING MEDITATION UNDER the Zen master Sengai. One of them used to arise at night, climb over the temple wall, and go to town on a pleasure jaunt.

Sengai, inspecting the dormitory quarters, found this pupil missing one night and also discovered the high stool he had used to scale the wall. Sengai removed the stool and stood there in its place.

When the wanderer returned, not knowing that Sengai was the stool, he put his feet on the master's head and jumped down into the grounds. Discovering what he had done, he was aghast.

Sengai said: "It is very chilly in the early morning. Do be careful not to catch cold yourself."

The pupil never went out at night again.

Zen

⋙⋘

THE ZEN MASTER HAKUIN WAS PRAISED BY NEIGH-bors as one living a pure life.

A beautiful Japanese girl whose parents owned a food store lived near him. Suddenly without any warning, her parents discovered she was with child.

This made her parents angry. She would not confess who the man was, but after much harassment at last named Hakuin.

In great anger the parents went to the master. "Is that so?" was all he would say.

After the child was born it was brought to Hakuin. By this time he had lost his reputation, which did not trouble him, but he took very good care of the child. He obtained milk from his neighbors and everything else the little one needed.

A year later the girl-mother could stand it no longer. She told her parents the truth—that the real father of the child was a young man who worked in the fishmarket.

The mother and father of the girl at once went to Hakuin to ask his forgiveness, to apologize at length, and to get the child back again.

Hakuin was willing. In yielding the child, all he said was: "Is that so?"

Zen

KEICHU, THE GREAT ZEN TEACHER OF THE MEIJI era, was the head of Tofuku, a cathedral in Kyoto. One day the governor of Kyoto called upon him for the first time.

His attendant presented the card of the governor, which read: Kitagaki, Governor of Kyoto.

"I have no business with such a fellow," said Keichu to his attendant. "Tell him to get out of here."

The attendant carried the card back with apologies. "That was my error," said the governor, and with a pencil he scratched out the words Governor of Kyoto. "Ask your teacher again."

"Oh, is that Kitagaki?" exclaimed the teacher when he saw the card. "I want to see that fellow."

Zen

A YOUNG MAN WHO HAD JUST COMPLETED HIS spiritual training and was eagerly intent on becoming a teacher moved to a new town. He tried to teach but no one came. The only spiritual interest in the town were the many followers of a wise and well-known rabbi. Frustrated, the young teacher devised a plan to embarrass the old master and gain students for himself. He captured a small bird and one day went to where the master was seated surrounded by many disciples.

Holding the small bird in his hand he spoke directly to the master. "If you are so wise, tell me now is this bird in my hand alive or is it dead?" His plan was this: If the master said the bird was dead he would open his hand, the bird would fly away, the master would be wrong, and students would come to him. If the master said the bird was alive, he would quickly crush the bird in his hand and open it and say, "See, the bird is dead." Again the master would be wrong and the young teacher would gain students.

He sat poised in front of the master demanding an answer. "Tell me, if you are so wise, is this bird alive or is it dead?" The master looked back at him with great compassion and answered quite simply, "Really, my friend, it is up to you."

Chassid

IT OFTEN HAPPENS THAT I AWAKE AT NIGHT AND begin to think about a serious problem and decide that I must tell the pope about it. Then I wake up completely and remember that I am the pope.

Pope John XXIII

❧❧

RABBI SHELOMO SAID: "IF YOU WANT TO RAISE A man from mud and filth, do not think it is enough to keep standing on top and reaching down to him a helping hand. You must go all the way down yourself, down into mud and filth. Then take hold of him with strong hands and pull him and yourself out into the light."

Chassid

❧❧

IT IS SAID THAT SOON AFTER HIS ENLIGHTENMENT, the Buddha passed a man on the road who was struck by the extraordinary radiance and peacefulness of his presence. The man stopped and asked, "My friend, what are you? Are you a celestial being or a god?"

"No," said the Buddha.

"Well, then, are you some kind of magician or wizard?"

Again the Buddha answered, "No."

"Are you a man?"

"No."

"Well, my friend, what then are you?"

The Buddha replied, "I am awake."

Buddhist

❧❧

Index

T HE PAGE ON WHICH A STORY BEGINS IS GIVEN IN boldface type. Authors of stories are listed by the page number where their story begins. Characters are often listed by title or first name as well as by last name. Example: Ramakrishna, Sri / Sri Ramakrishna.

Acknowledgments

The publishing of this book has been made possible by the great generosity of teachers and traditions of past and present, who through the ages have selflessly shared their wisdom with us. Every reasonable effort has been made to obtain appropriate permission to reproduce the stories included in this volume. We gratefully acknowledge the following authors and publishers for kindly granting us permission to retell tales that have been previously published.

"The Banyan Deer," "The Brave Little Parrot," "Great Joy the Ox," and "King Shiva" from *The Hungry Tigress* by Rafe Martin. Reprinted by permission of Parallax Press.

"Reading a Zen Story" from *Zen and the Ways* by Trevor Leggett. Reprinted by permission of Charles E. Tuttle Co., Inc.

Parables from *Zen Flesh, Zen Bones* by Paul Reps. Reprinted by permission of Charles E. Tuttle Co., Inc.

The introduction from *Peacemaking Day by Day* by Mary Lou Kownacki. Reprinted by permission of Pax Christi USA, Erie, PA.

1975, 1976 by Richard Selzer. Reprinted by permission of Simon & Schuster, Inc.

Excerpt from *And There Was Light* by Jacques Lusseyran, copyright © 1963 by Jacques Lusseyran, English translation copyright © 1963 by Little, Brown and Company. Reprinted by permission of Little, Brown and Company.

"A Kind Word Turneth Away Wrath" by Terry Dobson. Reprinted by permission of Richard Heckler, Lomi School Bulletin.

"A Visit from the Buddha," "A Creature of Contraction and Expansion," "What Do They Really Need," "The Great Silence," and "Boredom" from *Tales of a Magic Monastery* by Theophane the Monk, copyright © 1981 by Cistercian Abbey of Spencer, Inc. Reprinted by permission of Crossroad/Continuum Publishing Group.

Excerpt from *Chop Wood, Carry Water* by Rick Fields with Peggy Taylor, Rex Weyler, and Rick Ingrasci, copyright © 1984 by Jeremy P. Tarcher, Inc. Reprinted by permission of St. Martin's Press, Inc.

The Different Drum by M. Scott Peck, M.D., copyright © 1987. Reprinted by permission of Simon & Schuster, Inc.

"The Devil and Daniel Webster" by Stephen Vincent Benet from *Selected Works of Stephen Vincent Benet,* copyright © 1933 by The Curtis Publishing Company, copyright © 1964 by Thomas C. Benet, Stephanie B. Mahin, and Rachel Lewis Benet. Reprinted by permission of Brandt & Brandt Literary Agents, Inc.

"Lo, The Poor Cabdriver" from *Boston* magazine, February 1986, by Foster Furcolo. Reprinted by permission of author.

"Buddha & Mara" from *The Heart of Understanding* by Thich Nhat Hanh. Reprinted by permission of Parallax Press.

Three stories from *Rumi We Are Three* by Coleman Barks. Reprinted by permission of author.

Excerpt from *The Art of Living: Vipassana Meditation* by William Hart, copyright © 1987 by William Hart. Reprinted by permission of Harper & Row Publishers, Inc., and Francis Goldin, Literary Agent.